A Council for the Global Church

A Council for the Global Church

Receiving Vatican II in History

Massimo Faggioli

Fortress Press
Minneapolis

A COUNCIL FOR THE GLOBAL CHURCH
Receiving Vatican II in History

Cover image: Cardinals gathered for the Second Vatican Council. © Bruno Barbey/ Magnum Photos
Cover design: Tory Herman

Library of Congress Cataloging-in-Publication Data
Print ISBN: 978-1-4514-8456-4
eBook ISBN: 978-1-4514-9663-5

The paper used in this publication meets the minimum requirements of American National Standard for Information Sciences — Permanence of Paper for Printed Library Materials, ANSI Z329.48-1984.

Manufactured in the U.S.A.

This book was produced using PressBooks.com, and PDF rendering was done by PrinceXML.

Contents

Acknowledgments

This book is the fruit of a dozen years of reflection and exchanges about Vatican II between the fortieth anniversary of the liturgical constitution in 2003 and the fiftieth anniversary in 2015—quite a momentous change in the life of the Catholic Church, much of it having to do with the legacy of the Second Vatican Council. But the past decade coincides also with the beginning of a new phase in my experience as a scholar of church history and Catholicism, with the decision to move from Europe to America—a decision that enriched enormously the opportunities to understand a global phenomenon that is much more complex than any mono-disciplinary and non-historical approach can possibly grasp.

I want to thank here the many friends and colleagues who made possible the reflections developed in these essays, first of all the scholars of the Fondazione per le scienze religiose Giovanni XXIII (John XXIII Foundation for Religious Studies) in Bologna, especially Enrico Galavotti, Alberto Melloni, Giuseppe Ruggieri, Federico Ruozzi, and Silvia Scatena. In Bologna, other friends have given me ideas and suggestions at the journal *Il Regno* and the Catholic publishing company Edizioni Dehoniane. In Italy, Fr. Giovanni Cereti; Paolo Gamberini, SJ; Marcello Neri; Serena Noceti; the

Ecumenical Monastic Community of Bose and the Monastery of Camaldoli continue to be generous sources of ideas and friendship.

I am really grateful to Michael Gibson of Fortress Press for the encouragement he gave me in this project, which helped me look back at a very fruitful period of studies and, especially, of encounters. Here in America, other indispensable groups for the continuing reflection on Vatican II have been the "Vatican II Studies" and "Ecclesiological Investigations" groups at the American Academy of Religion. In these groups and beyond them, I would like to thank here Kevin Ahern; John Baldovin, SJ; Christopher Bellitto; Hans Christoffersen; James Coriden; Kathleen Cummings; Peter De Mey; Richard Gaillardetz; James L. Heft, SM; Cathleen Kaveny, James Keenan, SJ; Hervé Legrand, OP; Gerard Mannion; John O'Malley, SJ; Mark Massa, SJ; Ormond Rush; David Schultenover, SJ; Maureen Sullivan, OP; and Andrea Vicini, SJ. I thank finally Karen Schenkenfelder, my copy editor, who was very patient with a very impatient author.

This book is dedicated to our son, Gabriel Francis.

Minneapolis
October 11, 2014
Memorial of Saint John XXIII

Publication Credits

Some of the chapters of this book have appeared elsewhere. All of them have been revised and updated for the present book. I wholeheartedly thank the editors and publishers of the journals and books where they appeared originally.

Chapter 2
"Vatican II: The History and the 'Narratives.'" *Theological Studies* 73, no. 4 (December 2012): 749–67.

Chapter 3
"Verfahrensformen und Legitimierungsquellen während des Zweiten Vatikanischen Konzils" [Forms of procedure and sources of legitimacy in the Second Vatican Council]. Pages 187–201 in *Ekklesiologische Alternativen? Monarchischer Papat und Formen kollegialer Kirchenleitung (15.–20. Jahrhundert)*, edited by Bernward Schmidt and Hubert Wolf. Münster: Rhema, 2013.

Chapter 4
"The Post–Council of Basel and the Post–Vatican II Debate." Paper delivered at the American Cusanus Society, 45th International Congress on Medieval Studies, Kalamazoo, MI, May 14, 2010.

Chapter 5
"Sacrosanctum Concilium and the Meaning of Vatican II." *Theological Studies* 71, no. 3 (June 2010): 437–52.

Chapter 6
"The Battle over 'Gaudium et Spes' Then and Now: Dialogue with the Modern World after Vatican II." *Origins* 42, no. 34 (January 31, 2013): 545–51.

Chapter 7
"Il Vaticano II come 'Costituzione' e la 'recezione politica' del concilio" [The political significance of Vatican II and its "constitutional" value]. *Rassegna di Teologia* 50 (2009): 107–22.

Chapter 8
"Vatican II and the Church of the Margins." *Theological Studies* 74, no. 3 (September 2013): 808–18.

Chapter 9
"Is Vatican II Still Relevant?" Pages 7–19 in *Visions of Hope: Emerging Theologians and the Future of the Church*, edited by Kevin Ahern. Maryknoll, NY: Orbis, 2013.

Chapter 10
"The Regulation of Episcopal Conferences since Vatican II." *Japan Mission Journal* 68, no. 2 (Summer 2014): 82–96.

Chapter 11
"Institutions of Episcopal Synodality-Collegiality after Vatican II: The Decree Christus Dominus and the Agenda for Synodality-Collegiality in the 21st Century." *Jurist* 64, no. 2 (2004): 224–46.

Chapter 12
"Concili: Tra testi e contesti" [About Vatican II and women in the church: Councils and postconciliar ages in modern Catholicism]. Pages 75–83 in *Avendo qualcosa da dire: Teologi e teologhe rileggono il Vaticano II*, edited by Marinella Perroni and Hervé Legrand. Milan: San Paolo, 2014.

Chapter 13
"The Future of Vatican II: The Vision of the Council beyond the 'Narratives.'" Pages 7–26 in *Vatican II: A Universal Call to Holiness*, edited by Anthony Ciorra and Michael Higgins. New York: Paulist, 2012.

Chapter 14
"Europe and the Modern World in the Catholic Narrative during the 1960's: Migration, Decolonization and De-Europeanization." Pages 127–39 in *The Heart of Europe: The Power of Faith, Vision and Belonging in European Unification*, edited by Katharina Kunter. Hannover: Wehrhahn, 2011.

Chapter 15
"Cardinal Bernardin's 'Catholic Common Ground' Initiative: Can It Survive Current Political Cultures?" Lecture delivered for the 14th Joseph Cardinal Bernardin Annual Lecture at the University of South Carolina, Columbia, SC, October 7, 2013.

Introduction

Vatican II, Historicity of Theology, and Global Catholicism

This book collects and brings to a unity a series of my studies on Vatican II published in the last decade—a decade that has been quite momentous in the life of the Catholic Church and for the reception of the council. The succession of three popes (John Paul II, Benedict XVI, and Francis) and the first resignation of a pope in the modern era are, in fact, only symptoms of deeper changes in Catholicism and in particular in the debate about Vatican II, the most important event in the history of modern Catholicism after the Council of Trent. In this sense, the fiftieth anniversary of Vatican II (2012–2015) has been not just a celebratory date like previous anniversaries, but a stimulus to renewed attention to that moment of change and reform in a Church that was not expected to change.

For some, not only was Vatican II not supposed to change anything in the Church, but the official debate and doctrinal policy on Vatican II attempted to reinforce the idea that Vatican II was over and done with. For a few years, between 2000 and the election of Francis, Vatican II was treated as a kind of uncomfortable memory. It was uncomfortable for Catholic traditionalists because Vatican II proved that tradition in the Church also means transition. For

1

Catholic radicals, it was uncomfortable because Vatican II reminded them that change in the Church takes time and implies not only dialogue with the world outside, but also mediation and compromise within the Church. This uncomfortable memory of Vatican II was, of course, asymmetric, as the traditionalists quite successfully convinced high-level Church officials of the need to bend the debate on Vatican II toward a "hermeneutic of continuity," forgetting that Benedict XVI in his famous speech of December 22, 2005, spoke of "continuity and reform"—in other words, continuity and discontinuity.

In this sense, it is clear that the transition from Benedict XVI to Francis represents also a transition from one era in the debate on Vatican II to a new era, and not only because of the evident biographical differences between Benedict, the last pope who was at Vatican II, and Jorge Mario Bergoglio, the first pope who was ordained well after Vatican II, in 1969.[1] The event of the resignation of Benedict XVI and the beginning of Francis's pontificate was a practical demonstration of the necessity of the Second Vatican Council for the theological, spiritual, and intellectual viability of Catholicism today. The recentering of the papal office around the episcopal ministry as bishop of Rome, the need to reconsider the functions of the Roman Curia, the emphasis on the Synod of Bishops as part of a more synodal Church, the message on the poor and on a poor Church—all these key elements in the pontificate of Francis are simply unthinkable without Vatican II.

This demonstration of the deep conciliar identity of the Catholic Church happened, since February 2013, with very few explicit mentions of Vatican II. But far from being forgetfulness, Francis's lack or scarcity of direct mentions of Vatican II are part of the

---

1. See Massimo Faggioli, *Pope Francis: Tradition in Transition* (New York: Paulist, 2015).

new direction of the Vatican doctrinal policy about Vatican II (and not only). While the "pope theologian" Benedict XVI embraced the need to lead the debate, Francis leaves to historians and theologians the debate on the council. Benedict imagined a redirection of the reception of Vatican II, while Francis wants to speed up the reception and implementation of the pastoral council.

All this means not only a new start in the life of the Church along the trajectories drawn by Vatican II, an event that for the vast majority of contemporary Catholics happened before they were born. It means also a rediscovery of the profound historical nature of Christianity and of the Catholic Church in particular, and therefore the need for a renewed appreciation of historical theology, of Church history, and of the history of the Christian theological tradition as a fundamental way to understand Christianity.

Among the many changes brought by the papal transition of 2013, this is probably one of the most forgotten. The sensational change of pontificate has attracted attention once again to the protagonists of the council. This is hardly surprising in a mainstream culture that is anything but historically aware and is exclusively focused on the moment. But the present moment in the life of the Church contains enormously significant implications for the future of theological studies and for the role that theological studies can play in the future of Christianity at different levels.

1. The Role of History in the Study of Christianity and Catholicism

The first issue that arises from the alignment between the anniversary of Vatican II and the transition to the first non-European pope concerns methodology in the studies of Christianity and of Catholicism in particular. The twentieth century was the century of the encounter between Catholic theology and historical consciousness.[2] In the last few decades, part of the anti–Vatican II rhetoric has clearly been nourished by an anti-historical surge in the mode of neo-essentialism. There is no doubt that the state of the health of historical theology reflects the health of the memory of Vatican II and its accomplishments and shortcomings.

This is not new to those who remember how long the very possibility of writing a history of the Council of Trent had been a matter of contention in the Church: four centuries, until the beginning of Vatican II. For more than three centuries after the end of the council in 1563, the *acta* of Trent were not available to scholars. The publication of the first scholarly history of Trent had to wait for Hubert Jedin, after World War II;[3] the last volume of the complete edition of the documents of Trent was published only in 2001.[4] Similarly, there is no question that having a long and detailed *History of Vatican II* published just thirty years after the end of the council was unprecedented, and was even considered threatening in some quarters.[5] It is also not a coincidence that the Council of Trent

2. See Peter Hünermann, "Geschichtliches Denken und Reform der Kirche," *Cristianesimo nella Storia* 34, no. 3 (2013): 741–54.

3. See Hubert Jedin, *Geschichte des Konzils von Trient*, 4 vols. (orig. pub. Freiburg im Breisgau: Herder, 1949, 1957, 1970, 1975). English translation of the first two volumes by Ernest Graf, *A History of the Council of Trent* (London: T. Nelson, 1957 and 1961). Jedin's final two volumes were never translated into English.

4. See *Concilium Tridentinum: Diariorum, actorum, epistularum, tractatuum nova collectio*, ed. Görres-Gesellschaft (Freiburg i.B.: Herder, 1901–2001). About the relationship between historians of the councils and ecclesiastical authorities, see the new edition of Paolo Sarpi's *Istoria del Concilio Tridentino*, rev. ed., ed. Corrado Vivanti (Turin: Einaudi, 2011). The Venetian Sarpi's book was published in London in 1619 and immediately condemned to the Index of Prohibited Books.

5. See Giuseppe Alberigo, ed., *Storia del concilio Vaticano II*, 5 vols. (Bologna: Il Mulino; Leuven: Peeters, 1995–2001), published in English as *History of Vatican II*, ed. Joseph Komonchak (Maryknoll, NY: Orbis, 1995–2006). The *Storia del concilio Vaticano II* was published in Italian, English, French, German, Spanish, Portuguese, and Russian. It is often forgotten that the historiographical work on Vatican II fulfilled Paul VI's desire to have the council studied and analyzed with the help of the Archivio del concilio Vaticano II created by his decision immediately after the end of Vatican II. See "L'Archivio Vaticano II (1965–1999): Trentacinque

is being rediscovered precisely at this moment in the history of the reception of Vatican II.[6]

Here the historiographical work on Vatican II provided a sometimes-neglected service to Catholic theology as such at the turn of the twenty-first century. It is useful here to parallel with what Mark Juergensmeyer calls the "sociotheological turn" in religious studies. Juergensmeyer argues that the "sociotheological turn" represents "a third way—a path between reductionism (denying that religion can have any "real" importance) and isolationism (delinking religion from its social milieu)."[7] In a similar way, it can be said that Church history—at least the Church history that engaged Vatican II—represents a third way between "ecclesiastical history" (important for the Church as an institution, mostly in an apologetical attitude) and an "intellectual history of theological ideas" (potentially detached from the impact of theological thinking on the Church as a community, and tendentially uninterested in the institutional-juridical element of the Church).

There is no question that we have witnessed a certain weariness of the classic, nineteenth- to twentieth-century "critical Church history" in these last few years. Church history is perceived to be still too "confessional" for the scholars of religion using the methods of "social studies," and it is perceived as way too "secular" for theologians who think a nonhistorical approach is *the* way to be obedient to the Church. Vatican II—both the historical event and the historiography on Vatican II—disproves that weariness and is a powerful case for Church history as relevant both for the humanities

anni di inventari e pubblicazioni; Intervista a mons. Vincenzo Carbone," in *Centro Vaticano II: Ricerche e documenti*, vol. 1, no. 0 (2000): 42–46.

6. See John W. O'Malley, *Trent: What Happened at the Council* (Cambridge, MA: Belknap Press of Harvard University Press, 2013).

7. See Mark Juergensmayer, "The Sociotheological Turn," *Journal of the American Academy of Religion* (2013): 939–48.

and for theology. A historical approach to theological ideas is one of those instances on which official Catholic culture often forgets the countercultural potential of its own intellectual tradition vis-à-vis our antihistorical, detemporalized, and present-obsessed culture.

2. Vatican II and (Post)Modernity

There is also a second reason that reveals the relevance of reflecting on Vatican II, fifty years after its conclusion and in future perspective. The clash around Vatican II as "continuity" versus "discontinuity" in the Catholic tradition has been completely unfruitful from an intellectual point of view. One of the most notable features of the debate in the last few years has been the reaction against a "traditionalist" reading of Vatican II and especially against the creeping and silent acceptance of this "traditionalist" narrative of Vatican II by Catholic theology and Catholic leadership (including some quarters in the Roman Curia).[8] In other words, in the last few years, it has become more important than ever to monitor the exchanges between the traditionalist, anti–Vatican II milieu on the one side and official Catholicism on the other, in order to estimate the influence of traditionalism on official Catholic doctrinal policy and in order to verify how little mainstream Vatican II theology has penetrated the traditionalist camp.[9] What Alberto Melloni called "the third quest" in the studies on Vatican II during the decade 2003–2013 (between the fortieth and fiftieth anniversaries) gave a clear result in terms of the intellectual achievements of that debate, with the

8. See *Vatikan und Pius-Brüder: Anatomie einer Krise*, ed. Wolfgang Beinert (Freiburg i.B.: Herder, 2009). See also Klaus Schatz, "Ein kirchliches 1789? Zu einer traditionalistischen Sicht auf das Zweite Vatikanum," *Theologie und Philosophie* 88, no. 1 (2013): 47–71.
9. See especially Giovanni Miccoli, *La Chiesa dell'anticoncilio: I tradizionalisti alla riconquista di Roma* (Roma-Bari: Laterza, 2011).

names of Peter Hünermann; John W. O'Malley, SJ; and Christoph Theobald, SJ, standing out above all others.[10]

What is going to be more relevant, in a future perspective of a Catholic historiography that rejects the illusion of self-sufficiency, is the issue of periodization—namely, the position of Vatican II on the issue of modern versus postmodern. Vatican II was undoubtedly a modernizing council, of the Catholic Church and of Catholic theology, as Vatican II tried to come to terms with a modernity condemned during the "long nineteenth century."[11] Less explored is the triangular relationship between Catholic tradition, Vatican II, and postmodern culture. While Vatican II dealt with the huge changes in geopolitics (end of the empires, decolonization, de-Europeanization, and the Cold War), the cultural landscape of Western society after 1975 is affected by changes in "biopolitics" (abortion, contraception, homosexuality, bioethics).[12] In other words, the perception of the postmodern and of its relevance for Catholicism is much more evident today, at fifty years from Vatican II, than when the studies on Vatican II began in the mid-1980s.

Vatican II closes the anti-modern period of Catholic theology and magisterium, but what remains to be investigated is its relationship with postmodernity. A simple answer is, sometimes, to see in Vatican II and in the 1960s of Catholic theology the last breath of a modern world that has been abrogated by postmodernity. In this, the debate on Vatican II raises a serious methodological issue for Catholic culture and Catholic theology in postmodernity: that is, the issue of

---

10. See the introduction to the new edition of the *History of Vatican II* in Italian: Alberto Melloni, "Il Vaticano II e la sua storia: Introduzione alla nuova edizione," in *Storia del concilio Vaticano II*, ed. Giuseppe Alberigo, 2nd ed. (Bologna: Il Mulino, 2012), 1:ix–lvi, esp. 1:xlii–li.
11. John W. O'Malley, *What Happened at Vatican II* (Cambridge, MA: Belknap Press of Harvard University Press, 2008) 53–92.
12. See Stephen Schloesser, "Dancing on the Edge of the Volcano': Biopolitics and What Happened after Vatican II," in *From Vatican II to Pope Francis: Charting a Catholic Future*, ed. Paul Crowley (Maryknoll, NY: Orbis, 2014), 3-26.

the compatibility between understanding Vatican II (and Catholicism in the twentieth century, for that matter) and tending to deconstruct Church history in a series of narrower fields of "Catholic studies" defined by gender, ethnic-national culture, local versus global, etc. It is a legitimate question whether or not understanding Vatican II historically and theologically still needs a general, classical "Church history" kind of approach, which is less and less practiced in academia (both secular and ecclesiastical) for various reasons, without giving up the new methodological insights of postmodern historical and social studies. In other words, the studies on Vatican II are at crossroads where a tradition of historical and theological studies still done with a "universalistic" approach meets a postmodern approach to the subject.[13] But the debate on Vatican II needs more and more to be part of a long-term understanding of Church history and of the history of the ecumenical councils, as is clear from a recent book dedicated to the "idea of reform" in Church history.[14]

The research on Vatican II has made huge steps forward in these last twenty-five years, thanks to the variety of methodologies and approaches: theological history of Vatican II (history of ideas), biographical approach (prosopography of Vatican II), social history of Vatican II (groups of influence, think tanks), history of canon law, history of bureaucracy (of the Roman Curia and of the elites of the Church), history of the mass-media perception and transmission of

13. About this, see Laurie F. Maffly-Kipp, "The Burdens of Church History," *Church History* 82 (June 2013): 353–67.
14. See Christopher M. Bellitto and David Z. Flanagin, eds., *Reassessing Reform: A Historical Investigation into Church Renewal* (Washington, DC: Catholic University of America Press, 2012). *Reassessing Reform* can be read as a Festschrift for a book, in this case Gerhart Ladner's *Idea of Reform: Its Impact on Christian Thought and Action in the Age of the Fathers* (Cambridge, MA: Harvard University Press, 1960), but it has also clear implications for the debate on Vatican II: "The majority of the essays in this volume presume this narrative of *continuity with change* in the idea of reform. . . . The concept of *continuity with change* has implications not only for the medieval and early modern centuries, but also for the debates concerning Vatican II." Bellitto and Flanagin, *Reassessing Reform*, introduction, 9.

the event, and history of the "outsiders" (women of Vatican II, lay people, ecumenical observers, etc.). Church history as a discipline has a lot to learn from other methodologies, and this might well be the key for its survival as a historical discipline in the no-man's-land between historical theology, secular history, and social studies. But the studies on Vatican II also tell us a lot about the need to respect the object of study: an ecumenical council of the Catholic Church.

3. The History of Vatican II and Global Catholicism

A third reason for the importance of Vatican II concerns how a historical understanding of the Church and of theology is related to the global Church. From a theological perspective, the relevance of the historical studies about Vatican II and of historical theology in general also depends on how much of an impact historical thinking can have on the Church as an institution and as a community of believers. Far from being a completely detached discussion that takes place in the ivory tower, the theological and historiographical question on Vatican II has had an impact on the life of the Church. It is difficult to ignore the impact that O'Malley's book *What Happened at Vatican II* had in rescuing the memory of Vatican II.[15] In that year, in 2008, the project for the *History of Vatican II* had been concluded already for a few years (the last volume had been published in 2001), and most "Vatican II Catholics" and theologians considered the legacy of the council in grave danger.[16] Vatican II recovered the historical awareness of Catholic theology; in a similar way, in the most delicate moment in the reception of Vatican II half a century

---

15. O'Malley's *What Happened at Vatican II* has been translated into Italian, French, Spanish, Portuguese, and Polish.
16. About this, see Massimo Faggioli, "Council Vatican II: Bibliographical Overview 2007–2010," *Cristianesimo nella Storia* 32 (2011–12): 755–91; and "Council Vatican II: Bibliographical Survey 2010–2013," *Cristianesimo nella Storia* 24, no. 3 (2013): 927–55.

after its conclusion, historians rescued the council from the grip of an ideological debate fueled in some ecclesiastical quarters by persons interested in taming the council for political-ecclesiastical considerations in the name of an abstract "continuity" and in spite of the basic historical facts about the most important religious event in twentieth-century religious history.

This rescue is important not only because, in the words of Avery Dulles, "True theology must not panic when scholarly inquiry threatens to demolish what had previously been regarded as unassailable truth."[17] The historical dimension of Vatican II and its discontinuities are also necessary to recover the relationship between the council and the global identity of Catholicism. The attempts to de-historicize theology and to submit Vatican II to the ideology of "absolute continuity" lead necessarily to a re-Europeanization of Catholicism, which has become more global than ever. Here is where intellectual debate on theology meets the pastoral dimension.

The event of Vatican II is still having consequences, sometimes at a deep level. The discontinuities introduced by the council still emerge, not only with regard to the Church of the early twentieth century, but also concerning the epochal consequences of the council for the global Church. In the history of the Catholic Church, incidents are many, but events charged with consequences such as Vatican II are few. Vatican II is certainly a uniquely consequential event in the last four centuries of the Church's history.

17. Avery Dulles, *The Craft of Theology* (New York: Crossroad, 1999), 156.

PART I

The Debate on Vatican II in a Catholicism Made Global

1

Fifty Years of Debate on Vatican II

From Paul VI to Francis (1965–2015)

If the history of the conciliar event is necessary for the hermeneutics of Vatican II, also the history of the reception of the council is part of our understanding of it. Every Catholic has developed consciously or unconsciously an historical-theological framework where the position of Vatican II in Church history is located. The interpretation of Vatican II today cannot be disconnected from an interpretation of the history of the interpretations of Vatican II in these last fifty years.

1. Vatican II: Acknowledged, Received, Refused (1965–1970s)

On December 8, 1965, the end of Vatican II meant the return of bishops and theologians from Rome to their local churches, but it did not mean the conclusion of the debates or the end of the Roman Curia's attempt to control the final outcome of the council. This was in contrast to 1564, when not long after the end of the

Council of Trent, Pope Pius IV established the Congregation of the Council in charge of interpreting the decrees of the council and forbade the publication of any glosses or commentaries on them. In 1965, although the final texts of the council had been approved and solemnly promulgated by Pope Paul VI in order to be translated and spread in the Catholic Church, the conclusion of Vatican II did not entail a prohibition on commenting on the final texts. Hence the end of Vatican II did not imply that the Holy See and Roman Curia held a strict monopoly on the interpretation of the council texts.[1] Rather, the first opportunity for theologians to debate the council's final documents was given by a series of commentaries on the texts, published for theologians, priests, seminarians, and religious men and women, and also a broad readership eager to gain more familiarity with the texts of Vatican II.[2]

Of particular interest is that the most important of these commentaries came not from bishops who oversaw the drafting process but from theologians acting during Vatican II as consultants (*periti*) in the official commissions or as private theologians serving their bishops during the preparations for their interventions in the *aula*, the plenary meetings in St. Peter's basilica and in the council commissions. Some of the authors of these commentaries (for example, Yves Congar, Henri de Lubac, Joseph Ratzinger, and Edward Schillebeeckx) became the main characters of the debate about Vatican II from the 1970s on. What is important to note now is the eminently academic background of these

---

1. For a more complete history of the debate on Vatican II, see Massimo Faggioli, *Vatican II: The Battle for Meaning* (New York: Paulist, 2012).
2. For the first studies on the language of the final documents of Vatican II, see *Indices verborum et locutionum Decretorum Concilii Vaticani II*, 11 vols. (Bologna: Istituto per le Scienze Religiose, 1968–1986); Philippe Delhaye, Michel Gueret, and Paul Tombeur, eds., *Concilium Vaticanum II: Concordance, index, listes de fréquence, tables comparatives* (Louvain: CETEDOC, 1974).

commentators—theologians by profession and not always holders of ecclesiastical offices with direct pastoral duties.

In the meantime, the bishops were active on another level of the debate on Vatican II, having committed themselves to initiatives for an ecclesial reception of Vatican II through a significant wave of diocesan and national synods (Austria 1968–1971, the Netherlands 1970, and Germany 1972–1975) and the continental assemblies of bishops (for Latin America, the CELAM convened in Medellín in 1968). Moreover, the theological landscape of the first year of the post–Vatican II period began with a fruitful season of ecumenical dialogues.

This separation of tasks between theologians and bishops is a feature of the debate on Vatican II and a marker of post–Vatican II Catholicism, at least until the end of the pontificate of John Paul II. He acted as the last and only guarantee for Vatican II, sometimes in a rather nominalistic yet unequivocal intention to receive the legacy of the council. John Paul II revisited in a creative way some crucial teachings of Vatican II, such as, for example, ecumenism, in his encyclical *Ut Unum Sint* (1995) and interreligious dialogue beginning with the World Day of Prayer in Assisi (1986) and in his travels, especially in the Middle East. In contrast, the role of the bishops and of the national bishops' conferences in the interpretation of Vatican II in the life of the Church was reduced under John Paul II. A more significant and clearer change happened in April 2005 with the election of Benedict XVI, who as cardinal prefect for the Congregation for the Doctrine of the Faith (1981–2005) had been a powerful interpreter of Vatican II and not a mere enforcer of John Paul II's doctrinal policies. An analysis not only of Benedict's famous speech to the Roman Curia of December 22, 2005, but especially of the most important decisions of Benedict XVI is essential in order to understand the change happened in the approach of the papacy to Vatican II with the conclave of 2005.

The main commentaries on the final documents of the council represented an attempt to cast light on the deeper meaning of the texts against the background of the history of the debate, and to elaborate hypotheses on the Catholic Church's path after Vatican II. In the very first years after the council, the "ideological" spectrum of Catholic theologians on Vatican II seemed to be unanimous in their enthusiastic acceptance of the final documents and their view of the novelty of Vatican II, for example in ecclesiology, liturgy, biblical revival, ecumenism, religious freedom, and interreligious relations. The tensions between the "letter" and "spirit" of Vatican II did not play much of a role at that time, and neither did the supposed tension between the hermeneutics of "continuity" with the whole Catholic tradition and the awareness of a "discontinuity" from Catholicism of the past, especially of the "long nineteenth century" from Pius IX to Pius XII.[3]

Nevertheless, behind the acceptance of Vatican II as a major turning point, even in the ranks of theologians of the so-called majority, the nuances of how to read Vatican II—by applying, receiving, or interpreting it—could not conceal important differences. The focus on nuances of *how* to read could not conceal differences in thoughts about the content. That kind of theological unanimity about Vatican II, arising from the "moral unanimity" Paul VI sought for the approval of the final documents, would not last. Toward the end of the council, the debate concerning the content and the role of the pastoral constitution *Gaudium et Spes* revealed the division within twentieth-century theologians between the neo-

---

3. John W. O'Malley, *What Happened at Vatican II* (Cambridge, MA: Belknap Press of Harvard University Press, 2008) 53–92.

Augustinians (Daniélou, de Lubac, Ratzinger, von Balthasar) and the neo-Thomists (Chenu, Congar, Rahner, Lonergan, Schillebeeckx).[4]

The foundation of the journal *Concilium* in 1964 represented the most notable attempt to spread the message of Vatican II by a group of scholars representing the vast majority at Vatican II (Hans Küng, Yves Congar, Karl Rahner, Edward Schillebeeckx). By 1970, the group had already had important defections (Henri de Lubac, Hans Urs von Balthasar, Joseph Ratzinger), signaling a rupture in the theologians' attitude toward Vatican II. A new international review, *Communio*, was founded in 1972 by Joseph Ratzinger (elected Pope Benedict XVI in 2005), Hans Urs von Balthasar, and Henri de Lubac as an attempt to offset the progressive Dutch-based journal *Concilium* and to "scan the turmoil and confusion of battling ideologies and the clash of philosophies of life at the present day."[5]

The impact of 1968, a politically intense year around the world, on the Catholic Church and Paul VI's encyclical *Humanae Vitae* (1968) had its toll on the reception of Vatican II and produced the first revisions of the council's interpretations, inaugurating less enthusiastic and more wary views of the council. These revisions were also a way of reading the council that had more to do with ideological standpoints than with the history of theology and Church history. On one hand, the controversies of the early seventies for the Catholic Church did not bring together again the theologians of Vatican II, but contributed to an increasing rift between the interpretations of Vatican II. In particular, Paul VI's final defeat in drafting *Lex Ecclesiae Fundamentalis* (Fundamental Church Law), which tried to canonize a narrow ecclesiological interpretation of

---

4. See Joseph Komonchak, "Augustine, Aquinas, or the Gospel *sine glossa*? Divisions over *Gaudium et Spes*," in *Unfinished Journey: The Church 40 Years after Vatican II*, ed. John Wilkins (London: Bloomsbury, 2004), 102–118.

5. Hans Urs von Balthasar, "*Communio*—a Program," *Communio* 1 (1972): 3–12.

Vatican II, made the Holy See more and more wary toward some implementations of Vatican II. The debates on the need for this Fundamental Church Law between 1965 and the mid-1970s (a law that was never promulgated but was "recycled" in many parts of the 1983 Code of Canon Law) showed the variety of interpretations of Vatican II present inside the Roman Curia and within the former "progressive" majority at the council.

The former "conservative" minority at the council proved more coherent in its fight against Vatican II. The small sect created by Monsignor Marcel Lefebvre in 1970, the Society of Saint Pius X, represented quite effectively the awkward (to say the least) features of a contemporary Catholicism deliberately rejecting Vatican II and attached to a premodern theological culture and antidemocratic political worldview.[6] The excommunication of Monsignor Lefebvre in 1988 did not have significant effects on the debate about Vatican II, but at the beginning of 2009, Benedict XVI's lifting of the excommunications of the four bishops ordained by Lefebvre in 1988 cast significant light on a veiled yet very active rift within European and North American Catholicism concerning the role of Vatican II. On the other hand, the issue of modernity in Catholicism was going to be part of the most important pontificate in the post–Vatican II period. John Paul II's election in 1978 unleashed a new impulse for the reception of Vatican II by a bishop of Rome who, as bishop of Krakow, had been very active at Vatican II in the commission for the drafting of the pastoral constitution *Gaudium et Spes* and later as the author of a bulky commentary on Vatican II.[7]

---

6. See Marcel Lefebvre, *J'accuse le Concile!* (Paris: Clovis, 1976).
7. See Karol Wojtyla (Pope John Paul II), *U podstaw odnowy: Studium o realizacji Vaticanum II* (Krakow: Polskie Towarzystwa Teologicznego, 1972).

2. Vatican II Celebrated and Enforced (1980s–1990s)

In the 1980s and 1990s, the debate on Vatican II focused less on the contributions from academia and began to become more influenced by the doctrinal policy of the Holy See, especially by Pope John Paul II and Cardinal Joseph Ratzinger, prefect of the Congregation for the Doctrine of the Faith (appointed in 1981). Both were first-rank participants at Vatican II—the first a prominent bishop from Poland (the most Catholic country in the Soviet-controlled Eastern European bloc), and the second a theological counselor of Cardinal Frings of Cologne (one of the most important German bishops and a courageous critic of the Roman Curia during the debates on the floor of Saint Peter). These two men shaped a complex and sometimes contradictory Vatican policy toward the heritage of the council and its role for contemporary Catholicism.

After the theological interpretation of Vatican II that took place in the recodification of canon law, which led to the Code of 1983,[8] John Paul II convened an extraordinary assembly of the Synod of Bishops in 1985 on the twentieth anniversary of the conclusion of the council to overcome polarization and bring about greater consensus. The 1985 Extraordinary Synod of Bishops and its *Final Report* provided the debate with some guidelines for the interpretation of the council, without questioning the riches of Vatican II or its key role for the future of the Catholic Church. The synod's *Final Report* of 1985 affirmed that "the Council is a legitimate and valid expression and interpretation of the deposit of faith as it is found in Sacred Scripture and in the living tradition of the Church. Therefore we are determined to progress further along the path indicated to us by the Council." The synod was clear in recognizing the "deficiencies and

---

8. See Eugenio Corecco, "Aspects of the Reception of Vatican II in the Code of Canon Law," in *The Reception of Vatican II*, ed. Giuseppe Alberigo, Jean-Pierre Jossua, and Joseph Komonchak (Washington, DC: Catholic University of America Press, 1985), 249–96.

difficulties in the acceptance of the Council. In truth, there certainly have also been shadows in the post–council period, in part due to an incomplete understanding and application of the Council, in part to other causes. However, in no way can it be affirmed that everything which took place after the Council was caused by the Council."

Concerning the issue of how to interpret Vatican II, the 1985 synod was resolute in explaining that "it is not licit to separate the pastoral character from the doctrinal vigor of the documents. In the same way, it is not legitimate to separate the spirit and the letter of the Council." As for the relationships between the documents of Vatican II, the synod did not establish a clear hierarchy, even if "special attention must be paid to the four major Constitutions of the Council, which contain the interpretative key for the other Decrees and Declarations."

The synod pointed out the fact that "the theological interpretation of the conciliar doctrine must show attention to all the documents, in themselves and in their close inter-relationship, in such a way that the integral meaning of the Council's affirmations—often very complex—might be understood and expressed." As for the "continuity-discontinuity" issue, the *Final Report* did not take a position for or against theological or historiographical "schools," but reaffirmed the complex relationship between tradition and transition in Catholic theology.[9]

John Paul II's complex and sometimes contradictory orientation toward Vatican II, his decision to convene the Synod of 1985, and the overall result of the synod for the state of the debate on Vatican II were somehow overshadowed by *The Ratzinger Report*, timed to be published for the opening of the synod and aimed at exerting pressure on the bishops and on public opinion, in order to make

9. See *The Final Report of the 1985 Extraordinary Synod* (Washington, DC: National Conference of Catholic Bishops, 1986).

a case for rethinking the approach to Vatican II and to point out the responsibility of Vatican II in the crisis of post–Vatican II Catholicism.[10] However, the Synod of 1985 provided theologians and historians with the opportunity to reflect on the reception of Vatican II twenty years after its conclusion. The publication of important collections of studies between 1985 and 1987 showed an obvious plurality of opinions toward Vatican II and some differences between bishops and scholars, but not necessarily an unyielding tension and opposition between different hermeneutics of Vatican II.[11]

At the same time, the doctrinal policy of the Holy See toward some key issues of Vatican II, such as ecclesiology, began unfolding from the mid-1980s on, both through the Congregation for the Doctrine of the Faith and the International Theological Commission of the Holy See. The Congregation for the Doctrine of the Faith issued a new profession of faith (March 1, 1989) for the faithful who were called to exercise an office in the name of the Church, such as vicars general, episcopal vicars, rectors of a seminary, professors of theology and philosophy in seminaries and Catholic universities, and superiors in clerical religious institutes and societies of apostolic life. The letter to the bishops about the "ecclesiology of communion" (*Communionis Notio*, May 28, 1992), and the "declaration on the unicity and salvific universality of Jesus Christ and the Church" about the relationship between Christ, the Church, and the non-

---

10. Joseph Cardinal Ratzinger with Vittorio Messori, *The Ratzinger Report: An Exclusive Interview on the State of the Church*, trans. Salvator Attanasio and Graham Harrison (San Francisco: Ignatius, 1985).

11. See Alberic Stacpoole, ed., *Vatican II Revisited: By Those Who Were There* (Minneapolis: Winston, 1986); Alberigo et al., *The Reception of Vatican II*; Norbert Greinacher and Hans Küng, eds., *Katholische Kirche, wohin? Wider den Verrat am Konzil* (Munich: Piper, 1986); Timothy E. O'Connell, ed., *Vatican II and Its Documents: An American Reappraisal* (Wilmington Michael Glazier, 1986); René Latourelle, ed., *Vatican II: Assessment and Perspectives: Twenty-five Years After (1962–1987)*, 3 vols. (New York: Paulist, 1988–89); Lucien Richard with Daniel T. Harrington and John W. O'Malley, *Vatican II, the Unfinished Agenda: A Look to the Future* (New York: Paulist, 1987).

Christian religions (*Dominus Iesus*, August 6, 2000) marked two other important steps in the Roman reception of Vatican II. From the standpoint of the post–Vatican II governance of the Catholic Church, John Paul II's apostolic constitution *Apostolos Suos* (May 21, 1998) on the status and authority of episcopal conferences reinforced one of the basic assumptions of the International Theological Commission chaired by Cardinal Ratzinger—that is, the need to scale back some aspects of the post–Vatican II decentralization and empowerment of national bishops' conferences. It seemed that power was being reclaimed by the Church's head in Rome at the expense of the Church's body throughout the world.

3. Vatican II Historicized (1990s–2000s)

Notwithstanding the pressure of John Paul II's Vatican doctrinal policy on Catholic theologians, the most important wave of studies and research on Vatican II began in the late 1980s and early 1990s. In an international conference at the Centre Sèvres in Paris in December 1988, Giuseppe Alberigo started the enterprise that had its conclusion in 2001 with the five-volume *History of Vatican II*, subsequently published in seven languages.[12] Employing as a point of departure the first sources edited by Monsignor Vincenzo Carbone in the *Acta et Documenta* and *Acta Synodalia*,[13] the first commentaries[14] and

---

12. Giuseppe Alberigo, ed., *History of Vatican II*, 5 vols., English version ed. Joseph A. Komonchak (Maryknoll, NY: Orbis, 1995–2006), also published in Italian, French, German, Spanish, Portuguese, and Russian.

13. The official documents of the governing bodies of Vatican II (commissions, plenary assemblies) and of the participants were published in *Acta et documenta Concilio Oecumenico Vaticano II apparando,* series I, *Antepraeparatoria* (Vatican City: Libreria Editrice Vaticana, 1960–61); series II, *Praeparatoria* (Vatican City: Libreria Editrice Vaticana, 1964–94); *Acta Synodalia Sacrosancti Concilii Oecumenici Vaticani II* (Vatican City: Libreria Editrice Vaticana, 1970–99).

14. *Das Zweite Vatikanische Konzil: Konstitutionen, Dekrete und Erklärungen lateinisch und deutsch Kommentare,* Lexikon für Theologie und Kirche, 3 vols. (Freiburg i.B.: Herder, 1966–68), trans. Lalit Adolphus, Kevin Smyth, and Richard Strachan as Herbert Vorgrimler, ed., *Commentary*

historical-critical studies of the texts,[15] journalistic accounts, personal memoirs, and sociological approaches to the event of Vatican II,[16] an international network of scholars (theologians and historians from Europe, North America, and Latin America all working together) took the first steps toward a comprehensive history of Vatican II. This *History of Vatican II* aimed not at a new series of commentaries on the final documents, but at a scholarly reconstruction of the history of the council as historical event in a multivolume work, in a parallel yet independent way from some important syntheses[17] and proceedings of international conferences on Vatican II which took place after the Extraordinary Synod of 1985.[18]

on the Documents of Vatican II, 5 vols. (London: Burns & Oates, New York: Herder & Herder, 1967–69).

15. See Giuseppe Alberigo and Franca Magistretti, *Constitutionis dogmaticae Lumen Gentium Synopsis historica* (Bologna: Istituto per le scienze religiose, 1975); Antonio Acerbi, *Due ecclesiologie: ecclesiologia giuridica ed ecclesiologia di comunione nella "Lumen gentium"* (Bologna: EDB, 1975).

16. Rock Caporale, *Vatican II: Last of the Councils*, foreword by John J. Wright (Baltimore: Helicon, 1964); Giuseppe Caprile, *Il Concilio Vaticano II*, 5 vols. (Rome: Edizioni La Civiltà Cattolica, 1966–68); Yves Congar, *Vatican II: Le concile au jour le jour*, 4 vols. (Paris : Cerf, 1963–66); Henri Fesquet, *Le journal du Concile* (Forcalquier : Morel, 1966); René Laurentin, *L'Enjeu du Concile* (Paris: Seuil, 1962); Laurentin, *Bilan du Concile Vatican II* (Paris: Seuil, 1967); René Rouquette, *La fin d'une chrétienté: Chroniques*, 2 vols. (Paris: Cerf, 1968); Xavier Rynne, *Letters from Vatican City: Vatican Council II (First Session); Background and Debates* (New York: Farrar, Straus & Company, 1963); Rynne, *The Second Session* (New York: Farrar, Straus & Company, 1964); Rynne, *The Third Session* (New York: Farrar, Straus & Company, 1965); Rynne, *The Fourth Session* (New York: Farrar, Straus & Company, 1966); a revised version of Rynne's earlier books covering the four sessions of Vatican Council II, *Vatican Council II* (Maryknoll, NY: Orbis, 1999); Antoine Wenger, *Vatican II*, 4 vols. (Paris: Centurion, 1963–66); Ralph Wiltgen, *The Rhine Flows into the Tiber* (New York: Hawthorn, 1967; Rockford, IL: Tan, 1985).

17. See the synthesis by René Aubert, *The Church in a Secularised Society* (London: Darton, Longman & Todd, 1978), and by Otto Hermann Pesch, *Das Zweite Vatikanische Konzil, 1962–1965: Vorgeschichte, Verlauf, Ergebnisse, Nachgeschichte* (Würzburg: Echter, 1993).

18. See *Le Deuxième concile du Vatican (1959–1965)* (Rome: École française de Rome, 1989); Elmar Klinger and Klaus Wittstadt, eds., *Glaube im Prozess: Christsein nach dem II. Vatikanum; Für Karl Rahner* (Freiburg i.B.: Herder, 1984); René Latourelle, ed., *Vatican II: Assessment and Perspectives; Twenty-Five Years After (1962–1987)* (New York: Paulist, 1988–89); Wolfgang Weiss, ed., *Zeugnis und Dialog: die Katholische Kirche in der neuzeitlichen Welt und das II. Vatikanische Konzil* (Würzburg: Echter, 1996).

The *History of Vatican II* represented a major scholarly and historiographical exploration of the debate on Vatican II. On one side, the undertaking, coordinated by Giuseppe Alberigo and the John XXIII Foundation for Religious Studies in Bologna, called for a major effort in the search for undiscovered and unused archives of primary sources all over the world and in gaining access to the official sources (unpublished sources such as the acts of the preparatory phase, acts of the council commissions and committees, and reports and letters between the council's various bodies), which the Holy See held in the Archive of Vatican II.[19] On the other side, the international and multidisciplinary character of the team provided the debate on Vatican II with many new questions, issues, and places for comparing perspectives, results, and paths of research.[20] The main hermeneutical principles that guided Alberigo in the enterprise were the idea of the council as an "event," John XXIII's intention in announcing the council, the "pastoral" nature of Vatican II, *aggiornamento* as the main goal of the council, and the importance of compromise in understanding the council's final documents.[21]

The five-volume *History of Vatican II* was surrounded and followed by many other volumes produced and published by the same international team, focusing on individual constitutions and decrees and on specific issues debated at the council. But the most important result was the spreading of a debate and the enlivening of the international debate on Vatican II in Latin America,[22] Europe,[23]

---

19. See Massimo Faggioli and Giovanni Turbanti, *Il concilio inedito: Fonti del Vaticano II* (Bologna: Il Mulino, 2001).

20. See Joseph Famerée, "Vers un histoire du Concile Vatican II," *Revue d'Histoire Ecclesiastique* 89 (1994): 638–41; Alois Greiler, "Ein Internationales Forschungsprojekt zur Geschichte des Zweitens Vatikanums," in *Zeugnis und Dialog: die Katholische Kirche in der neuzeitlichen Welt und das II. Vatikanische Konzil* (Würzburg: Echter, 1996), 571–78.

21. See Giuseppe Alberigo, "Criteri ermeneutici per una storia del Vaticano II," in *Il Vaticano II fra attese e celebrazione*, ed. Giuseppe Alberigo (Bologna: Il Mulino, 1995), 12–23, also in Giuseppe Alberigo, *Transizione epocale: Studi sul concilio Vaticano II* (Bologna: Il Mulino, 2009), 29–45.

America,[24] and all over the world,[25] in journals and reviews and among theologians, historians, and lay women and men.

Immediately after the completion of the *History of Vatican II*, Peter Hünermann, the theologian from Tübingen, launched another major project aimed at a new series of commentaries on the final documents of Vatican II intended to replace the three-volume *Zweite Vatikanische Konzil, Dokumente und Kommentare* published in the series *Lexicon für Theologie und Kirche* between 1966 and 1968. In contrast to the *History of Vatican II*, the new five-volume *Kommentar zum Zweiten Vatikanischen Konzil* was a project entirely funded and produced in the German-speaking world,[26] but aimed at providing the international theological community with a major contribution on the council forty years after its end, a theological contribution based on the results of the historical research on Vatican II in the previous two decades.

22. See José Oscar Beozzo, ed., *Cristianismo e iglesias de America Latina en vísperas del Vaticano II* (San José, Costa Rica: Cehila, 1992); Beozzo, *A Igreja do Brasil no Concílio Vaticano II (1959–1965)* (São Paulo and Rio de Janeiro: Paulinas, 2005).

23. See Franz-Xaver Kaufmann and Arnold Zingerle, eds., *Vatikanum II und Modernisierung: Historische, theologische und soziologische Perspektiven* (Paderborn: Schöningh, 1996); Peter Hünermann, ed., *Das II. Vatikanum. Christlicher Glaube im Horizont globaler Modernisierung: Einleitungsfragen* (Paderborn: Schöningh, 1998); Hubert Wolf, ed., *Die deutschsprachigen Länder und das II. Vatikanum* (Paderborn: Schöningh, 2000).

24. See, for example, Joseph A. Komonchak, "Vatican II as Ecumenical Council," in *Commonweal*, November 22, 2002, and the debate between Dulles and O'Malley in *America* in 2003: Avery Dulles, "Vatican II: The Myth and the Reality," and John W. O'Malley, "The Style of Vatican II," *America*, February 24, 2003; Avery Dulles, "Vatican II: Substantive Teaching," and John W. O'Malley, "Vatican II: Official Norms," *America*, March 31, 2003.

25. See, for example, Ormond Rush, *Still Interpreting Vatican II: Some Hermeneutical Principles* (New York: Paulist, 2004).

26. Peter Hünermann and Bernd Jochen Hilberath, eds., *Herders theologischer Kommentar zum Zweiten Vatikanischen Konzil*, 5 vols., (Freiburg i.B.: Herder, 2004–06); Peter Hünermann, ed., *Das Zweite Vatikanische Konzil und die Zeichen der Zeit heute* (Freiburg i.B.: Herder, 2006).

4. The Polemics against the Historiography of Vatican II

The fortieth anniversary of the conclusion of Vatican II in 2005 did not have a significant impact on the theological debate surrounding the council. Rather, the year was marked by the death of John Paul II, the conclave, and the election of Benedict XVI. But the death of John Paul II—the last bishop participant at council Vatican II to be elected bishop of Rome—and the election of Benedict XVI constituted undoubtedly two important elements in the broad theological and ecclesiastical landscape of the debate on Vatican II in the last few years.

The change of pontificate also nourished the journalistic and political dispute about Vatican II, its history, and its legacy, and not only the historiographical and theological debate. Since Benedict XVI's election on April 19 2005, during the fortieth anniversary of the end of Vatican II, his teachings increasingly renewed both ecclesiastical and public scrutiny on the council, bound up with the question about the legacy of the "Vatican II era" in the vitality of the contemporary Catholic Church and its impact on the Western world.

After Benedict XVI's address to the Roman Curia in December 2005, the Vatican document (released June 29, 2007) on the ecclesiology and interpretation of "subsistit in," subsists in (the dogmatic constitution on the Church *Lumen Gentium*, n. 8) contributed to the feeling of a new age. Benedict XVI's teachings have refired a debate about the long-taken-for-granted role of the council in the Catholic Church, leaving the impression of a Roman "attitude review" (if not policy review) of the council.

That feeling was strengthened between 2005 and 2007, when some public discussions in Rome brought to light a long-lasting dispute with the *History of Vatican II*. The so-called Bologna school and its director Giuseppe Alberigo were accused of writing the history of the Council not on the basis of the final documents voted for by the conciliar fathers and approved by the pope, but on the basis of an ideologically biased and "modernist" interpretation of the "spirit of Vatican II." After John Paul II's death, the conservative reckoning of the Bologna school appeared more and more popular inside some conservative think tanks and journalistic milieus, yet the conservatives' ability to provide a constructive contribution to the historiography of Vatican II goes no further than some harsh and biased book reviews.[27]

In any case, the polemics proved somewhat useful, as they sparked a new interest in the hermeneutics of Vatican II by echoing an argument on the hermeneutics of the council rooted in its final "documents" versus in its "spirit," and by making room for a new series of studies focusing on "what happened at Vatican II."[28] At the fortieth anniversary of the council in 2005, it had become clear that the historiography on Vatican II had already brought significant results and made a significant step from the state of the art on the council in the 1980s, the decade that encompasses two major decisions for the reception of Vatican II: the new Code of Canon Law (1983) and the Extraordinary Synod of Bishops on Vatican II (1985). It was also clear that the speech of Benedict XVI in December 22, 2005, was also a response to the new contributions to the debate and the attempt to reconcile hermeneutics—in particular, a response to the historicizing made by the *History of Vatican II* in five volumes edited by Giuseppe Alberigo and the new German commentary (also

27. See Agostino Marchetto, *Il Concilio ecumenico Vaticano II: Contrappunto per la sua storia* (Vatican City: Libreria Editrice Vaticana, 2005).

28. See Christoph Theobald, ed., *Vatican II sous le regard des historiens* (Paris: Médiasèvres, 2006); Raymond F. Bulman and Frederick J. Parrella, eds., *From Trent to Vatican II: Historical and Theological Investigations* (Oxford: Oxford University Press, 2006); David G. Schultenover, ed., *Vatican II: Did Anything Happen?* (London: Bloomsbury, 2007); O'Malley, *What Happened at Vatican II*. For a reductionist interpretation of the council, see Matthew L. Lamb and Matthew Levering, eds., *Vatican II: Renewal within Tradition* (Oxford: Oxford University Press, 2008).

in five volumes) edited by Peter Hünermann.[29] The pope's speech was not an isolated episode: it had been preceded, in early December 2005, by an article in *L'Osservatore Romano* of Karl Josef Becker, SJ, professor at the Pontifical Gregorian University and consultant of the Roman Curia, on conciliar hermeneutics and the ecclesiology of *Lumen Gentium*.[30]

From 2005 onward, the trend toward a reopening of the debate hermeneutic by Benedict XVI called into question what had been acquired, especially in terms of methodology of the historical and theological studies on the Second Vatican Council, by the international scientific community over the last fifteen years at least. Benedict XVI also started to programmatically remove from the doctrinal policy of the Vatican those openings that allowed Catholic theologians not to speak of a complete repudiation of Vatican II by John Paul II.[31]

The Regensburg speech on September 12, 2006, although not directly focused on the conciliar hermeneutics, revealed Benedict XVI's parameters for the relationship of Christianity and the Catholic Church with its Greek and European heritage. What emerged more and more obviously was a growing re-Europeanization of the Church of Benedict XVI, in a clear opposition to the theology of Vatican II as a council of the global Catholic Church, especially of the non-European churches, for which the role of the Second Vatican

---

29. Especially Peter Hünermann, "Der Text: Werden—Gestalt—Bedeutung; Eine Hermeneutische Reflexion," in *Herders Theologischer Kommentar zum Zweiten Vatikanischen Konzil* (Freiburg i.B.: Herder, 2005), 5:5–101. The implicit but clear criticism by Benedict XVI of the five-volume *Kommentar* has been confirmed by Peter Hünermann himself in Margit Eckholt and Regina Heyder, eds., *"In der Freiheit des Geistes leben": Peter Hünermann im Gespräch* (Ostfildern: Matthias-Grünewald, 2010).

30. See Karl Josef Becker, SI, "Subsistit in" [*Lumen Gentium*, 8], in *L'Osservatore Romano*, December 5–6, 2005, pp. 1, 6–7.

31. See Pierre Bordeyne and Laurent Villemin, eds., *Le concile et la théologie: Perspectives pour le XXIe siècle* (Paris: Cerf, 2006).

Council is more a condition of existence for their *Sitz im Leben* than an argument or rhetoric of revenge against internal enemies.

The leading role of Benedict XVI's interpretation thus reopened the debate on the council, sometimes providing support for the criticisms against the historicizing of Vatican II. It even contributed increasingly to his being read as the pope of the *revanche* against the council—in spite of his having been a theologian of Vatican II.

5. Vatican II and Francis, the First Pope of the Postconciliar Church

From 2005 onward, the polarity between continuity and reform on the one extreme and discontinuity and rupture on the other became also a mantra in the Catholic Church, especially at the level of theological studies and seminaries, but not only at that level. The argument of "continuity with the tradition of the council," which had been presented at the beginning as an argument against the Lefebvrian thesis of Vatican II as a rupture with the Catholic tradition, soon showed the real objectives of the controversy according to the interpreters of that speech of Benedict XVI. Even in a portion of the Catholic Church far away from the dome of Saint Peter's, the obvious implication is a mutual exclusivity of the two terms "continuity vs. discontuinuity" and the "Catholicity" of the category of continuity with respect to the idea of a discontinuity in the tradition.

But also the life experiences and personality of Pope Benedict XVI played a role in the interpretation of Vatican II, as it did for John Paul II, but in a completely opposite way. The reception of the council by Pope John Paul II was placed in an oblique and transverse opposite to the expectations of academic theology, often surprising for the openings to the papacy *ad extra*. Ratzinger's conciliar hermeneutics developed instead in programmatic contrast with the historiographical consensus on Vatican II and the theological and ecclesial reception of that event, invoking a counterreception that has precise ecclesiastical and ideological referents. The identification of the work of historiography and hermeneutics of Vatican II (especially Giuseppe Alberigo, Peter Hünermann, and John O'Malley) with the idea of "rupture" led in some cases to a *damnatio* of the council itself. In fact, in the clichés of the curiae of ecclesiastical power (the Roman Curia and the diocesan *curiae* worldwide), the Ratzingerian interpretation of the council lends itself perfectly to feed, especially in the West and in the North American continent, the theological side of the "culture wars" that envelops the discourse on the role of religion in American society and politics. The phenomenon of "political conversions" to Catholicism in North America is not immune from this debate.[32]

But it is also clear that the Second Vatican Council has become more and more a fundamental element—in the negative—for the culture of nostalgia in Western Catholicism, a theological tradition downgraded sometimes as the home of choice for conservative thought. The thought of Benedict XVI has been used by the feeling of intransigents and nostalgics in order to launch a takeover bid on the Church of Rome.[33] In this sense, it is not a coincidence that the focus of interpretation of the council by Pope Benedict XVI is obviously moved by "political-ecclesiastical considerations."[34]

---

32. See Joseph P. Chinnici, "An Historian's Creed and the Emergence of Postconciliar Culture Wars," *Catholic Historical Review* 94 (2008): 219–44; Joseph P. Chinnici, "Reception of Vatican II in the United States," *Theological Studies* 64, no. 3 (2003): 461–94.

33. Especially Roberto de Mattei, *Il Concilio Vaticano II: Una storia mai raccontata* (Turin: Lindau, 2010), translated in other languages.

34. Lieven Boeve, "'La vraie réception de Vatican II n'a pas encore commencé': Joseph Ratzinger, Révélation et autorité de Vatican II," in *L'autorité et les autorités: L'herméneutique théologique de Vatican II,* ed. Gilles Routhier and Guy Jobin (Paris: Cerf, 2010), 13–50, esp. 28.

Not surprisingly, it was noteworthy under Pope Benedict to see a growing divergence between the curial mantras about Vatican II and the most recent contributions to the debate on the historicity and history of the council, on the dynamics of interpretation between the various final documents of the council in the light of their history,[35] on the reception of Vatican II at the level of Church institutions and canon law,[36] and on the relationship between the authority of the conciliar texts and authority in the Church. The public debate in the Church among theologians and the bishops seemed to have been replaced by a creeping schism created by the ones who see in the interpretation of Vatican II a sticking point now more symbolic than textual: from this point of view, we were now well beyond the dialectic of letter versus spirit or event versus documents. No longer just the spirit or the event, but also the same letter and the documents of Vatican II were now under the influence of revisionism and revanchism conducted perhaps even more in the Western peripheries of global Catholicism than in Rome.

The center of gravity of the public debate shifted from theological debate on the Second Vatican Council as a starting point for the reform of the institutions of the Church to an institutional and official hermeneutics, in which the issue of the authority interpreting Vatican II became much more relevant than the issues under interpretation. In this sense, the intuition of Peter Hünermann on the "constitutional character" of the council and its texts has become even more evident since the lifting of the excommunication of the Lefebvrite bishops in January 2009. Benedict's rejection of "Vatican II's constitutional value" was argued by creating an opposition between continuity and discontinuity, reform and rupture, but

---

35. See Christoph Theobald, *La réception du concile Vatican II: Vol. I. Accéder à la source* (Paris: Cerf, 2009).
36. See Ladislas Orsy, *Receiving the Council: Theological and Canonical Insights and Debates* (Collegeville, MN: Liturgical, 2009).

without ever touching the nerve of "traditionalism" and its dangers for the Catholic idea of tradition.[37]

The election of Pope Francis on March 13, 2013, has indubitably changed the landscape of the Catholic Church and especially of the debate on Vatican II. In his first months of pontificate, Pope Francis showed a full and unequivocal reception of Vatican II. This is also thanks to the theological and ecclesial debate on Vatican II, which in these last fifty years never ceased to be part of the real life of the universal Church.

Pope Francis inaugurated a new phase in the reception of Vatican II, and not only for the sudden and complete disappearance of the traditionalist, anti–Vatican II issues from the agenda of Pope Francis. The pontificates of the last seventy years have all been defined (in different measures) by the historical-theological debate in relation to the council: Pius XII failed to reconvene Vatican I and he was the pope most cited in the documents of Vatican II. John XXIII was the convener of the council. Paul VI was explicitly elected to continue the council, which led him to the conclusion at the cost of significant compromises with some of the aspirations that emerged from the council during the council itself. John Paul I was a "second row" council father. John Paul II, the last pope who had been a member of Vatican II, was a key figure of Vatican II and at the same time a stabilizer of the council. Benedict XVI was one of the most important *periti* of Vatican II and as pope and cardinal was the most important theological "reviewer" of the council and its interpretations. Pope Francis does not belong in this line of popes involved in Vatican II for biographical reasons (he was ordained priest in 1969). But there is also the specific heritage of the Catholic Church in Latin America and the legacy of Vatican II for Latin American Catholicism in these

---

37. See Peter Hünermann, ed., *Exkommunikation oder Kommunikation? Der Weg der Kirche nach dem II: Vatikanum und die Pius-Brüder* (Freiburg i.B.: Herder, 2009).

last 50 years. It is clear that the Argentine Jesuit Bergoglio perceives Vatican II as a matter that should not be reinterpreted or restricted, but implemented and expanded.[38]

Many elements that marked the beginning of his pontificate are integral parts of a Vatican II Church. In the words addressed to the people in Saint Peter's Square after the election, in the evening of March 13, 2013, Francis presented himself as the "bishop of Rome." On March 16, in the meeting with journalists, recalling the first moments after the election and the words put to him by Brazilian cardinal Claudio Hummes, Francis claimed to want "a poor Church and for the poor."[39] The Mass of inauguration of the pontificate, March 19, marked a visible difference in terms of liturgical style from that of his predecessor: at the celebration was present, for the first time, the Ecumenical Patriarch Bartholomew of Constantinople, whom Francis would later meet with twice between 2013 and 2014. On March 20, 2013, hearing from the fraternal delegates from other churches and religions, Francis mentioned for the first time the Second Vatican Council and in particular the declaration *Nostra Aetate* (1965) on non-Christian religions.

A core theme of Francis is that of the poor and their role in the Church and in society. Faithful to the intuitions of Vatican II (expressed in only a partial manner in the final documents of the council), Francis speaks to a part of the theological value of spiritual poverty as a condition of accepting the gospel of Jesus Christ; at the same time, he proposes a radical and continuous need for the Church and Christians to be next to the poor, in the sense of existential and economic poverty. This emphasis on social justice is part of Francis's ecclesiology, an ecclesiology of the people of God that has clear

38. About this, see Massimo Faggioli, *Pope Francis: Tradition in Transition* (New York: Paulist, 2015).
39. See also Austen Ivereigh, *The Great Reformer. Francis and the Making of a Radical Pope* (New York: Holt and Company, 2014) 363.

implications also on the level of a more conciliar style and structure of Church government. Francis talks about a greater collegiality with the bishops and synodality at various levels in the Church. A month after the election, on April 13, 2013, Francis created a council of eight cardinals (from various parts of the world, with one Italian member of the Curia) to help him in government of the universal Church and in particular the reform of the Roman Curia. The council of the eight meets regularly every two to three months starting from the meeting of October 1–3, 2013. The Synod of Bishops—created by Paul VI in September 1965 before the Second Vatican Council presented its own proposal in this regard—receives greater attention from Francis than it did from his predecessors. In October 2013, Francis called an extraordinary synod on the family, so that the Catholic Church celebrates the two assemblies of the synod on the same subject in the twelve months between October 2014 and 2015.

Francis also reclaims the role of the papacy in ecumenism opened by John XXIII's decision to create the Secretariat for Christian Unity in 1960, continued by Paul VI's pilgrimage to the Holy Land in January 1964, and expanded by the interreligious sensibility of John Paul II. The reform of the papacy under way with Francis is part of the ecumenical *rapprochement* as well as legacy of the ecclesiological turn of Vatican II. The destinations of Francis's travels indicate a correspondence between the ecclesiological vision of a Church that must go forth to the peripheries and the geopolitics of the pontificate. For Francis, a full reception of Vatican II is an integral part of the Catholic Church as a "world Church." It is not surprising that this new era in the reception of Vatican II coincides with the election of the pope coming "from the end of the world"—as Francis famously said in his first appearance from the loggia balcony of St. Peter's in the evening of March 13, 2013.

Francis's new awareness of the deep consequences of Vatican II is certainly not the end of the debate on Vatican II. The theological method of the council—attention to history, valuation of experience—cannot be renounced. On the plane of lived faith, Catholics worldwide live Vatican II every day, albeit sometimes unconsciously. To choose to celebrate the council fifty years after its opening implies the possibility of becoming more conscious of the theological praxis of the Catholic Church, and also of the questions that were left unresolved by the council and await a response.

2

The History and the "Narratives" of Vatican II

Who controls the past controls the future;
who controls the present controls the past.
—George Orwell[1]

In the development of the Christian theological tradition, history plays a major role—the Christian theological tradition is a history. Consequently, an historical perspective should be fundamental for the hermeneutics of major events that have shaped new teachings of the Church. Instead, in recent times Catholic theology has been tempted to cling to "narratives" instead of "history," especially for the interpretation of Vatican II.[2]

---

1. The "party slogan" in Orwell's novel *1984* (published 1949).
2. This chapter was published originally as "Vatican II: The History and the 'Narratives,'" *Theological Studies* 73, no. 4 (December 2012): 749–67.

1. Memory and Institutional Amnesia in Church History

Vatican II is a complex event from a historical point of view, given its global dimension, its duration, its agenda, and its long-term consequences for the Catholic Church and for our world. But Vatican II is complex also in terms of "institutional memory": memory of an event of the Church that has changed the Church. It is indeed clear that institutional memory is often not the contrary, but instead the companion or other side of institutional amnesia—the need for institutions to forget some aspects of their past in order to maintain integrity and cohesion. However, memory is not always helped by the process of memorialization, that is, the culture of constructing festivities, rituals, monuments, and memorials intended to shape and remind us of our national and political identities around a given interpretation of major events in our recent history.[3]

Even so, after Vatican II, the Catholic Church took unambiguous steps in order to help Catholics remember the council. Paul VI's decision to create the Archive of Vatican II immediately after the conclusion of the council and to make it available to scholars was an act of trust in the ability and the will of theologians and historians to build an institutional memory.[4] Paul VI trusted Monsignor Vincenzo Carbone (former aide of the powerful secretary general of Vatican II, Monsignor Pericle Felici) to collect and publish the proceedings of the plenary congregations celebrated in the Basilica of Saint Peter, the different schemata in the redaction history of each final conciliar document, and the minutes of the conciliar and preconciliar commissions.

---

3. For a very different kind of event, see Harold Marcuse, "Holocaust Memorials: The Emergence of a Genre," *American Historical Review* 115, no. 1 (2010): 53–89.
4. See Vincenzo Carbone, "L'archivio del Concilio Vaticano II," *Archiva Ecclesiae* 34–35 (1991): 57–68.

After the completion of the publication of the *Acta Synodalia*,[5] the recent (in 2002) decision to move that archive within the Vatican Secret Archive to make it even more available to scholars signaled the institution's continuing trust in the community of scholars of Vatican II.[6] This fact is often taken for granted, but it is indeed remarkable, because Vatican II is still changing the Church, and a particular institutional interpretation of the council is still able to influence the effect of the council on the Church. Vatican II was not only a religious event, but also an institutional event, and the "political" implications of the historiography on that event are not quite like other religious events that are less monopolized by the organizational dominance of one center of power that announces the event, manages it, and when it is ended, is in charge of the process of evaluating and concretizing the resolutions of the event.[7]

Usually the starting point for this discussion is Vatican II as an event of Church history that has both a textual dimension and a culture surrounding it—or, in other words, a "letter" and a "spirit," as the existence of both and their relationship has been defined by the Extraordinary Synod of Bishops of 1985.[8] Both these elements

5. *Acta et documenta Concilio Oecumenico Vaticano II apparando*, series I, *Antepraeparatoria* (Vatican City: Typis Polyglottis Vaticanis, 1960–61); series II, *Praeparatoria* (Vatican City: Typis Polyglottis Vaticanis, 1964–94); *Acta Synodalia Sacrosancti Concilii Oecumenici Vaticani II* (Vatican City: Typis Polyglottis Vaticanis, 1970–99).

6. See Sergio Pagano, "Riflessioni sulle fonti archivistiche del concilio Vaticano II: In margine ad una recente pubblicazione," *Cristianesimo nella Storia* 24, no. 3 (2002): 775–812. For the availability of the archive of Vatican II in the Vatican Secret Archives, see the index carefully edited by Piero Doria in "Heritage," *Archivum Secretum Vaticum*, http://www.archiviosegretovaticano.va/en/patrimonio/.

7. See John O'Malley, *What Happened at Vatican II* (Cambridge, MA: Belknap Press of Harvard University Press, 2008), 311.

8. See *The Final Report of the 1985 Extraordinary Synod* (Washington, DC: National Conference of Catholic Bishops, 1986); Avery Dulles, "The Reception of Vatican II at the Extraordinary Synod of 1985," in *The Reception of Vatican II*, ed. Giuseppe Alberigo, Jean-Pierre Jossua, and Joseph A. Komonchak (Washington, DC: Catholic University of America Press, 1987), 349–63; Jean-Marie Tillard, "Final Report of the Last Synod," in *Synod 1985: An Evaluation*, ed. Giuseppe Alberigo and James Provost (Edinburgh: T. & T. Clark, 1986), 64–77.

have to be part of every hermeneutical effort, and the history of the interpretations of Vatican II at fifty years of age has been somewhat marked by this complex relationship between text and context of the council.

Far less explored so far has been the issue of the role of Vatican II as a historical event in the Church's memory-building effort in these last fifty years. In other words, it is now clear that for the Church arises the issue of finding in Vatican II a "usable past" in a rapidly changing world and in an even more rapidly changing and global Catholicism.[9] The imagery, symbols, and data the public discourse in the Church associates with Vatican II are very powerful markers of Vatican II itself, especially for the future generations of Catholics who will not be able to connect directly with the generation of Catholics who lived through the council.

What the Church of today makes of Vatican II depends on what the transmitters of the memory of the council are able and willing to transmit. In the process of reception, the perception of Vatican II as such—the "whole thing"—is no less important, rather more important than the reception of a single document (e.g., the constitution on the Church, *Lumen Gentium*) or of a single passage in a document (e.g., the *subsistit in* in *Lumen Gentium* 8).

What we have seen emerge in these last few decades is a new prominence for narratives about Vatican II and about the shape of contemporary Catholicism that take no account of the historical research on the council produced during this same period. We are

---

9. See William J. Bouwsma, *A Usable Past: Essays in European Cultural History* (Berkeley and Los Angeles: University of California Press, 1990), esp. 421–30 ("The History Teacher as Mediator"). The title of Bouwsma's book derived from Nietzsche's *On the Uses and Disadvantages of History for Life* (*Vom Nutzen und Nachteil der Historie für das Leben*, 1874). About the consequences of the "usable past" for contemporary Church history, see Joseph P. Chinnici, "An Historian's Creed and the Emergence of Postconciliar Culture Wars," *Catholic Historical Review* 94, no. 2 (April 2008): 219–44.

left with narratives innocent of historical studies and even inimical to them.

2. Narrative and Narratives of Vatican II

The concept of narrative is relatively new and comes from linguistics and literary science. Between the 1960s and the 1970s, the works by Tzvetan Todorov and Émile Benveniste, among others, have stressed the distinction between "story" and "discourse" or "narrative," and between the "narrator" and the "recipient of the narration."

Narratology was born as a development of structuralism, whose first principle is that "meaning-making is a rule-governed activity."[10] Narrative is a formal system but also an ideological instrument; it is a way to decode the rules of social communication, but also the effort to read the text not in the context that produced it, but in the context of the consequences supposedly created by the text.

Lately the relevance of the "narrative" has gone beyond the academic study of narrative. In recent times, the pervasiveness of the concept of narrative has changed the way major historical events are offered to the public:

> We are living in the age of the Narrative Turn, an era when narrative is widely celebrated and studied for its ubiquity and importance. Doctors, lawyers, psychologists, business men and women, politicians, and political pundits of all stripes are just a few of the groups who now regard narrative as the Queen of Discourses and an essential component of their work. These groups acknowledge narrative's power to capture certain truths and experiences in ways that other modes of explanation and analysis such as statistics, descriptions, summaries, and reasoning via conceptual abstractions cannot.[11]

10. Robert Scholes and Robert Kellogg, *The Nature of Narrative* (London: Oxford University Press, 1966); Robert Scholes, James Phelan, and Robert Kellogg, *The Nature of Narrative*, 40th anniv. ed., rev. and expanded (Oxford: Oxford University Press, 2006), 287.
11. See Scholes and Kellogg, *The Nature of Narrative*, 285.

Theology has adopted the narrative theory, and in these last few years, narratology has become, especially in the French-speaking world, an important way of theology to understand and transmit the revelation in the Scripture.[12]

Outside the field of theological narratology, the idea of a narrative has imposed itself also when it comes to understanding and explaining what happened at Vatican II and after Vatican II. One of the phenomena typical of these last few decades in the Church of Vatican II has been not only the growing separation and mistrust between theologians and magisterium, but also the gap between Catholic Church historians on one side (and historians of the councils in particular) and theologians, magisterium, and "secular historians" on the other side.[13] But for the understanding of Vatican II, the problem is even more acute in the separation between historians and "narrators."

Usually the macronarratives are identified as the "conservative" and the "liberal" interpretation of Vatican II: the first one embodying the skeptical view of the new openness of the council vis-à-vis modernity and modern world, and the second one advocating a more positive view of the council as a necessary step to unlock Catholic theology from the reaction against modernity that was typical of the nineteenth and early twentieth centuries. In addition, a third narrative might be called "neoconservative" or "neoliberal." But

12. See Jean-Noël Aletti, *L'art de raconter Jésus Christ: L'écriture narrative de l'évangile de Luc* (Paris: Seuil, 1989); *La Bible en récits: L'exégèse biblique à l'heure du lecteur*, ed. Daniel Marguerat (Geneva: Labor et Fides, 2003).

13. About the relationship between Church historians and Catholic theology in the decades before Vatican II and during the council, see Daniele Menozzi and Marina Montacutelli, eds., *Storici e religione nel novecento italiano* (Brescia: Morcelliana, 2011); Giuseppe Alberigo, "Hubert Jedin storiografo (1900–1980)," *Cristianesimo nella Storia* 22, no. 2 (2001): 315–38; and "Concili," in *Dizionario del sapere storico-religioso del Novecento*, ed. Alberto Melloni (Bologna: Il Mulino, 2010), 540–56; Heribert Müller, "Konzilien des 15. Jahrhunderts und Zweites Vatikanisches Konzil: Historiker und Theologen als Wissenschaftler und Zeitgenossen," in *Historie und Leben: Der Historiker als Wissenschaftler und Zeitgenosse; Festschrift für Lothar Gall zum 70. Geburtstag*, ed. Dieter Hein, Klaus Hildebrand, and Andreas Schulz (Munich: Oldenbourg, 2006), 117–35.

behind these macronarratives are other subnarratives that have marked these years of reception of the council. Others have already tried to catalog them, and we will just begin here a work of decoding of the public discourse of and on Catholicism of Vatican II that will be a task for the future historians of the Catholic Church.[14]

A first narrative trying to undermine the legitimacy of the council, which emerged already during Vatican II and is more and more influential in the Church, is the traditionalist narrative of the Lefebvrites, the Society of Saint Pius X founded in 1970 by archbishop Monsignor Marcel Lefebvre (1905–1991), the most famous group that denounces Vatican II as heretical. This narrative sees Vatican II as a product of early-twentieth-century theological "modernism" condemned by Pius X in 1907. This allegedly modernist theology took over Catholic theology and rehabilitated the worst enemies of modern Catholicism: among others, Protestantism, liberalism, communism, and Freemasons. The definition of Vatican II as the ultimate and final moment of early-twentieth-century modernism has almost become, at the beginning of the twenty-first century, common language in the neotraditionalist movement within contemporary Catholicism.[15] The view of Vatican II as the French Revolution in the Church was fundamental in shaping Lefebvre's historical perception of the council, especially for a French bishop, such as Lefebvre, faithful to the idea of a chain of "modern errors" (the sixteenth-century Reformation followed by the

---

14. A few years ago, Peter Steinfels described these tendencies active in American Catholicism: Vatican II as a tragic mistake (ultraconservative narrative), Vatican II misinterpreted and distorted (conservative), Vatican II as the needed change and reconciliation with the world (liberal), and Vatican II as a false revolution (ultraliberal). See Peter Steinfels, *A People Adrift: The Crisis of the Roman Catholic Church in America* (New York: Simon & Schuster, 2003), 32–39.

15. For an example of such a mind-set, see Dominique Bourmaud, *Cent ans de modernisme: Généalogie du concile Vatican II* (Étampes: Clovis, 2003), trans. Brian Sudlow and Anne Marie Temple as *One Hundred Years of Modernism: A History of Modernism, Aristotle to the Second Vatican Council,* (Kansas City, MO: Angelus, 2006).

Enlightenment, the French Revolution, liberalism, and socialism, and culminating in twentieth-century communism). Lefebvre—who had expressed support in the 1940s for the "Catholic order" of the authoritarian French Vichy régime (which collaborated with Nazi Germany), in the 1970s for authoritarian governments and military dictatorships (in Spain, Portugal, Chile, and Argentina), and in the 1980s for the French far-right party National Front—added Vatican II as the final link in this chain of "modern errors." In his *Open Letter to Confused Catholics* (1986), Lefebvre described this chain of events: "The parallel I have drawn between the crisis in the Church and the French Revolution is not simply a metaphorical one. The influence of the *philosophes* of the eighteenth century, and of the upheaval that they produced in the world, has continued down to our times. Those who injected that poison admit it themselves."[16]

Lefebvre's assessment of the state of the Church after Vatican II was inextricably connected with his firm attachment to a very narrow idea of pontifical magisterium that developed after the French Revolution and to the "ultramontanist" mind-set typical of nineteenth-century Catholicism. He identified the idea of Church teaching with the contents and forms of nineteenth-century papal magisterium, culminating in Pius X's encyclical *Pascendi Dominici Gregis* (1907), which had condemned modernism and brought about the most dramatic purge of theologians in the modern history of the Catholic Church. For Lefebvre, Vatican II represented the decisive point in the development of Catholicism in the modern world, a path that went from "Christian democracy" to "Christian socialism" and concluded with "Christian atheism" in which "dialogue" had become the most dangerous attitude: "The adulterous union of the Church

---

16. Marcel Lefebvre, *An Open Letter to Confused Catholics* (Herefordshire, England: Fowler Wright for the Society of St. Pius X, 1986), 105, translation of *Lettre ouverte aux catholiques perplexes* (Paris: Albin Michel, 1985).

and the Revolution is cemented by 'dialogue.' Truth and error are incompatible; to dialogue with error is to put God and the devil on the same footing."[17] According to Lefebvre, Vatican II had become the work of the devil against the Church: "There is no more any Magisterium, no dogma, nor hierarchy; not Holy Scripture even, in the sense of an inspired and historically certain text. Christians are inspired directly by the Holy Spirit. The Church then collapses."[18]

This ultratraditionalist narrative is all but dead in the public discourse of Catholicism today: typical of the spirit of revanche against Vatican II and propagating a view of Vatican II in its texts as clearly discontinuous from the tradition, the recent publication by self-appointed apologists very close to some Roman circles has gone far beyond the usual boundaries of the debate "texts versus spirit of Vatican II." Among them, Roberto de Mattei, a renowned apologist of ultratraditionalist Catholicism and a biographer of the Brazilian revanchist Plinio Corrêa de Oliveira, sees in Vatican II the triumph of modernism and the result of the infiltration of communism and Freemasonry in Catholic theology. De Mattei's hermeneutical effort provides interesting results in terms of archival discoveries from the ultratraditionalist Lefebvrians, but it is most interesting (and disconcerting) in the attempt to present itself as the historiographical translation of the call of Benedict XVI for a renewed interpretation of Vatican II. In de Mattei's work, the rejection is not only of the "spirit" of Vatican II, but also of the very texts of the council, thus retrieving the conspiracy-driven Lefebvrian interpretation of Vatican II and proving essentially useless for developing a hermeneutical approach to Vatican II.[19]

17. Lefebvre, *An Open Letter to Confused Catholics*, 117.
18. Ibid., 118.
19. See Roberto de Mattei, *Il Concilio Vaticano II: Una storia mai raccontata* (Turin: Lindau, 2010). Translations in other languages are forthcoming.

A second narrative that has become more vigorous in these last few years is the narrative that sees in Vatican II a council whose major accomplishments were fatally weakened since the very beginning by excessive compromises between the reformers and the conservative forces in the Roman Curia and in the leadership of the Church. This narrative maintains that Vatican II was devoid of its major results even before its work was accomplished. What has happened after Vatican II is only the logical consequence of what had happened already at the council. The most important promoter of this narrative is Hans Küng, whose disappointment with Vatican II began during the council, when he refused the invitation to become involved as a *peritus*, as an expert in the work of a conciliar commission. Recently, Küng characterized the accomplishments of the council in a belittling way, in light of "what Vatican II should have said," due to the alleged disconnect between the wishes of the council fathers and the texts of the documents approved by the council:

> There is absolutely no decree that completely satisfies me and certainly even most bishops. Much of what the Council Fathers wanted was not included in the decrees. And much of what was accepted in the decrees the Council Fathers did not want. What is lacking almost everywhere in the doctrinal decrees is a solid exegetical and historical foundation—I have often lamented as a fundamental defect the almost total absence of historical-critical exegesis in the council. Often very difficult issues such as Scripture, tradition, or primacy-collegiality have been plastered over by diplomatic compromise.[20]

---

20. My translation from Hans Küng, *Erkämpfte Freiheit: Erinnerungen* (Munich: Piper, 2002), 577 ("Es gibt überhaupt kein Dekret, das mich und doch wohl auch die meisten Bischöfe ganz befriedigte. Vieles, was die Konzilsväter wollten, ist nicht in die Dekrete aufgenommen worden. Und vieles, was aufgenommen wurde, wollten die Konzilsväter nicht. Fast überall felht mir gerade in den Lehrdekreten—die fast totale Abwesenheit der historisch-kritischen Exegese im Konzil habe ich oft als grundlegenden Mangel beklagt—ein solides exegetisches und historisches Fundament. Öfters sind gerade schwierigste Punkten wie Schrift/Tradition oder Primat/Kollegialität durch diplomatische Kompromisse überkleistert worden"). Küng's assessment of the council runs in this volume between pp. 230 and 580.

A few years after Vatican II (and a few years after his book on papal infallibility),[21] Hans Küng had expressed already his views about the "betrayal" of Vatican II by Pope Paul VI: "The bishops present there—advised and prompted by theologians—spoke a lot at that time about the breathing of the Holy Spirit; but under another Pope [Paul VI] they returned to their old surroundings and the papal curia tried to correct the mistakes of the new Pope's predecessor and to consolidate afresh its tottering rule over the Roman Empire."[22] In the 1980s, Küng's criticism of Vatican II as a betrayal continued, as he responded to the Extraordinary Synod of 1985: "Has the Second Vatican Council been forgotten, superseded, betrayed? . . . The ecclesiastical bureaucracy is fostering a restoration movement such as has taken hold of other churches, religions, and nations."[23] More recently, Küng substantially rejected the historians of Vatican II, accusing them not only of failing to see Küng's contribution to the formation of the council agenda (his books *Konzil und Wiedervereinigung*, 1959, and *Strukturen der Kirche*, 1962) but also of being compromised with Rome and the papacy, and thus unable to perceive the real Vatican II.[24]

A third narrative emerged in the 1980s but only recently, after the death of John Paul II and the election of Benedict XVI, invaded the discourse of Catholics on Vatican II. The neoconservative or neoliberal narrative of Vatican II merges elements of the two master narratives, the ultratraditionalist and the ultraliberal. The ultratraditionalist elements come from a very narrow view of the "tradition" that allows neoconservatives to propagate an

21. See Hans Küng, *Unfehlbar? Eine Anfrage* (Zürich: Einsiedeln; Cologne: Benziger, 1970), trans. Edward Quinn as *Infallible? An Inquiry* (Garden City, NY: Doubleday, 1983).

22. Hans Küng, *On Being a Christian*, trans. Edward Quinn (New York: Doubleday, 1976), 37.

23. Hans Küng, "On the State of the Catholic Church—or Why a Book like This Is Necessary," in *The Church in Anguish: Has the Vatican Betrayed Vatican II?*, ed. Hans Küng and Leonard Swindler (New York: Harper & Row, 1987), 1.

24. Küng, *Erkämpfte Freiheit*, 501, 541.

interpretation of Catholicism according to the theological and cultural markers of the "long nineteenth century"[25] and, accordingly, of Vatican II as some kind of "pacifist-communist" takeover of Catholicism. The ultraliberal elements come from a "Jacobin-Leninist" conception (typical of the neoconservative mind-set) of the role of theologians and intellectuals in the Church: an avant-garde that is entitled to move the state of the debate in the Church according to a specific and idiosyncratic agenda, championing the rule of an elite over a Catholic population that will never be able to understand their intellectual masters.

The neoconservative narrative on Vatican II is embodied by Michael Novak, Richard John Neuhaus, and George Weigel, and their philosophical inspiration comes from Irving Kristol, particularly from Kristol's engagement with the philosopher Leo Strauss.[26] This narrative surfaced in the 1980s, at the same time as the emergence of a new breed of neo-Catholics in the United States. For at least two decades, it did not manage to rise and infiltrate the leadership of the Catholic Church, thanks to the personal-biographical contribution of John Paul II to the Church's interpretation of Vatican II, especially in the issues *ad extra* (ecumenism, interreligious dialogue, and global justice). But during the pontificate of John Paul II, a staunch defense of the council in the name of the personal experience of the pontiff as a council father did not exclude a sometimes casual labeling of phenomena, movements, and theological insights as the direct "fruit

---

25. See O'Malley, *What Happened at Vatican II*, 53–92.

26. About the intellectual roots of neoconservatives, see Irving Kristol, *The Neoconservative Persuasion: Selected Essays, 1942–2009* (New York: Basic, 2011), esp. "Taking Religious Conservatives Seriously" (1994, pp. 292–95), where Kristol defined that "the three pillars of modern conservatism are religion, nationalism, and economic growth." For the personal experience with Vatican II of one of the leaders of neoconservative discourse in America, see William F. Buckley Jr., "Disruptions and Achievements of Vatican II," ch. 6 in *Nearer, My God: An Autobiography of Faith* (New York: Doubleday, 1997). About Novak, see the autobiography *Writing from Left to Right: My Journey from Liberal to Conservative* (New York: Image, 2013).

of Vatican II," thus endorsing a kind of Vatican II nominalism coming from John Paul II. On the other side, the doctrinal policy of Cardinal Ratzinger never disavowed a clearly conservative reading of Vatican II in the name of literalism: an interpretation of the literal texts of Vatican II aimed at countering the liberal interpretation of the council allegedly based on the pure spirit of Vatican II.

For many years, the Vatican was the expression of a contradiction between two partially conflicting visions of Vatican II: John Paul II's fundamentally positive view of the council and Cardinal Ratzinger's acutely pessimistic reading of the post–Vatican II period. This "dialogue" of interpretations, at the beginning under some control of the pope, gave place gradually to a more important role for Cardinal Ratzinger's views. The conclave of 2005 put an end to the dialogue between the two most important interpreters of Vatican II in the first fifty years of its reception and opened a new phase, in which the Church could not count anymore on the fact that Ratzinger's interpretation was balanced by John Paul II.

The change of pontificate inaugurated with the election of Benedict XVI in 2005 helped move this neoconservative narrative into the vocabulary of the governing elites of Western Catholicism (European and North Atlantic especially). This transatlantic migration of the neoconservative narrative (in the opposite direction of the history of the migrations of Catholics in North America) has multiple consequences; most of them are still invisible and so far underappreciated. But the starting point of this approach to the issue of the presence of Catholicism in the modern world finds in the attack against Vatican II one of its favorite markers. These new breed of "public theologians" (in some cases, recent converts to Catholicism as their home of choice fit for their social and political conservatism) made the case for the fundamental need to restore the interpretation of Vatican II, building a new narrative against what Richard John

Neuhaus called "the councils called Vatican II." In his 1987 book *The Catholic Moment*, Neuhaus took off from *The Ratzinger Report* (published in 1985) to attack the interpretation of Vatican II coming from "the party of discontinuity." The need to attack these "councils in conflict" comes largely, for Neuhaus, from the fact that

> The cultural, intellectual, and political leadership of the country [the United States] is interested in American Catholicism because it has a stake in American Catholicism. The Catholic wars are surrounded by, and indeed are part of, the larger cultural warfare within American society. Those who view with anxiety the resurgence of fundamentalist and evangelical religion in the public arena view with undisguised alarm the possibility that that resurgence may converge with similar directions in American Catholicism. For such people "Vatican II," however vaguely understood, has become a totem, the last remaining and institutionally most formidable redoubt of a liberalism under conservative assault. . . . In all the changing definitions of sides and alignments, the contest over the interpretation of Vatican II constitutes a critical battlefront in our society's continuing cultural wars.[27]

George Weigel inaugurated the political anti–Paul VI narrative of Vatican II, seeing the positive basically only in Vatican II's teaching on religious freedom, and portraying John Paul II's offensive against liberation theology as the much-needed correction against the social teaching of Paul VI and against the thread between the pastoral constitution *Gaudium et Spes* and the encyclical *Populorum Progressio* (1967).[28] This effort needed to be accompanied by the push against "revisionist" Catholic historiography.[29] In the name of an *aggiornamento* carried by *ressourcement*, Weigel advocated a new

---

27. Richard John Neuhaus, *The Catholic Moment: The Paradox of the Church in the Postmodern World* (San Francisco: Harper & Row, 1987), 61.
28. For Weigel's comparison between the "glumness" of Paul VI and John Paul II and their interpretations of the social message of Vatican II, see George Weigel, *Catholicism and the Renewal of American Democracy* (Mahwah, NJ: Paulist, 1989), 27–44.
29. See George Weigel, *Freedom and Its Discontents: Catholicism Confronts Modernity* (Washington, DC: Ethics and Public Policy Center, 1991), esp. 43, 57, 87, 134–49.

"Americanist" reading of Vatican II. This new reading entitles itself the right to push back the social and intellectual agenda of theologians and bishops in the United States in the two decades between 1965 and 1985.[30]

A similar identification of Vatican II with the neoconservative gospel of economic freedom is to be found in Michael Novak, once an enthusiast of Vatican II and a student of Bernard Lonergan at the Pontifical Gregorian University in Rome in the late 1950s.[31] The assessment of Vatican II in the eyes of a former enthusiast of it could not be starker: "The very meaning of Catholicism as a coherent people with a coherent vision has been threatened. What the barbarian invasions, centuries of primitive village life, medieval plagues and diseases, wars, revolutions, heresies and schisms had failed to do, the Second Vatican Council succeeded in doing."[32]

3. The Narratives and the History of Vatican II

These narratives about Vatican II were all created in the first twenty years after the council, but also *before* these last twenty years, that is, before the publication of the most significant contributions of the community of theologians and historians to the scholarship on Vatican II. While the ultratraditionalist narrative kept going as if nothing happened between 1965 and the beginning of the twenty-first century, both the ultraliberal and the neoconservative narratives

30. See also George Weigel, *The Courage to Be Catholic: Crisis, Reform, and the Future of the Church* (New York: Basic, 2002), esp. 44–47, 220.
31. For a comparison with the early positions of Michael Novak, see *The Open Church: Vatican II, Act II* (New York: Macmillan, 1964), a journalistic account of the events of the second session of the council. It is interesting that in the apologetical "Introduction to the Transaction Edition" (New Brunswick, NJ: Transaction, 2002), Novak accuses "the spirit of Vatican II" but also—quite inconsequently—says that "for the history of Vatican II, there is no more thorough and scholarly source than the *History of Vatican II*, whose general editor is Giuseppe Alberigo, and whose American editor is Joseph Komonchak" (p. xxxvii).
32. Michael Novak, *Confessions of a Catholic* (San Francisco: Harper & Row, 1983), 8.

were fueled—the former by the pivotal moment of the Extraordinary Synod of Bishops of 1985 and the debate surrounding the synod and its conclusions, and the latter by the changing role of Catholics in growingly secularized societies in Europe and North America.

But the Synod of 1985 was also the chronological starting point for the major scholarly work about Vatican II, the *History of Vatican II* edited by Giuseppe Alberigo,[33] and it is remarkable to see how little these narratives have been touched and modified by the amount of new information made available by this accomplishment carried out by an international team of historians and theologians. In the mid-1980s, the project for a *History of Vatican II* was formed in the Institute of Bologna as an attempt at "historicization" (and not memorialization) of Vatican II. Leading the project was the consideration that the epochal change taking place in contemporary Catholicism was "the cause and purpose of Vatican II," the council being "an experience of communion in search of action in the human story that not only affects a few preferred, but involves the church as such."[34]

The first step of the project was around the types of sources for the history of Vatican II. A need emerged to resort to historical sources along with the official ones, in order to develop the most complete and comprehensive possible reconstruction of a complex event and to articulate how the council actually happened. The project therefore used not only the monumental official documentation published by the Holy See (the *Acta et Documenta* and the *Acta Synodalia*), but also the unofficial documentation, political and diplomatic sources, and the private records of bishops and theologians (projects, draft

---

33. Giuseppe Alberigo, ed., *Storia del concilio Vaticano II*, 5 vols. (Leuven: Peeters; Bologna: Il Mulino, 1995–2001), ed. and trans. Joseph Komonchak, *The History of Vatican II* (Maryknoll, NY: Orbis, 1996–2006); translated also into French, German, Spanish, Portuguese, and Russian.
34. Giuseppe Alberigo, "Il Vaticano II nella storia della chiesa," *Cristianesimo nella Storia* 6, no. 2 (1985): 441–44, quotation at 443.

plans, diaries, and correspondence)—thus expanding the sources that had been used for the edition of the acts of the Council of Trent, the thirteen-volume *Concilium Tridentinum*: "acta, epistulae, diarii" (proceedings, letters, diaries).[35] In the early stages of this research, the historians working in Alberigo's team uncovered, researched, and made available more than one hundred unofficial archives, after having inquired about the existence of archival sources kept by more than seven hundred potential persons and institutions.[36]

The intention of Giuseppe Alberigo and the team around him was to build the project around Vatican II as a multiyear research effort, with no apologetic or polemical purposes, aimed at writing a critically rigorous history of the council, based on historical sources, as a historical event. This work aimed to write a multidimensional history of the council, and that required an interdenominational and intercontinental collaboration in order to achieve a perception of the "internal" aspects of Vatican II in their relationship with the "external" factors: "It is time to work on a historicization of Vatican II not to relegate it to a distant past, but to facilitate the overcoming of the apologetical phase of its reception."[37] Alberigo's training under Hubert Jedin in Bonn in the early 1950s, and his firsthand experience of the work on and the reception of Jedin's four-volume *History of the Council of Trent* made Alberigo superbly qualified to attempt a history of Vatican II just three decades after its completion.[38]

Alberigo had developed a reflection on the "hermeneutical criteria for the history of Vatican II" that would accompany his work as

35. See *Concilium Tridentinum: Diariorum, actorum, epistularum, tractatuum*, ed. the Görres-Gesellschaft, 18 tomes in 13 vols. (Freiburg im Breisgau: Societas Gorresiana, 1901–2001).

36. See Massimo Faggioli and Giovanni Turbanti, *Il concilio inedito: Fonti del Vaticano II* (Bologna: Il Mulino, 2001).

37. Giuseppe Alberigo, "Per la storicizzazione del Vaticano II," in *Per la storicizzazione del Vaticano II*, ed. Giuseppe Alberigo and Alberto Melloni, "Cristianesimo nella Storia" 13, no. 3 (1992): 473.

38. See Hubert Jedin, *Geschichte des Konzils von Trient*, 4 vols. (Freiburg i.B.: Herder, 1949–75).

a historian—in the last three decades dedicated to the council by Alberigo as a scholar, teacher, and Christian. These were his criteria, developed between the late 1980s and the mid 1990s:

- *The council-event as a canon of interpretation.* Vatican II is much more than the sum of its decisions, since the nature of the assembly and the council have an important role for understanding and for the reception of the council itself. Vatican II is an "event" also, because the council was a celebration in the liturgical sense. Trying to understand it without taking into account the nature of the gathering misses the point completely.
- *The intention of John XXIII.* Pope John XXIII was planning to convene a council that could set the Church again in a position to speak to modern men and women, without sacrificing the essentials of his message and his tradition, but by updating older forms in order to make the announcement of the gospel more effective in the modern world.
- *The pastoral nature of the council.* Vatican II was not to proclaim new dogmas. Vatican II put at the center of theology the pastoral nature of Church teaching. Vatican II did teach, but the pastoral nature of the council made the *salus animarum* (salvation of souls), not the conservation of the old ways, the ultimate goal of theology.
- Aggiornamento *(updating) as the key goal of the council.* As the goal for the council, "update" means the effort to know and renew and reform the cultural, theological, and spiritual patrimony of the Church, in order to come back to talk to men and women of our time.
- *The importance of compromise for interpreting the documents of Vatican II.* No decision of the council is a unique source of mind, a school, or a doctrine. The search for compromise by

the council fathers and council committees, in order to reach, where possible, a consensus (at least a moral consensus) of the council about the texts under discussion, has greatly influenced the formulas of the final documents.[39]

The five-volume *History of Vatican II* (and the many other volumes of the series published as a corollary of the five-volume *History*) changed much of what the Church knows about specific and greatly important issues regarding the "continuity/discontinuity" of Vatican II with the previous recent tradition. This is especially thanks to the following new discoveries, among others:[40]

- The history of the preparation of the council (1960–1962) and the debate on the rejection of the preparatory schemata drafted by the Roman Curia;[41]
- The history of the individual documents of Vatican II (constitutions, decrees, and declarations), from their first draft to the final version, through the work in the conciliar commission and the debate on the floor of the aula of Saint Peter;[42]

39. Giuseppe Alberigo, "Critères herméneutiques pour une histoire de Vatican II," in *À la Veille du Concile Vatican II: Vota et Réactions en Europe et dans le Catholicisme oriental* (Leuven: Peeters, 1992), 12–23, republished in Italian in Giuseppe Alberigo, *Transizione epocale: Studi sul concilio Vaticano II* (Bologna: Il Mulino, 2009), 29–45.

40. See also Giuseppe Alberigo, "*L'Histoire du Concile Vatican II*: Problèmes et perspectives," in *Vatican II sous le regard des historiens*, ed. Christoph Theobald (Paris: Médiasèvres, 2006), 25–48.

41. Especially Antonino Indelicato, *Difendere la dottrina o annunciare l'Evangelo: Il dibattito nella Commissione centrale preparatoria del Vaticano II* (Genoa: Marietti, 1992); Joseph A. Komonchak, "The Struggle for the Council during the Preparation of Vatican II (1960–1962)," in *History of Vatican II*, ed. Giuseppe Alberigo and Joseph A. Komonchak, vol. I, *Announcing and Preparing Vatican Council II: Toward a New Era in Catholicism* (Maryknoll, NY: Orbis; Leuven: Peeters, 1995), 167–356.

42. About this, see Massimo Faggioli, "Concilio Vaticano II: Bollettino bibliografico (2000–2002)," *Cristianesimo nella Storia* 24, no. 2 (2003) 335–60; "Concilio Vaticano II: Bollettino bibliografico (2002–2005)," *Cristianesimo nella Storia* 26, no. 3 (2005): 743–67; "Council Vatican II: Bibliographical Overview 2005–2007," *Cristianesimo nella Storia* 29, no. 2 (2008): 567–610; "Council Vatican II: Bibliographical Overview 2007–2010," *Cristianesimo nella Storia*

- The fundamental contribution provided to the work of the commissions and to the document by the intersession periods (January–August 1963, January–August 1964, and January–August 1965), which until the 1990s had been underestimated, if not neglected, by the scholarship on Vatican II;[43]
- The influence of non-Roman and nontheological factors in the decision-making process regarding major documents of Vatican II.[44]

4. Church History and the Church of Vatican II

Understanding the importance of the councils in Catholic theology requires much more than historical studies: *traditio* is not just *historia*. But if the *traditio* of the teachings of a council in the Church goes beyond the passing down of the historical memory of the council as an event, this *traditio* is surely not detached from the kind of historical studies dedicated to the councils and cultivated by the Church that celebrated that council. In these last thirty years, the historiography on Vatican II has offered the global community of

32, no. 2 (2011): 755–91; "Council Vatican II: Bibliographical Survey 2010–2013," *Cristianesimo nella Storia* 24, no. 3 (2013): 927–55.

43. See Jan Grootaers, "The Drama Continues between the Acts: The 'Second Preparation' and Its Opponents," in *History of Vatican II*, ed. Giuseppe Alberigo and Joseph A. Komonchak, vol. 2, *The Formation of the Council's Identity: First Period and Intersession, October 1962–September 1963* (Maryknoll, NY: Orbis; Leuven: Peeters, 1997), 359–514; Evangelista Vilanova, "The Intersession," in *History of Vatican II*, ed. Giuseppe Alberigo and Joseph A. Komonchak, vol. 3, *The Mature Council: Second Period and Intersession, September 1963–September 1964* (Maryknoll, NY: Orbis; Leuven: Peeters, 2000), 347–490; Riccardo Burigana and Giovanni Turbanti, "The Intersession: Preparing the Conclusion of the Council," in *History of Vatican II*, ed. Giuseppe Alberigo and Joseph A. Komonchak, vol. 4, *Church as a Communion: Third Period and Intersession, September 1964–September 1965* (Maryknoll, NY: Orbis; Leuven: Peeters, 2003), 453–615.

44. See especially Alberto Melloni, *L'Altra Roma: Politica e S. Sede durante il Concilio Vaticano II, 1959–1965* (Bologna: Il Mulino, 2000); Stephen Schloesser, "Against Forgetting: Memory, History, Vatican II," *Theological Studies* 67 (2006): 275–319.

the Catholic Church a valuable patrimony of studies necessary to know and understand what happened at Vatican II. But the narratives—especially the previously mentioned three master narratives: the ultratraditionalist, the ultraliberal, and the neoconservative—have not changed a bit. Their spin on the council has been untouched by what we now know about Vatican II—something that we did not know before and when those narratives were crafted.

On the contrary, these narratives have only become louder in these last few years, because of the struggle to control the recent past of the Church, as it happened already in the years after Vatican I. It is worth remembering what Francis Oakley wrote recently about the need to remember the "repressed memory" of conciliarism (the theological foundations of the councils of the fourteenth to fifteenth century who saved the Church from a papacy gone astray with the Great Western Schism) against the "papalist narrative" dominant until the 1950s: "But in so doing I am acutely conscious of the fact that I will be arguing in the teeth of the high papalist constitutive narrative successfully installed, in the wake of Vatican I, not only in Catholic historiography but also in our general histories at large. Only in the past forty to fifty years at most has the revisionist process begun finally to gain traction and to succeed in calling into question that established narrative."[45] All that has become evident in today's theological debate, as well as in the public posture of the Holy See toward the topic of Vatican II between the end of John Paul II's pontificate and the beginning of Benedict XVI's. Already in 1997, members of the entourage of the Roman Curia, feeling more secure in the decline of John Paul II's pontificate, began expressing more

---

45. Francis Oakley, "The Conciliar Heritage and the Politics of Oblivion," in *The Church, the Councils, and Reform: The Legacy of the Fifteenth Century*, ed. Gerald Christianson, Thomas M. Izbicki, and Christopher M. Bellitto (Washington, DC: Catholic University of America Press, 2008), 82–97, quotation at 85.

vocally their prior criticism of the volumes of the *History of Vatican II* edited by Giuseppe Alberigo, because the *History of Vatican II* challenged the favored narrative.[46]

This initially quiet reaction against the international, multiauthored, and respected historiographical work on Vatican II (polemically labeled "the Bologna school") became gradually more visible over time and especially after 2005, but it never acquired a real scholarly standing as an alternative to the international research on Vatican II. The absence of Roman Curia theologians from the debate has been replaced by the political interpretation of Vatican II given by Roman Curia officials—high-ranking members and cardinals included. Only a few historians and theologians active at the Vatican in Rome have taken part in a serious debate.

A growing radicalization of positions around the council was perceivable during the pontificate of Benedict XVI: both the anti–Vatican II sentiment typical of traditionalism, closer and closer to the Lefebvrian narrative about the council as a total "rupture,"[47] and the radicals' disappointment with Vatican II as a failed promise[48] became typical of these times. The indirect, silent, and benevolent approval by some cardinals and bishops of the Lefebvrites' narrative on Vatican II was undoubtedly a side effect (much wished for by

---

46. See Agostino Marchetto's book review of the second volume of the *History of Vatican II*, in *Osservatore Romano*, November 13, 1997, and in *Apollinaris* 70 (1997): 331–51, now republished in Agostino Marchetto, *Il Concilio Ecumenico Vaticano II: Contrappunto per la sua storia* (Vatican City: Libreria Editrice Vaticana, 2005), 102–19. All the other historians and theologians had reviewed favorably the *History of Vatican II*: in the same "Roman milieu," see, for example, Giacomo Martina, in *La Civiltà Cattolica* 147, no. 2 (1996): 153–60; and in *Archivum Historiae Pontificiae* 35 (1997): 356–59. On the reception of the *History of Vatican II*, see Alberto Melloni, "Il Vaticano II e la sua storia: Introduzione alla nuova edizione, 2012–2014," in *Storia del concilio Vaticano II*, ed. Giuseppe Alberigo, 2nd ed. (Bologna: Il Mulino, 2012), 1:ix–lxx.

47. See *Penser Vatican II quarante ans après*. Actes du VIe congrès théologique de "Sì Sì No No" (Versailles: Courrier de Rome, 2004); and Dominic Bourmaud, *Cent ans de modernisme: Généalogie du concile Vatican II* (Étampes: Clovis, 2003).

48. Typical of this sentiment are some passages of Hans Küng's memoirs, *My Struggle for Freedom* (Grand Rapids, MI: Eerdmans, 2003).

some in Rome and in Catholic traditionalist quarters) of the reconciliation talks with the Society of Saint Pius X, especially since 2009.[49] Quite recently, Catholic ultratraditionalist intellectuals, ideologically much closer to the Lefebvrites than to the Roman "official" interpretation of Vatican II as an event of "continuity and reform," have been given honors and venues by prelates of the Roman Curia.[50]

The rise of the narratives in today's Church has weakened intellectually the awareness of Vatican II as a historical event. Even worse, "politically" (that is, from the Church government standpoint), the rise of the narratives is weakening the idea of Vatican II as a "reform council."[51] For the ultratraditionalist narrative, Vatican II was a council of complete and illegitimate rupture with the past; for the ultraliberal narrative, it was a totally failed promise; for the neoconservative narrative, it was merely the usher of an agenda of economic freedom. This crisis of the consensus around Vatican II is a crisis for the authority of the council that has spilled over to touch the credibility of the Church as such.[52]

What is happening to the role of Vatican II in today's Church and to the appreciation of the council as a decisive moment to tackle the challenges facing Catholicism today has many roots. Here it is possible only to make some hypotheses.

One first possible cause is the backlog of post–Vatican II reformism that has been piling up between the pontificates of Paul VI and

49. See *Exkommunikation oder Kommunikation? Der Weg der Kirche nach dem II. Vatikanum und die Pius-Brüder*, ed. Peter Hünermann (Freiburg i.B.: Herder, 2009).

50. About this, see Giovanni Miccoli, *La Chiesa dell'anticoncilio: I tradizionalisti alla riconquista di Roma* (Rome: Laterza, 2011), 234–334.

51. O'Malley, *What Happened at Vatican II*, 300.

52. See Andreas Battlogg, "Ist das Zweite Vatikanum Verhandlungsmasse?," *Stimmen der Zeit* 227, no. 10 (October 2009): 649–50; Wolfgang Beinert, "Nur pastoral oder dogmatisch verpflichtend? Zur Verbindlichkeit des Zweiten Vatikanischen Konzils," *Stimmen der Zeit* 228, no. 1 (January 2010): 3–15.

John Paul II: for example, the stop-and-go about the reform of the Roman Curia and the role of the papacy in the Church (especially after John Paul II's encyclical *Ut Unum Sint*, 1995) in the direction of decentralization in a growingly globalized Catholicism. So many expectations regarding the power of Vatican II to reform the Church have been disappointed that it has become easy for the ones who never believed in Vatican II as a real reform council to blame Vatican II for what happened *after* Vatican II.

A second probable reason is that the end of the first "global pontificate," John Paul II's, has given way to a surge in the new occidentalization of the Catholic Church. This development and the crisis of the theory of secularization have left Catholicism with no defense against the outbreak of a theologically worded "culture war." The so-called *revanche de Dieu*, "God's comeback," in Western Catholicism (especially among the younger generations of seminarians and priests) has taken the form of a *revanche contre*, a revenge against Vatican II.

Thirdly, one difference between the force of the ideological narratives about Vatican II and the historical narratives about the previous councils is that Vatican II and contemporary theological discourse in Catholicism operate in a completely new environment: we live in a "mass society" and a "mass culture" that make historical scholarship more exposed to ideological manipulation—and that meets an idea of the Church that was rephrased by Vatican II in a more embracing and participative fashion. In this new self-understanding of the Church, the power of the old elites (Catholic bishops, theologians, and historians included) is weaker than before. This makes the history of Vatican II a more debated project, not a shared enterprise as it was for previous councils.

Finally, the crisis of the historical awareness of Catholics about Vatican II is a symptom of the crisis of Church history as an academic discipline cultivated in pontifical universities, theological seminaries, departments of Catholic theology and religious studies, but also in history departments of non-Catholic academic institutions of higher education and research. The debate between Giuseppe Alberigo and Hubert Jedin about the status of Church history as a "theological discipline" has now, at the beginning of the twenty-first century, very few descendants still dealing professionally with Church history.[53] The crisis of Church history in Catholic culture, compared with the golden age of Church historians between Vatican I and Vatican II, means the escalating risk of leaving recent Church history, and especially Vatican II, in the hands of "theological pundits" (journalists in the best of cases, bloggers in the worst) whose agenda is far more influenced by nontheological factors. The fact that Church history has its own specificity but is part of global history is now rejected by many—as if it were intellectually possible to go back to the apologetics of *historia ecclesiastica*—on the grounds of a neo-Augustinian ecclesiology that sees the Church not *in* the modern world, but only opposed to it.

In these last fifty years after Vatican II, there have been not conflicting *histories*, but conflicting *narratives* at work on the interpretation of the council.[54] All the experts know that there is no trustworthy alternative, at least so far, to the history of Vatican II written in these last twenty years and represented by the names of Giuseppe Alberigo, Joseph Komonchak, and John O'Malley. In this cultural and theological environment, Church historians have been accused of "discontinuism," of being uninterested in the tradition,

---

53. See Hubert Jedin, *Chiesa della fede: Chiesa della storia* (Brescia: Morcelliana, 1972), esp. "Storia della chiesa come storia della salvezza," 35–40, and "La storia della chiesa è teologia e storia," 51–65. *Contra* Jedin's view of Church history as a theological discipline, see Giuseppe Alberigo, "Conoscenza storica e teologia," *Römische Quartalschrift* 80 (1985): 207–22; and "Méthodologie de l'histoire de l'Église en Europe," *Revue d'Histoire Ecclésiastique* 81 (1986): 401–20.

54. About the development of the debate, see Massimo Faggioli, *Vatican II: The Battle for Meaning* (New York: Paulist, 2012).

that is, in the past of Catholicism. But it is clear now, at fifty years from the opening of Vatican II, that the ones not interested in recovering the past—as well as tradition in its entirety—are actually the ideologues of the "narratives" on Vatican II, and certainly not Church historians.[55]

Church history as a "public utility" is far from being without problems and contradictions, but certainly it does not have more problems than the apparently more neutral "religious history." The conscience of serving the community of the faithful by discovering and publishing what happened at Vatican II was and is part of the intention of Church historians researching Vatican II.[56] In this moment of passage between the *memory* of Vatican II and a dangerously sterilized *memorialization* of it,[57] Church historians try, with their own scientific method, to remind the Church "how much purposeful forgetting—repression or amnesia—is required to make a case for continuity."[58] The main difference between the history and the narratives of Vatican II is that the former keeps track also of the forgotten things.

---

55. "Some modern intellectuals believe, like many social historians, that, as Alan Megill put it, we are now 'under the reign of discontinuity': that, in short, to be 'modern' means, among other things, to recognize the irrelevance of the past. This sense of a break with the past, particularly on the part of alienated intellectuals, is not, however, to be confused with discontinuity itself; indeed, as a repetition of similar attitudes, for example among Renaissance humanists, it reflects, in a radical form, one possible attitude to the past perhaps unique to Western culture." Bouwsma, *A Usable Past*, 6.

56. See Hervé Legrand, "Relecture et évaluation de l'Histoire du Concile Vatican II d'un point de vue ecclésiologique," in *Vatican II sous le regard des historiens*, ed. Christoph Theobald (Paris: Médiasèvres, 2006), 49–82; John W. O'Malley, "Vatican II: Did Anything Happen?," in *Vatican II: Did Anything Happen?*, ed. David G. Schultenover (New York: Continuum, 2008), 52–91, esp. 52–59.

57. See Enrico Galavotti, "Le beatificazioni di Benedetto XVI e il mausoleo del Vaticano II," *Il Margine* 30, no. 2 (2010): 22–33.

58. Schloesser, "Against Forgetting: Memory, History, Vatican II," 277.

3

Forms of Procedure and Sources of Legitimacy in the Second Vatican Council

In the last fifty years, there has been no shortage of publications on the major religious event of the twentieth century.[1] Theologians and historians can rely on a series of studies on the history of the council and on commentaries on the final documents of the council.[2] For Church historians, the history of Vatican II is not a secret anymore. But for the public at large, the historicity of Vatican II could become

---

1. This chapter was published originally in German: "Verfahrensformen und Legitimierungsquellen während des Zweiten Vatikanischen Konzils," in *Ekklesiologische Alternativen? Monarchischer Papat und Formen kollegialer Kirchenleitung (15.–20. Jahrhundert)*, ed. Bernward Schmidt and Hubert Wolf (Münster: Rhema, 2013), 187–201.
2. See Massimo Faggioli, "Concilio Vaticano II: Bollettino bibliografico (2000–2002)," *Cristianesimo nella Storia* 24, no. 2 (2003): 335–60; Massimo Faggioli, *Concilio Vaticano II: Bollettino bibliografico (2002–2005)*, *Cristianesimo nella Storia* 26, no. 3 (2005): 743–67; Massimo Faggioli, "Council Vatican II: Bibliographical Overview 2005–2007," *Cristianesimo nella Storia* 29, no. 2 (2008): 567–610; Massimo Faggioli, "Council Vatican II: Bibliographical Overview 2007–2010," *Cristianesimo nella Storia* 31, no. 1 (2011): 755–91; Massimo Faggioli, "Council Vatican II: Bibliographical Survey 2010–2013," *Cristianesimo nella Storia* 24, no. 3 (2013): 927–55.

one of the best-kept secrets. The return to a tendency to interpret Vatican II only with a "literalist" approach, stopping short of any intellectual effort to understand the value and the meaning of its documents in the light of "what happened at Vatican II," is clear. In this respect, the rediscovery of the ever-existing and natural distance between the text of a conciliar document and its hermeneutics in the history of the Church needs to tap resources that have so far not been fully developed—that is, the "symbolism" of Vatican II.

Despite Vatican II's understatement in comparison to the heavy use of the symbols of Church power during Pius XII's pontificate, which made rich use of the symbols of papal power during World War II and in the postwar period,[3] a correct hermeneutics of the council must address the role of "symbolic moments" in the making of the conciliar event. We will not consider the highly ecclesiological symbols relating to Vatican II,[4] not only because many of them were soon absorbed in the "political mechanics" of the debate at the council, but also because the cautious use of symbols during Vatican II was a kind of late acceptance of the historical fact of the end of the Papal State and the beginning of a new era in the relationship between papacy and the Church, and between the Church and modern world.

Nevertheless, it is possible to identify symbolic moments that are representative of different, but not always competing, sources of the legitimacy of Vatican II and that build the hermeneutical framework for the interpretation of the council. Between the announcement

---

3. For the history of the debate on Pius XII, see Angelo Persico, *Il caso Pio XII: Mezzo secolo di dibattito su Eugenio Pacelli* (Milan: Guerini e Associati, 2008).

4. These include the opening ceremony of Vatican II; the placement and the order of precedence between cardinals and Eastern patriarchs; the placement of the "ecumenical observers"; the profession of faith expressed by John XXIII at the beginning of the council (and not in the "new formula" drawn up at the wish of the Holy Office); Paul VI's formula of promulgation of the council documents; the pope's travel in the Holy Land, India, and to the United Nations headquarters in New York during the council.

of the council by John XXIII on January 25, 1959, and the end of the council in December 1965, it is possible to identify at least five moments in which the nature and the symbolism of the actions of the players of the council show different sources of legitimacy. These moments are necessary in order to understand the connection between what happened at Vatican II and a correct hermeneutics of the council:

1. Calling of the council and *legitimacy of papal inspiration:* the speeches of John XXIII on January 25, 1959, and October 11, 1962;
2. Formation of the agenda and *legitimacy of the consultation of the Church:* the *vota* of the preparatory phase, 1959–1960;
3. Forms of the debate and *legitimacy of the coherence of the council's work:* John XXIII's decision about the schema on the revelation, November 21, 1962;
4. Decision-making procedures and *legitimacy of the council's consensus:* the votes on collegiality and episcopacy, October 30, 1963;
5. "Fixing" the council's decisions and creating postconciliar institutions, and *legitimacy of the papal hermeneutics of the council:* the *Nota Explicativa Praevia* to *Lumen Gentium* (November 16, 1964) and the motu proprio *Apostolica sollicitudo* (September 15, 1965).

1. The Calling of the Council and the Legitimacy of Papal Inspiration

John XXIII's decision to call the twenty-first ecumenical council was a genuinely personal decision, as is now well known and witnessed by the pope's private journal.[5] His decision was communicated to the cardinals, gathered in the Basilica of Saint Paul Outside-the-Walls, on January 25, 1959. To the surprise of the cardinals, the pope communicated a decision that, given the "electoral mandate" of a newly elected seventy-seven-year old pope, he was not supposed to make.[6]

Strange as it may appear, the calling of the council by the pope alone—as it was clearly stated in the *Code of Canon Law*[7]—represents a typical feature of only the last two ecumenical councils: the "modernity" of Vatican II is also to be found in the new independence of the Catholic Church in calling a council without consulting with the emperor.[8] John XXIII was acutely aware of the solitude necessary for this decision, and he consulted with the secretary of state five days before the announcement, when the pope was already sure of his decision.[9]

There are no accounts of this first act of Vatican II, except for the pope's memory, which he shared only two years later, of the

5. See Giuseppe Alberigo, ed., *History of Vatican II*, vol. 1, *Announcing and Preparing Vatican Council II: Toward a New Era in Catholicism*, English version ed. Joseph A. Komonchak (Maryknoll, NY: Orbis, 1995); Angelo Giuseppe Roncalli - Giovanni XXIII, *Pater amabilis: Agende del pontefice, 1958–1963*, ed. Mauro Velati (Bologna: Fondazione per le scienze religiose, 2007).

6. See Alberto Melloni, "Prodromi e preparazione del discorso d'annuncio del Vaticano II," *Rivista di Storia e Letteratura Religiosa* 27 (1992): 607–43.

7. "Dari nequit Oecumenicum Concilium quod a Romano Pontifice non fuerit convocatum," *Codex Iuris Canonici* (1917), can. 222, 1.

8. See Giuseppe Alberigo, ed., *Storia dei concili ecumenici* (Brescia: Queriniana, 1993); Klaus Schatz, *Allgemeine Konzilien: Brennpunkte der Kirchengeschichte* (Paderborn: Schöning, 1997).

9. "Giornata *albo signanda lapillo*. Nella udienza col Segretario di Stato Tardini, per la prima volta, e, direi, come a caso mi accadde di pronunciare il nome di *Concilio*, come a dir che cosa il nuovo Papa potrebbe proporre come invito ad un movimento vasto di spiritualità per la S. Chiesa e per il mondo intero. Temevo proprio una smorfia sorridente e sconfortante come risposta. Invece al semplice tocco, il Cardinale – bianco in viso, e smorto – scattò con una esclamazione indimenticabile ed un lampo di entusiasmo: 'Oh! Oh? Questa è un'idea, questa è una grande idea.' Devo dire che *viscera mea exultaverunt in D.no* [Sal 84(83), 3]: e tutto fù chiaro e semplice nel mio spirito: e non credetti di dover aggiungere parola. Come se l'idea di un Concilio mi sorgesse in cuore con la naturalezza delle riflessioni più spontanee e più sicure. Veramente *a D.no factum est istud et est mirabile oculis meis* [Mt 21,42]." Roncalli - Giovanni XXIII, *Pater amabilis*, 25.

"impressive, devout silence" of the cardinals' reaction. In his private journal, Roncalli noted that the cardinals who could be present in Saint Paul Outside-the-Walls numbered *twelve*.[10] The anomaly of the gathering of the cardinals, like an ancient *consistory* (in the words of John XXIII annotated by Cardinal Tardini), was clear.[11]

John XXIII described the decision of calling the council as an inspiration: "I do not like to appeal to special inspirations. I am satisfied with the orthodox teaching that everything is from God. In light of that teaching I regarded the idea of a Council as likewise an inspiration from heaven."[12] The decision making about the council saw the pope acting alone, avoiding consultations with the Roman Curia. His decision was final, and it was not a poll of cardinals' views on the idea: "Trembling with a little emotion but at the same time humbly resolute in my purpose."[13] A confirmation of this estrangement of the Roman Curia from the decision about the council was the reaction of the newspaper of the Holy See: "In Rome the 'Osservatore Romano' never published the text of the allocution in Saint Paul's, only a short bulletin, whereas the announcement created widespread interest among the public."[14]

Giuseppe Alberigo listed, in a seminal article, the "intention" of John XXIII as the first hermeneutical criteria for the understanding of Vatican II.[15] Since then, the calling of the council by John XXIII has become, for the hermeneutics of Vatican II, *the first source of the legitimacy of the council, that is, papal inspiration*. This speech has

---

10. Ibid., 26. But there were seventeen cardinals: see the list in Alberto Melloni, *Papa Giovanni: Un cristiano e il suo concilio* (Turin: Einaudi, 2009), 215.

11. See Melloni, *Papa Giovanni*, 215.

12. *Discorsi Messaggi Colloqui del Santo Padre Giovanni XXIII* (Vatican City: Libreria Editrice Vaticana, 1963), 4:609, quoted in *History of Vatican II*, 1:7.

13. See *History of Vatican II*, vol. 1, 1.

14. See ibid., 1:17.

15. See Giuseppe Alberigo, "Criteri ermeneutici per una storia del Vaticano II," now in Giuseppe Alberigo, *Transizione epocale: Studi sul concilio Vaticano II* (Bologna: Il Mulino, 2009), 29–45.

become important for the interpretation of Vatican II because of the literary genre of the announcement speech, a literary genre that will be typical of the final documents of the council. The announcement of the council is "a speech that explains,"[16] the first leg of the major contribution of John XXIII to the council, because the second leg was the opening speech *Gaudet Mater Ecclesia,*[17] "a mosaic-fashioned speech,"[18] and the address to the faithful gathered in Saint Peter's Square on the evening of October 11, 1962.

The pope's speeches clearly mark the beginning (January 1959) and the end (October 1962) of the preparation of the council, and they are John XXIII's only "long interventions" in the council. In them, there is no antagonism between the council and its pope, and there is no possible hint at the role of the Roman Curia in the making of the council: from an ecclesiological point of view in this creative act of Pope John XXIII, bishops and local churches are called to gather for the council.[19]

John XXIII's announcement was "the act that generated Vatican II";[20] therefore, his intention and concrete expression in the speeches have been considered a hermeneutical principle for the comprehension of the council and its final documents.[21]

16. For the importance of the literary genre of the documents of Vatican II, see John W. O'Malley, *What Happened at Vatican II* (Cambridge, MA: Belknap Press of Harvard University Press, 2008); Ann Michele Nolan, *A Privileged Moment: Dialogue in the Language of the Second Vatican Council 1962–1965* (Bern-Berlin: Peter Lang, 2006). For the analysis of the text of the speech, see Melloni, *Papa Giovanni*, 217–24.
17. See Christoph Theobald, *La réception du concile Vatican II: vol. 1. Accéder à la source* (Paris: Cerf, 2009), 235–58.
18. See O'Malley, *What Happened at Vatican II*, 94–96; *History of Vatican II*, vol. 2, *The Formation of the Council's Identity, First Period and Intersession, October 1962–September 1963* (Maryknoll, NY: Orbis, 1997), 14–18; Melloni, *Papa Giovanni*, 264.
19. So Melloni, *Papa Giovanni*, 269–70.
20. Giuseppe Alberigo, "Il Vaticano II nella tradizione conciliare," now in Alberigo, *Transizione epocale*, 553–74.
21. See Giuseppe Alberigo, "Fedeltà e creatività nella ricezione del concilio Vaticano II: Criteri ermeneutici," now in *Transizione epocale*, 47–69.

2. The Formation of the Agenda and the Legitimacy
of the Consultation

On June 30, 1959, the letter with the questionnaire for the *vota* of the bishops, modified and approved by John XXIII, was sent (with the date of June 18) to the secretary of state for his signature and to be mailed to the bishops, the superior-generals of the religious orders of men, and the institutions of higher education around the world that held papal charters.[22] The change in the form of the letter was a personal decision of the pope, who wanted no questionnaire, but only a simple letter, asking the opinions of the recipients on the agenda of the council.[23]

The shift from a multiple-choice questionnaire to a letter meant a greater deal of freedom for the respondents and marked a significant step in the preparation of a council as John XXIII had thought about it. The responses were not only a clear sign against the attempts of the Roman Curia to shape the preparation of Vatican II as an unsettling experience for the status quo, but also a first step in the direction of the new language of the council, in the "style" of Vatican II: "the center-periphery issue thus blends into the style issue."[24]

The consultation of the bishops marked a significant difference from the councils of the first millennium, in which the agenda was a matter of agreement between the pope and the emperor (or between the council and the emperor), and of the second millennium of Christianity, where councils were "consultative bodies" of the pope's authority. The preparation of Vatican II was much different from the preparation of Vatican I, where the model for the creation of

22. *History of Vatican II*, 1:55–166 and 97–135; O'Malley, *What Happened at Vatican II*, 19–20.
23. See Giuseppe Alberigo, "Passaggi cruciali della fase antepreparatoria (1959–1960)," in *Verso il Concilio Vaticano II, 1960–1962: Passaggi e problemi della preparazione conciliare*, es. Giuseppe Alberigo and Alberto Melloni (Genova: Marietti, 1993), 22–23.
24. O'Malley, *What Happened at Vatican II*, 305.

the agenda was Trent and the Fifth Lateran Council.[25] It was also different from the consultation prepared for the "council of Pius XII" in 1949, which wanted to consult only with a few dozen bishops carefully selected by Rome.[26]

The final result of the *vota* of the bishops was condensed by the Roman Curia in the *quaestiones* (July 1960). Therefore, the consultation for the preparation of Vatican II oriented not much the preparation of the schemata, but it did orient the "narrative" of the council and provided a binding interpretive framework for the work ahead during Vatican II: "the style of the council was invitational."[27]

This procedure for the formation of the agenda of the council provides a second key element for the understanding of the legitimacy of Vatican II: that is, the fact that the bishops were given a voice well before the beginning of the council about their idea of the council's focus. In this idea of legitimacy of Vatican II as a consultation, there is also Roncalli's idea of the council as "representative" of the Church.[28] Roncalli was not as worried as other popes about the return of conciliarism, and he seemed to share the pre-council optimism about the future relations between the pope and the council that was witnessed by that the insertion of the decrees of Constance and Basel in the first edition of the Bologna–based *Conciliorum Oecumenicorum Decreta*, the collection of all the decrees of the ecumenical councils from Nicaea to Vatican I.[29]

---

25. See Klaus Schatz, *Allgemeine Konzilien*.

26. See Giuseppe Caprile, "Pio XII e un nuovo progetto di Concilio ecumenico," *La Civiltà Cattolica* 117, no. 3 (1966): 209–22.

27. John W. O'Malley, "The Style of Vatican II," *America*, February 24, 2003, pp. 12–15.

28. See Giuseppe Alberigo, "Concili e rappresentanza," in Repraesentatio: *Mapping a Keyword for Churches and Governance*, ed. Massimo Faggioli and Alberto Melloni (Berlin: LIT, 2006), 99–124, esp. 120; Theobald, *La réception du concile Vatican II*, 1:149.

29. See Giuseppe Alberigo, ed., *Conciliorum Oecumenicorum Decreta* (Freiburg i.B.: Herder, 1962; 1973, 2nd ed.; 1991, bilingual ed.). See also Heribert Müller, "Konzilien des 15. Jahrhunderts und Zweites Vatikanisches Konzil: Historiker und Theologen als Wissenschaftler und Zeitgenossen," in *Historie und Leben: Der Historiker als Wissenschaftler und Zeitgenosse, Festschrift*

3. Forms of the Debate and Legitimacy of the Coherence of the Council's Work

The results of the vote of November 20, 1962, concerning the debate on the preparatory schema about the divine revelation, had been in favor of discontinuing the debate, but the majority was 105 votes short of the two-thirds majority that the council regulations required for a decision of this kind. John XXIII's decision on November 21, 1962 (on the proposals of a number of cardinals) to restart the debate on the constitution on the revelation was "the turning point" in the history of Vatican II.[30]

The pope made the decision, but through an interpretation of the debate on the floor of Saint Peter in which the vast majority of speakers had indicated the inconsistency between John XXIII's "Gaudet Mater Ecclesia" and the schema "De fontibus revelationis" (On the sources of revelation) of the Theological Commission led by Cardinal Ottaviani of the Holy Office.[31] Bishop De Smedt especially had explained the importance of the "style" of the schema in relation to the ecumenical goal of the council, as it had been expressed by John XXIII in the opening speech of Vatican II, "Gaudet Mater Ecclesia."[32]

In this moment of Vatican II, some observers saw that the dam broke: the decision of the pope, which was interpreting the debate on the floor of Saint Peter and which produced a reversal of the preparation of the schema on revelation by the Theological Commission, meant "the end of the Counter-Reformation."[33] The

---

für Lothar Gall zum 70. Geburtstag, ed. Dieter Hein, Klaus Hildebrand, and Andreas Schulz (Munich: Oldenbourg, 2006), 117–35.

30. O'Malley, *What Happened at Vatican II*, 141.

31. See Riccardo Burigana, *La Bibbia nel concilio: La redazione della costituzione Dei verbum del Vaticano II* (Bologna: Il Mulino, 1998), 150–71.

32. See *History of Vatican II*, 2:258–66.

33. See O'Malley, *What Happened at Vatican II*, 141–52.

appeal of the conciliar majority for a new text on the revelation was indeed much more than a push for a schema alternative to the one prepared by the Roman Curia, and the decision to create a new mixed commission for the new schema on revelation was more than "fixing" a loophole in the council's regulations.[34] Especially during the crisis of November 1962, Vatican II made a step forward in the direction of a mature awareness of the connection between the intention of John XXIII and the theological orientation of the council: "The rules of procedure of Vatican II and its interpretation by John XXIII reflect a real progress in the understanding of the Gospel."[35]

November 21, 1962, was the strongest indication of the importance of the *legitimacy of the coherence of the council's work with the intention of John XXIII.* It was an appeal to the coherence between the intention of John XXIII in calling the council, the pope's speech at the beginning of the council, and the expectations of the world from the council.[36] It means much more than a self-awareness of the council vis-à-vis the Roman Curia or the conservative minority. It is clear here that the decision of the pope fits the idea of the "constitutional" characteristics of Vatican II as a council with unambiguous theological features,[37] considering the "constitutional" elements given by John XXIII's announcement of the council and the consultative nature of the preparation of the council.

34. See Giuseppe Alberigo, "Dinamiche e procedure nel Vaticano II: Verso la revisione del Regolamento del Concilio (1962–1963)," now in Alberigo, *Transizione epocale*, 183–228.
35. Theobald, *La réception du concile Vatican II*, 1:13: "le règlement de Vatican II et son interprétation par Jean XXIII nous semblent enregistrer une réelle avancée de la conscience évangelique."
36. Melloni, *Papa Giovanni*, 275–79.
37. See Peter Hünermann, "Der Text: Werden—Gestalt—Bedeutung: Eine hermeneutische Reflexion," in *Herders Theologischer Kommentar zum Zweiten Vatikanischen Konzil*, ed. Hans Jochen Hilberath and Peter Hünermann, 5 vols. (Freiburg i.B.: Herder, 2004–2005), 5:5–101, esp. 11–17, 85–87.

4. Decision-Making Procedures and the Legitimacy of the Council's Consensus

The "five votes" of 30 October 1963 on the ecclesiological debate represented a turning point not only for the history of the debate on *Lumen Gentium*, but also for the history of the council as an assembly. The votes on the major issues of chapter II of the schema *De Ecclesia* (episcopal consecration, collegiality of the bishops and the pope, diaconate)[38] went beyond the written regulations of the council, which allowed only a vote on a chapter as such and not on the specific topics within a chapter. The procedure of "straw votes" (*voti orientativi*) was proposed by the four moderators of the council (Cardinals Agagianian, Lercaro, Döpfner, and Suenens) and accepted by Paul VI in order to ascertain the will of the majority and to give direction to the commission. The votes on the five questions showed that a clear and overwhelming majority of the council fathers agreed in principle on some critical issues.[39]

The history of the "five votes" shows the increased awareness of the council fathers about the stakes of the council, and the assertion of the authority of the council on the Roman Curia. October 30, 1963, marked "a dramatic and vitally important transition. . . . The Council fathers grew in their convictions and awareness during that October of discussions and exchanges. They understood themselves not as a majority on the basis of power, but as an agreement on the matters at issue."[40] In O'Malley's words, "The bishops had actually experienced

38. The results of the votes: (1) the episcopacy as the highest level of the sacrament of orders: 98.42 percent *placet*, 1.58 percent *non placet*, (a no vote); (2) episcopal consecration, by which there is communicated the *potestas* (power in the Church): 95.13 percent *placet*, 4.83 percent *non placet*; (3) succession of the bishops to the apostolic college: 84.17 percent *placet*, 15.64 percent *non placet*; (4) divine right of the episcopacy: 80.13 percent *placet*, 19.08 percent *non placet*; (5) the restoration of the diaconate: 74.91 percent *placet*, 24.76 percent *non placet*.

39. See Peter Hünermann, "Theologischer Kommentar zur dogmatischen Konstitution über die Kirche Lumen Gentium," in *Herders Theologischer Kommentar zum Zweiten Vatikanischen Konzil*, vol. 2, esp. 346–50.

collegiality. It was for them now part of their lived reality. The two weeks that had intervened between October 15 and 30 gave the bishops time to reflect and to cast an even more considered vote."[41]

The symbolic victory of the conciliar majority on October 30, 1963, has been linked to the emergence of a "Pyrrhic syndrome."[42] The votes of October 1963 had solved the clash between the Theological Commission and the council, but they did unveil the upcoming issue of the relationship between the council and the pope that later became the most important issue for the third and fourth sessions of Vatican II.

But the votes of October 1963 represent the most visible moment in the creation of the *legitimacy of the council's consensus* because it made the bishops profoundly aware of the specificity of the council. Already in the regulations of the council, the relationship between rules and consensus was clear: "Legislative procedures are subject to their purpose, that is, the manifestation of consensus in the liturgy of the public sessions [...] Without being considered as a source of law, the consensus is clearly hereinafter referred to as the ultimate goal."[43]

In these votes, collegiality became the symbol of the conciliar experience: "Collegiality was at the same time the issue on the ballot and the conscience of the voters."[44] In Giuseppe Dossetti's words, the votes of October 1963 produced a decisive shift in the mechanics of the council, given that "the vote has inaugurated a new method: so

40. Alberto Melloni, "The Great Ecclesiological Debate," in *History of Vatican II*, vol. 3, *The Mature Council: Second Period and Intersession, September 1963–September 1964*, ed. Giuseppe Alberigo, English version ed. Joseph A. Komonchak (Maryknoll, NY: Orbis, 2000), 106.
41. O'Malley, *What Happened at Vatican II*, 184.
42. Melloni, "The Great Ecclesiological Debate," in *History of Vatican II*, 3:106.
43. Theobald, *La réception du concile Vatican II*, 1:148: "les procédures législatives sont subordonnées à leur finalité, la manifestation du consensus dans la liturgie des sessions publiques [...] Sans être considéré comme source du droit, le *consensus* est donc clairement désigné ici comme a visée ultime."
44. Alberto Melloni, "Procedure e coscienza conciliare al Vaticano II. I 5 voti del 30 ottobre 1963," in *Cristianesimo nella storia: Saggi in onore di Giuseppe Alberigo*, ed. Alberto Melloni, Daniele Menozzi, et al. (Bologna: Il Mulino, 1996), 387.

far the conciliar commissions had not *served* the council, but instead they wanted to *dominate* it."[45]

The ecclesiological debate and the votes of October 30, 1963 show on one side the intimate connection between the procedural issues and the doctrinal issues in a council,[46] thus revealing a new dimension in the "political and juridical" dimension of the decision-making procedures in the Catholic Church in a Kelsenian view of the tight relationship between the form of the procedure and the content of the decision, without going to the extreme of a "legal positivism" in a council, such as Vatican II, very much aware of the place of revelation and tradition in the life of the Church. On the other side, these votes represent the symbol of the maturity of Vatican II as a collegial experience. This is why, for the rest of the council until 1965, the minority, and especially the Holy Office and the ultraconservative Coetus Internationalis Patrum (Ottaviani, Browne, Marcel Lefebvre, Carli), attacked the legitimacy of the votes of October 30, 1963, saying the vote was merely "indicative" and, in the final analysis, invalid.

5. "Fixing" the Council's Decisions and Creating Postconciliar Institutions: The Legitimacy of the Papal Hermeneutics of the Council

From the beginning of Vatican II, during the preparatory phase but especially during the ecclesiological debate in the second session (October 1963), several conciliar fathers expressed an interest and

---

45. "Il voto di stamane inizia un nuovo metodo: sinora le Commissioni—e in esse tre-quattro persone—invece di servire il concilio volevano comandarlo." Giuseppe Dossetti, personal notes of October 30, 1963, quoted in Melloni, "Procedure e coscienza conciliare al Vaticano II," 383.

46. See Giuseppe Alberigo, "Dinamiche e procedure nel Vaticano II: Verso la revisione del Regolamento del concilio (1962–1963)"; and "Giuseppe Dossetti al concilio Vaticano II," in Alberigo, *Transizione epocale*, 183–228, esp. 225; 393–502, esp. 434–37.

made proposals for the creation of a new body at the level of the central Church government. The most interesting among these proposals called for the creation of a core and permanent board of a few bishops who would be in charge of the government of the Roman Catholic Church, in communion with and in cooperation with the pope and *above* the Roman Curia. One of the strongly emerging themes during Vatican II, especially during the preparatory phase and the second session, was the necessity of a reform of the dicasteries of the central government of the Roman Catholic Church.[47]

The richness of the proposals on this matter coming from the conciliar fathers and national episcopates can only partially be perceived in the wording of the conciliar decree "Christus Dominus," at paragraph 5. One of the most unclear and, until recently, obscure passages in the history of Vatican II is the genesis of the institution of the "Synodus Episcoporum," of the Synod of Bishops by Paul VI in September 1965,[48] and therefore of paragraph 5 of "Christus Dominus," which depends on that pontifical act, although originally the text of the conciliar commission "de episcopis," on the bishops' role in the Church, was supposed to be the basis for the new synod.

According to the logic of the conciliar agenda, until the beginning of the fourth session, the commission "de episcopis" did not have the responsibility of supporting, a posteriori, the Synod of Bishops designed by Paul VI and by some other curia bishops close to the pope, and created in a different way from the council's proposals for the formation of a "synodal board." The timing of the pontifical intervention, in anticipation of the commission's proceedings, was

47. For the change in pontificate in 1963 and the relationship between Paul VI and the Roman Curia, see Paul VI's address to the cardinals and personnel of the Roman Curia, September 21, 1963, in *Acta Apostolicae Sedis* 55 (1963): 793.
48. See Paul VI, *motu proprio Apostolica sollicitudo*, September 15, 1965, in *Acta Apostolicae Sedis* 57 (1965): 775–80.

perceived as less scandalous than in other cases. The effect of Paul VI's interventions on the text on ecumenism, on the final text of *Lumen Gentium* with the *nota praevia*, and on the text on religious freedom during the so-called black week (*settimana nera*) at the end of the third session (November 1964) also plays a significant role in one's understanding of the final text of *Christus Dominus* and the effects of its implementation.

In fact, the first reactions of the conciliar fathers and of non-Catholic observers to the new synod after the publication of *Apostolica sollicitudo* (September 15, 1965) were mostly positive. Only a few members, after their initial surprise, perceived that the timing of the *motu proprio* and the synod's structure meant a substantial undercutting of Vatican II's authority and the conciliar intention to create a new body representing the bishops' will and articulating their voice to the pope.[49]

Actually, the Synod of Bishops was an institutional innovation, which originated from the conciliar debate and which could be a turning point from multicentury centralizing tendencies and the Roman practice of Church government. But other passages in the text on the new bishops' synod remained undisputed by the conciliar fathers and hidden to the conciliar fathers. Forty-five years after the end of Vatican II, it is possible to identify the real differences between the mind of the conciliar fathers about the problems of Church government and the actual solution provided—that is, the bishops' synod and therefore *Christus Dominus* n. 5.[50]

---

49. Massimo Faggioli, *Il vescovo e il concilio: Modello episcopale e aggiornamento al Vaticano II* (Bologna: Il Mulino, 2005), 403–22 and 451–542.

50. See Massimo Faggioli, "Institutions of Episcopal Synodality-Collegiality after Vatican II: The Decree 'Christus Dominus' and the Agenda for Synodality-Collegiality in the 21st Century," *Jurist* 64, no. 2 (2004): 224–46; Gilles Routhier, "Vatican II: The First Stage of an Unfinished Process of Reversing the Centralized Government of the Catholic Church," *Jurist* 64, no. 2 (2004): 247–83.

Paul VI's intervention for the creation of the bishops' synod over the head of the council illustrates only one of the episodes in which the "red pencil" of the pope influenced the outcomes of the council.[51] The same *crayon rouge* had intervened already in 1964 in the text of *Lumen Gentium* through the *Nota Explicativa Praevia* to chapter III of the constitution on the Church, as well as in the documents on ecumenism and religious freedom. This act did not only proved in Paul VI "a type of understanding of the papal magisterium closer to the minority, which shows low sensitivity for a certain 'democratic' ethos." But it shows also "Paul VI's clear conscience on the difference between the time of the council and the time after the council, and the difference between the extraordinary magisterium which is expressed in the meeting and the ordinary government of the universal church under its own authority."[52]

The subtraction of the issue of the Synod of Bishops from the hands of the conciliar commission represented the beginning of the postconciliar period in the creation of a new, different kind of legitimacy credited to the council: *the legitimacy of the papal hermeneutics of the council*, in which the pope interprets the council, but through attributing to the council the intention the papacy is enacting in institutional reforms. This kind of hermeneutics became more and more important because it was an anticipated end of the council and an anticipated translation of the council's mind in the

51. "The creation of the Synod of Bishops severed collegiality, the doctrine empowering the periphery, from institutional grounding. The 'Preliminary Explanatory Note,' whatever its correct interpretation, certainly did not strengthen the statement on collegiality in chapter three in the Constitution on the Church. Collegiality, the linchpin in the center-periphery relationship promoted by the majority, ended up an abstract teaching without point of entry into the social reality of the church. It ended up an ideal, no match for the deeply entrenched system." O'Malley, *What Happened at Vatican II*, 311.

52. Theobald, *La réception du concile Vatican II*, 349 and 353: "un type de compréhension du magistère pontifical, plus proche de la minorité, qui se montre peu sensible . . . à un certain *éthos* 'démocratique'" [and Paul VI's] "clair conscience de Paul VI quant à la différence entre 'l'heure' du Concile et le temps qui suit, entre le magistère extraordinaire qui s'exprime dans l'assemblée et le gouvernement ordinaire de l'église universelle qui relève de sa propre autorité."

form of a defense of the primacy. The act of the creation of the bishops' synod in September 1965 stands not only for the symbol of the institutional continuity, but also for the papacy's selective interpretation of the "spirit of the council."[53]

6. Conclusions

On the eve of the fiftieth anniversary of the beginning of Vatican II, more than ever a new look at the historicity of Vatican II is needed: not only because of the generational shift within Catholicism, but also because of the "hermeneutical policy" on Vatican II that is based on an approach to the final documents that is filtered by a clear "doctrinal policy" typical of the post–Vatican II period. With the perception of the history of Vatican II, the symbolic dimension of the council also seems to be forgotten. But the epoch-making value of Vatican II became possible not through a thorough analysis of the texts of Vatican II (not even for the council's fathers), but through the widespread appreciation of the symbolic value of Vatican II as an experience of inspiration, consultation, coherence, and consensus. The symbolic moments of Vatican II provided the Catholic Church with a new conscience of the times, and that is why they are now relevant for a correct hermeneutics of Vatican II.

6.1. Symbolic Moments of Vatican II, Legitimacies and Conciliar Hermeneutics

Every hermeneutical approach to Vatican II has indeed a different set of preferences about the symbolical moments of the legitimacy

---

53. See Massimo Faggioli, "Council Vatican II between Documents and Spirit: The Case of the New Catholic Movements," in *After Vatican II: Trajectories and Hermeneutics*, ed. James L. Heft with John O'Malley (Grand Rapids, MI: Eerdmans, 2012), 1–22.

of the council. Some interpretations stress more the intention of the announcement of the council by John XXIII; others focus more on the consensus of the council fathers around the major issues. But it is clear that every hermeneutics of Vatican II that is faithful to the history of the council takes into account the first four legitimacies—papal inspiration, consultation of the Church, coherence of the council's work, and council's consensus—and builds a consistent hermeneutical approach.[54]

But the last of these legitimacies, the legitimacy of the papal hermeneutics of the council, is also the most controversial among the practical hermeneutics of Vatican II, because it contradicts the other four legitimacies and casts a shadow on the council as an experience of collegiality and the role of Paul VI: "He pored over council documents with a meticulous 'red pencil' in hand, and he edited them as they were in the making, a papal action unprecedented in the annals of ecumenical councils. He firmly kept four issues off the agenda—priestly celibacy, birth control, reform of the Curia, and the mechanism to implement collegiality at the center."[55]

The specificity of Vatican II is not based only on the literary genre of the final documents of the council, but first of all on the procedures that made Vatican II possible: "the evangelical coherence in the ways of the Second Vatican Council must play a role of theological criterion for assessing the weight of a particular meeting in the Christian theological tradition."[56] In this sense, Paul VI's interventions, especially the one aimed at building the new Synod

---

54. See Giuseppe Alberigo, "Criteri ermeneutici per una storia del Vaticano II"; Giuseppe Alberigo, "Fedeltà e creatività nella ricezione del concilio Vaticano II," in *Transizione epocale*, 47–69.

55. O'Malley, *What Happened at Vatican II*, 294.

56. Theobald, *La réception du concile Vatican II*, 121: "la cohérence évangélique des 'manières de procéder' doit pouvoir jouer un rôle de critère théologique pour évaluer le poids de telle ou telle assemblée dans la tradition."

of Bishops stands out as a different legitimacy of the council's work. Besides influencing the final documents of Vatican II, Paul VI's interventions produced a new kind of legitimacy of the council that became, after the end of the council, typical of the "doctrinal policy" of the Roman Curia in the application and interpretation of the council. For the sake of the "hermeneutics of the continuity," the interpreters of Vatican II gave credit to Vatican II for many postconciliar developments but merely on the basis of the papal hermeneutics of Vatican II.

6.2. Symbols, Liturgy, and Political Mechanics of Vatican II

The symbolism at play at Vatican II has not been analyzed so far, and this paper has not addressed the "symbols" of Vatican II in terms of objects, formulations, or images carrying a specific meaning in reference to the council. Taking the symbols of Vatican II as the primary source of the interpretation of the council could easily reduce the council "to a celebration of organized moral unanimity [which] would forget its status of deliberative assembly inevitably crossed by conflict."[57] Moreover, from a theological point of view, the most important symbol of Vatican II was the centrality of the liturgy celebrated in Saint Peter's at the beginning of every general congregation, the inthronization of the Gospels in the aula, and the recentering of the theological debate at the beginning of the council around the discussion of the liturgical reform.[58] It is clearly possible to see in the recentering on the liturgy and in the "symbolic minimalism" of Vatican II a reaction to the "political liturgies" of

---

57. Theobald, *La réception du concile Vatican II*, 354–55: "à une célebration de l'unanimité morale qui ferait oublier son statut d'assemblée délibérante inévitablement traversée par des conflits."

58. See Giuseppe Alberigo, "Sinodo come liturgia?," *Cristianesimo nella storia* 28, no. 1 (2007): 1–40; Massimo Faggioli, "Sacrosanctum Concilium and the Meaning of Vatican II," *Theological Studies* 71 (June 2010): 437–52.

the "political religions" of the twentieth century[59] and the dryness of the symbolic language of modern deliberative assemblies: in short, Vatican II "takes a moderate parliamentarian shape."[60]

But Vatican II, "a language event,"[61] lived also through symbolic moments. The different symbolic moments chosen in this paper are important in order to understand not only the different phases in the history of Vatican II, but also the different kinds of legitimacy that are credited to the council, both *concilio durante* and in the post–Vatican II period. These symbolic moments and kinds of legitimacy are clearly related to different kinds of interpretations of Vatican II in the now fifty-year-long history of the debate about the council. In the middle, we have a range of different hermeneutical approaches trying to balance the different "symbolic moments" of Vatican II in order to build a correct interpretation of the council as something more than its final documents. They may differ in the different attention given to the role of John XXIII's inspiration, to the consultation of the Church, to the coherence of the council's documents, and to the role of the consensus within the council, but they all acknowledge the existence of a complex set of legitimacies at work. But there are exceptions to this acceptance of the council as an effort to understand it in the light of its different moments, actors, and results. On one side, there is one extreme, which denies any legitimacy to any of these "symbolic moments" of Vatican II (the Lefebvrian rejection of Vatican II). On the other side is the extreme of the interpreters who see the legitimacy of Vatican II only in the last moment, that is, Paul

---

59. See Emilio Gentile, *Le religioni della politica: Fra democrazie e totalitarismi* (Roma-Bari: Laterza, 2001).

60. About the comparison between the assembly of Vatican II and the parliaments of democratic and nondemocratic states (like the Communist regimes in Russia and Eastern Europe during the Cold War), see Philippe Levillain, *La mécanique politique de Vatican II. La majorité et l'unanimité dans un concile* (Paris: Beauchesne, 1975), 445–47.

61. O'Malley, *What Happened at Vatican II*, 306: "Its style of discourse was the medium that conveyed the message."

VI's guidance of Vatican II, and in the postconciliar hermeneutics of the popes of the message of the council.

6.3. The Different Legitimacies of Collegiality and Synodality at Vatican II

At the Second Vatican Council, a new self-awareness of the Catholic Church emerged in terms of a new, more collegial, and shared governance, but it also saw the resilience of different, more traditional elements. In particular the difference, still very clear at the council, between the "collegial" (episcopal) element and the "synodal" element stands out. In the contemporary debate about the council, Vatican II is still identified with collegiality, but the original meaning of the term *collegial* is closer to the corporative power of the *ordines* in the council of the Middle Ages than to the modern idea of participation of the faithful to the decision-making process in the life of the Church. But the identification of Vatican II with collegiality is correct because the symbolically strongest moments of Vatican II were connected to the renewed awareness of the bishops as the collegial actors of Vatican II deciding on collegiality.

The history of the symbolic moments of Vatican II reveals that collegiality had been burdened with a load of expectations unable to be represented by the history of the debate on collegiality. However, Paul VI was the only one who used the term *synod*, exercising his primatial power of government of the universal Church, and moments of true "synodality" (involving bishops, clergy, and laity) were practically absent at Vatican II. *Synodality* as such had no place in the ecclesiological debates of Vatican II, but it was not absent in the council fathers' ideas of the postcouncil institutional and canonical "translations" of the new ecclesiology.

Nevertheless, the only synodal institutions created by Vatican II at the local level (diocese and parish) were the fruit of the commission's work without any direct intervention of the aula. On the other side, the creation of the Synod of Bishops by Paul VI was the symbol of the beginning of post–Vatican II in the way the pope took away from the council a matter still being debated. In the end, the *communio* ecclesiology of *Lumen Gentium* was overshadowed by the clash around the third chapter on the hierarchy and became soon dated when confronted with the expectations of the post–Vatican II period.

If the legitimacy of collegiality stayed strong following Vatican II, thanks to the symbolic moments of the history of the council, the calls for "synodality" in the Church could count only on a hermeneutics of the council's final documents—crippled by the resurgence of the legitimacy of the papal hermeneutics of the council. In this respect, it is clear that if the weakness of collegiality is due to the disconnect between the strong symbols of collegiality at the council and the overcautious wording of the documents about collegiality, the difficulty of arguing synodality in the Church on the basis of Vatican II is due both to the wording of the documents and to the lack of a true synodal experience at the council.

4

The Post–Vatican II Debate and the
Post–Council of Basel Period

Conciliarism and Constitutionalism

I grew up in Ferrara, in Northern Italy—the city where Pope Eugene IV called a council in 1438—and for five years I taught at the University of Bozen in Brixen, the city that received Nicholas of Cusa as its bishop in 1450.[1] Therefore, it is not surprising that the relationship between conciliarism and Vatican II is part of my biography and not only of my historiographical and theological endeavors. In a first step, I will try to frame the relationship between the post–Basel and the post–Vatican II debate, tracing the historiographical debate after 1959. In a second step, I will focus on the issues at stake in the comparison between the post–Basel and the post–Vatican II period.

---

1. This chapter originally was a paper delivered at the session of the American Cusanus Society at the 45th International Congress of Medieval Studies (Kalamazoo, MI, May 14, 2010).

1. The Rediscovery of Conciliarism during and after Vatican II

Well before their meeting in the papal residence of Castel Gandolfo in the summer of 2005, Hans Küng and Joseph Ratzinger had debated during Vatican II about the usefulness and validity of the Council of Constance and of conciliarism. In his book *Strukturen der Kirche* (1962), Küng had talked about conciliarism not only as a historically pivotal moment in the development of the structure of the Church, but also as a necessary element for the balancing of the infallibility decreed at the First Vatican Council. Also, the future Pope Benedict XVI, at the time theological adviser to the Cardinal of Cologne, Frings, engaged conciliarism and defined the decree *Haec Sancta* an "emergency measure" (*Notstandsmaßnahme*[2]) but not at all meaningless for the Catholic Church of today.[3]

The Second Vatican Council and the postconciliar period have surely sparked a new interest in conciliarism, as we can see from the books by Remigius Bäumer, Ansgar Frenken, Johannes Helmrath, and others.[4] The early post–Vatican II historical and theological research "rehabilitated" conciliarism and the conciliarist idea—to say the truth, in continental Europe (Germany[5] and Italy but not France)—at least a decade after Brian Tierney's *Foundations of the*

---

2. This term was introduced by Hubert Jedin in polemics with Hans Küng. See Heribert Müller, "Konzilien des 15. Jahrhunderts und Zweites Vatikanisches Konzil: Historiker und Theologen als Wissenschaftler und Zeitgenossen," in *Historie und Leben: Der Historiker als Wissenschaftler und Zeitgenosse; Festschrift für Lothar Gall zum 70. Geburtstag,* ed. Dieter Hein, Klaus Hildebrand, and Andreas Schulz (Munich: Oldenbourg, 2006), 117–35.

3. See Hans Küng, *Strukturen der Kirche* (Freiburg i.B.: Herder, 1962); Joseph Ratzinger, *Das neue Volk Gottes: Entwürfe zur Ekklesiologie* (Düsseldorf: Patmos, 1969).

4. Remigius Bäumer, *Die Entwicklung des Konziliarismus* (Darmstadt: Wissenschaftliche Buchgesellschaft, 1976); Remigius Bäumer, *Das Konstanzer Konzil* (Darmstadt: Wissenschaftliche Buchgesellschaft, 1977); Ansgar Frenken, *Die Erforschung des Konstanzer Konzils (1414–1418) in den letzten 100 Jahren* (Paderborn: Schöningh, 1994); Johannes Helmrath, *Das Basler Konzil 1431–1449: Forschungsstand und Probleme* (Cologne: Böhlau, 1987).

5. See Hermann Josef Sieben, *Traktate und Theorien zum Konzil vom Beginn des Grossen Schismas bis zum Vorabend der Reformation (1378–1521)* (Frankfurt am Main: Knecht, 1983).

Conciliar Theory.[6] A confirmation of this rehabilitation was the insertion of the decrees of Constance and of Basel in the first edition of the Bologna–based *Conciliorum Oecumenicorum Decreta.*[7]

The foundation of the international theological journal *Concilium* in 1965 was also an implicit rediscovery of the conciliar idea. But the split between the founders of *Concilium* on one side and the foundation of the more conservative journal *Communio* in 1972 and the theological approach given by Brandmüller to the new series of "Konziliengeschichte" on the other side are also the signs of the times for the fortune of the conciliar idea in post–Vatican II Catholicism.

Two poles of the connection between Basel and Vatican II have been especially analyzed so far: the thought of Nicholas of Cusa and the relationship between conciliarism and modern political thought. In this attempt, we will try to expand on the second issue and on other similarities between the first forty-five years of reception of Vatican II and its connections with the post–Basel period.[8]

2. Conciliarism and Constitutionalism

Francis Oakley opened a path for the understanding of the relationship between conciliarism and political thought in the seventeenth century.[9] Similarly, Brian Tierney emphasized the role of Gerson and the discovery of constitutionalism and individual rights,[10]

---

6. Brian Tierney, *Foundations of the Conciliar Theory: The Contribution of the Medieval Canonists from Gratian to the Great Schism* (Cambridge: Cambridge University Press, 1955; new ed. Leiden: Brill, 1998).

7. *Conciliorum Oecumenicorum Decreta*, ed. Giuseppe Alberigo (Freiburg i.B.: Herder, 1962). See also Giuseppe Alberigo, *Chiesa conciliare: Identità e significato del conciliarismo* (Brescia: Paideia, 1981).

8. See Joachim W. Stieber, *Pope Eugenius IV, the Council of Basel and the Secular and Ecclesiastical Authorities in the Empire: The Conflict over Supreme Authority and Power in the Church* (Leiden: Brill, 1978).

9. See Francis Oakley, "On the Road from Constance to 1688: The Political Thought of John Major and George Buchanan," *Journal of British Studies* 1, no. 2 (May 1962): 1–31.

so that the relationship between conciliarism and constitutionalism has become a major subject.

That has not happened for Vatican II. The debate about the relationship between the ecclesiology of Vatican II and political thought has not been addressed so far, for various reasons, including the rise and decline of liberation theology between the late 1960s and the mid-1980s, and the disappearance or elimination by Ratzinger's doctrinal policy of "political theology" from the cultural landscape of post–Vatican II Catholic theology.[11]

But in the last few years, and paradoxically immediately before the election of the German Pope Benedict XVI, from Germany has come a new political-constitutional interpretation of Vatican II—that is, Vatican II as a "constitution" for the Catholic Church. In the most important commentary of the documents of Vatican II published following the publication of the new wave of historical studies on the council, the dogmatician of Tübingen, Peter Hünermann developed a new analysis of the corpus of Vatican II: "If one looks for an analogy along the lines of a first approach to the outline of the text of the Second Vatican Council, with the goal of characterizing the decisions of the council, what results is a certain similarity with constitutional texts as drawn up by representative constitutional assemblies. This similarity is expressed in a particular way in the texts of Vatican II and appears in a form that is highly indirect and condensed as compared to the Council of Trent or Vatican I."[12] If it is true that there is a "Road from Constance to 1688,"[13] for Vatican II it is fair to say that

---

10. See Brian Tierney, *The Idea of Natural Rights: Studies on Natural Rights, Natural Law, and Church Law 1150–1625* (Atlanta: Scholars Press for Emory University, 1997).

11. See Hansjürgen Verweyen, *Joseph Ratzinger–Benedikt XVI: Die Entwicklung seines Denkens* (Darmstadt: Primus, 2007).

12. For the constitutional characteristics of Vatican II, see Peter Hünermann, "Der Text: Werden—Gestalt—Bedeutung: Eine Hermeneutische Reflexion," in *Herders Theologischer Kommentar zum Zweiten Vatikanischen Konzil*, ed. Bernd Jochen Hilberath and Peter Hünermann (Freiburg i.B.: Herder, 2005), 5:5–101, esp. 11–17 and 85–87, quotation at 12.

there is a completely different road,[14] and in some respects, it is not clear yet where this road is going to lead. But if we look at the reactions (from France and Germany especially[15]) against Benedict XVI's lifting of the excommunications against the Lefebvrian bishops in January 2009,[16] it is clear that there is some parallel between the "political reception" of conciliarism by the *Pragmatic Sanction* in France (1438) and by the *Acceptatio* of Mainz (1439) in Germany[17] on one side, and the "political reception" of Vatican II's "change" by the political culture of the Western world on the other side.

3. Ecclesiology and Relationship between Pope and Council

The history of the Church in these last five centuries can be seen also as a fight between constitutionalism and papalism, as Francis Oakley reminds us: "It is nothing other than this: how and why that essentially constitutionalist ecclesiology came to perish in the latter half of the nineteenth century, yielding the field to the victorious

13. See also Gerald Christianson, "The Conciliar Tradition and Ecumenical Dialogue," in *The Church, the Councils, and Reform: The Legacy of the Fifteenth Century*, ed. Gerald Christianson, Thomas M. Izbicki, and Christopher M. Bellitto (Washington, DC: Catholic University of America Press, 2008), 17–19.

14. See John W. O'Malley, *What Happened at Vatican II* (Cambridge, MA: Belknap Press of Harvard University Press, 2008).

15. It is worth remembering the parallel between German and French leadership at Basel and at Vatican II, but after Vatican II, we have the "rejection" of the French-German connection by anticonciliar Catholics and the rupture of this alliance around the debate on *Gaudium et Spes*. See Joseph A. Komonchak, "Le valutazioni sulla *Gaudium et Spes*: Chenu, Dossetti, Ratzinger," in *Volti di fine concilio: Studi di storia e teologia sulla conclusione del Vaticano II*, ed. Joseph Doré and Alberto Melloni (Bologna: Il Mulino, 2000), 115–53.

16. See Massimo Faggioli, "Il Vaticano II come 'costituzione' e la 'recezione politica' del concilio," *Rassegna di Teologia* 50 (2009): 107–22; Massimo Faggioli, "Die kulturelle und politische Relevanz des II. Vatikanischen Konzils als konstitutiver Faktor der Interpretation," in *Exkommunikation oder Kommunikation? Der Weg der Kirche nach dem II. Vatikanum und die Pius-Brüder*, ed. Peter Hünermann (Freiburg i.B.: Herder, 2009), 153–74; Massimo Faggioli, "Vatican II Comes of Age," *Tablet*, April 11, 2009, pp. 16–17.

17. See Francis Oakley, *The Conciliarist Tradition: Constitutionalism in the Catholic Church 1300–1870* (Oxford: Oxford University Press, 2003), 50.

champions of an imperial papacy, and, in so doing, leaving so very little trace on our historical consciousness."[18]

From an ecclesiological point of view, there is a parallel between the conciliarist ecclesiology of the mystical body and the development at Vatican II of Pius XII's *Mystici Corporis*. Likewise, there is a parallel between the ecclesiology of the conciliarist movement and the idea of collegiality in chapter III of the constitution on the Church *Lumen Gentium* at Vatican II. The parallel extends also to the end of Vatican II and the post–conciliar period, with the defeat of the new equilibrium of power in the Church that had been engineered and voted by Vatican II.

But the difference is that if at Basel an entrenchment between council and pope grew progressively,[19] at Vatican II the relationship between pope and council never got to that point—not even in the wake of the release of the *Nota Explicativa Praevia* to chapter III of *Lumen Gentium* in November 1964.[20] In the post–Basel period, we have a final victory of the papacy over conciliarism with the decree of union with *Laetentur Coeli* (1439)[21] and in the *horror concilii*, the "dread of the council" in the following decade. In the case of Vatican II, we have that, in some respects, the papacy won already *concilio durante*, during the council, and managed to impose a post–Vatican II ecclesiological balance of power in favor of the papacy, without

---

18. Francis Oakley, "The Conciliar Heritage and the Politics of Oblivion," in Christianson et al., *The Church, the Councils, and Reform*, 97.

19. See Giuseppe Alberigo, "The Conciliar Church," in Christianson et al., *The Church, the Councils, and Reform*, 271–90; Oakley, *The Conciliarist Tradition*, 46.

20. See Luis A. Tagle, "The 'Black Week' of Vatican II (November 14–21, 1964)," in *History of Vatican II*, vol. 4, *Church as Communion: Third Period and Intersession, September 1964–September 1965*, ed. Giuseppe Alberigo, English version ed. Joseph A. Komonchak (Maryknoll, NY: Orbis, 2003), 388–452.

21. Hubert Jedin called *Laetentur coeli* "the magna carta of the papal restoration." Hubert Jedin, *History of the Council of Trent*, vol. 1 (St. Louis: B. Herder, 1957).

changing—from a canonical and practical point of view—the final outcome of Vatican I.[22]

4. Libertas Ecclesiae *and Reform*

Both Basel and Vatican II tried to strike a new balance between powers in the Church through institutional reforms, because both conciliarism and Vatican II had to deal with two major problems for the public standing of the Church. The first of these was politicization of the Church, that is, the political alignment between Catholicism and the Western Hemisphere during the Cold War. The second was transformation of the idea and praxis of "ecclesiastical office" (*beneficium*).[23] About this second point, there are many possible similarities to consider.

From a political point of view, at Vatican II the procedure for the appointment of bishops could not be reformed, because in 1964 the reform proposal was stopped by the secretary of state with a letter to the commission in charge of the conciliar decree *de episcopis*.[24] In this respect, the Secretary of State used *libertas ecclesiae* (the medieval term used to defend "the freedom of the Church" from imperial interference) to stop the attempt at reforming ecclesiastical practices and traditions that had been built in the previous centuries through the history of the concordats (starting with the Concordat of Bologna

---

22. For a history of post–Vatican II ecclesiology, see Christoph Theobald, *La réception du concile Vatican II*, vol. 1, *Accéder à la source* (Paris: Cerf, 2009), 547–654; Ladislas Orsy, *Receiving the Council: Theological and Canonical Insights and Debates* (Collegeville, MN: Liturgical, 2009); Massimo Faggioli, "Prassi e norme relative alle conferenze episcopali tra concilio Vaticano II e post–concilio (1959–1998)," in *Synod and Synodality: Theology, History, Canon Law and Ecumenism in New Contact*, ed. Alberto Melloni and Silvia Scatena (Münster: LIT, 2005), 265–96.

23. See Oakley, *The Conciliarist Tradition*, 22.

24. See Massimo Faggioli, *Il vescovo e il concilio: Modello episcopale e aggiornamento al Vaticano II* (Bologna: Il Mulino, 2005), 300–304.

with France, in 1516, which cut a deal between the papacy and the king of France in exchange for the abrogation of the Pragmatic Sanction of Bourges and the defeat of French conciliarists).[25]

Vatican II tried a reform *de beneficiis*, of the benefit system connected to ecclesiastical ministry; but from an ecclesiological point of view, Vatican II could not overcome the emphasis (very much present in the 1959–1960 proposals for the preparation of Vatican II) on the "rights" and "power" of every bishop in his own diocese. The council's interest in an emphasis on the "collegial authority" of the bishops in the universal Church grew significantly during the council, but not as much as the interest of every bishop in the "autonomy" from the Roman Curia while governing his own diocese. In this sense, we can talk also of "corporate features" in the ecclesiology of Vatican II, as we can speak of the "normative ecclesiology of the conciliar movement."[26]

The similarities between post–Basel and post–Vatican II periods arise in the "papal appropriation" of the council's attempt to reform the ecclesiastical institutions (and *de beneficiis* especially). What Christianson has affirmed for Basel—that is, that for Basel, we have a papal interpretation of the council not as *libertas* from the empire, but as *libertas* from the council[27]—is true also for Vatican II. In the post–Vatican II period, it became even more evident that the papal power was to be used to reform the Church but could not be reformed.[28] In other terms, Vatican II has been often used to advocate

25. See Oakley, *The Conciliarist Tradition*, 56; Oakley, "The Conciliar Heritage and the Politics of Oblivion," in Christianson et al., *The Church, the Councils, and Reform*, 93.

26. Alberigo, "The Conciliar Church," in Christianson et al., *The Church, the Councils, and Reform*, 282.

27. See Gerald Christianson, "Annates and Reform at the Council of Basel," in *Reform and Renewal in the Middle Ages and the Renaissance: Studies in Honor of Louis Pascoe, S.J.*, ed. Thomas M. Izbicki and Christopher M. Bellitto (Leiden: Brill, 2000), 193-207.

28. The failed promise of John Paul II's encyclical *Ut Unum Sint* (1995) is exemplary. See Massimo Faggioli, "Note in margine a recenti contributi per una riforma ecumenica del papato," *Cristianesimo nella Storia* 22, no. 2 (2001): 451-72.

libertas ecclesiae (e.g., for a procedure of bishops' appointment free from governments' rights typical of the premodern and preconcordat era vis-à-vis the modern world), but not to implement a new idea of *libertas in ecclesia*.

It is too early to tell that for Vatican II is true what K. A. Fink said of conciliarism: in conciliarism, Rome dodged a reform but got a Reformation. But on one side, it is certainly true that in the post–Vatican II Church, the relationship between Curial emphasis on *libertas ecclesiae* and openness to Church reform has been inversely proportional.[29] On the other side, if it is true that the failure of the Roman Catholic Church to deal with Luther was delayed also for the "horror concilii," "the dread of the council" in the Church of the early sixteenth century,[30] we should ask ourselves what kind of consequences could bring the post–Vatican II "horror concilii." After Basel, conciliarism in the Church had become a taboo, and now the conciliar tradition might be again a "repressed memory."[31]

5. "Winners" and "Losers" of the Post-Council Period

Considering the relationship between *libertas ecclesiae* and Church reform in the post–Vatican II period, another similarity with the post–Basel period emerges: the role of the bishops as the real losers of the ecclesiological fight. What makes the case of Vatican II interesting, though, is the fact that Vatican II has been marked by the ecclesiological debate concerning and the new definition of the role and theology of bishops in the Church—a new definition that had

29. See Alberto Melloni and Christoph Theobald, eds., *Vatican II: A Forgotten Future?* (*Concilium*, no. 4 [2005]; London: SCM, 2005); David G. Schultenover, ed., *Vatican II: Did Anything Happen?* (New York: Continuum, 2007).

30. See Oakley, *The Conciliarist Tradition*, 58.

31. Oakley, "The Conciliar Heritage and the Politics of Oblivion," in Christianson et al., *The Church, the Councils, and Reform*, 85.

been taken as a victory of the bishops over the hypertrophic papacy crafted by Vatican I.

The history of post–Vatican II period tells a different picture. The bishops of Vatican II have been "outvoiced," especially in the last thirty years, by a theologically activist papacy. They have been replaced by a new draft of more obedient bishops, who have tried—in vain—to present themselves as the forefront of the orthodoxy, with the result of weakening or destroying a delicate balance of power within the Church. In Montesquieu's words,

> The most natural subordinate power is that of the nobility. Nobility enters in some way, in the essence of the monarchy, whose fundamental maxim is: "No monarch, no nobility; no nobility, no monarch; and instead there is a despot."[32]

What makes the post–Vatican II scenario even more interesting is that the formulation of infallibility of Vatican II involves the bishops without giving them the opportunity to take responsibility for the affirmations strengthened by the infallibility or quasi-infallibility of the contemporary papacy. In sum, if during Vatican II the bishops were seen as winners of Vatican II, immediately after they became the losers of the post–Vatican II period when we consider the infallibility they do not share and cannot protect from itself.[33]

---

32. Charles de Montesquieu, "Des lois dans leur rapport avec la nature du gouvernement monarchique," ch. 4 in "Des lois qui dérivent directement de la nature du gouvernement," book 2 in De l'esprit des lois (1748): "Le pouvoir intermédiaire subordonné le plus naturel, est celui de la noblesse. Elle entre, en quelque façon, dans l'essence de la monarchie, dont la maxime fondamentale est, Point de monarque, point de noblesse; point de noblesse, point de monarque; mais on a un despote."

33. See Hervé Marie Legrand, "Les évêques, les églises locales et l'église entière: Évolutions institutionnelles depuis Vatican II et chantiers actuels de recherche," Revue de Sciences philosophiques et théologiques 85 (2001): 461–509; Hermann J. Pottmeyer, Towards a Papacy in Communion: Perspectives from Vatican Councils I and II, trans. Matthew J. O'Connell (New York: Crossroad, 1998); Klaus Schatz, Papal Primacy: From Its Origins to the Present, trans. John A. Otto and Linda M. Maloney (Collegeville, MN: Liturgical, 1996), orig. pub. Der päpstliche Primat (Würzburg: Echter, 1990).

6. Changes of Direction by the Two Councils' Main Characters

The post–Basel period saw a change in the leading theological and ecclesiastical elites of the Church, according to a sort of spoils system in favor of the papacy. In other words, the post–Vatican II has created a post–Vatican II episcopate that is significantly different culturally and theologically from the bishops of Vatican II. The paradox of Vatican II is that the early post–Vatican II period saw the rise of a new leadership of bishops and theologians (also thanks to new norms for the turnover of diocesan bishops, forced by the decree *Christus Dominus* to resign at the age of seventy-five, and the new norms for cardinal electors in the conclave, after Paul VI's *motu proprio Ingravescentem Aetatem*, 1970, ended their right to elect the new pope when they reached the age of eighty). It can be said that after Vatican II, all the aggressively conservative cardinals and bishops were replaced by those loyal to Vatican II, only to be replaced later by a new generation of bishops skeptical of Vatican II.

Thus, after Basel, we had the cases of Enea Silvio Piccolomini and Nicholas Cusanus, and after Vatican II, Joseph Ratzinger shifted allegiances–in both situations from the reformist majority to the "moderates."[34]

---

34. See Joseph Ratzinger with Vittorio Messori, *The Ratzinger Report: An Exclusive Interview on the State of the Church*, trans. Salvator Attanasio and Graham Harrison (San Francisco: Ignatius, 1985).

PART II

Ecclesiology and Intertextuality at Vatican II

5

The Liturgical Reform and the Meaning of Vatican II

Vatican II has a theological integrity; minimizing one document minimizes all the documents.[1] That is especially true of the liturgical constitution, *Sacrosanctum Concilium*, the council's chronological and theological opening. In what follows, I argue that any attempt to relativize the liturgical debate at the council, the liturgical constitution, and the liturgical reform originating from the constitution entails diminishing the significance of Vatican II and its role in the life of the Catholic Church.

The hermeneutics of Vatican II's *Sacrosanctum Concixlium* in the Church's life is far from purely theoretical. In the endless debate over the meaning of the constitution in recent years, it is difficult to distinguish the debaters who are aware of what is at stake from the theologians who deal with liturgical reform as just one issue

1. This chapter was published originally as "*Sacrosanctum Concilium* and the Meaning of Vatican II," in *Theological Studies* 71, no. 3 (June 2010): 437–52.

among many. In this respect, the awareness of the ongoing debate on liturgy is now, fifty years after John XXIII's announcement of the council, not very different from the state of awareness of most bishops and theologians regarding this issue on the eve of Vatican II.[2] Nonetheless, the fortieth anniversary of the solemn approval of *Sacrosanctum Concilium* had stirred debate about the role of liturgy in the Church of Vatican II.[3] More recently, Benedict XVI's *motu proprio Summorum Pontificum* (July 7, 2007) concerning the liturgy has revived interest in the destiny of the *Sacrosanctum Concilium*, the first document debated and approved by the council on November 22, 1963—with a majority vote of 2,162 to 46 after a debate that featured 328 oral interventions.

1. The Nemesis of the Liturgical Reform

Although it may sound peculiar, looking at the spectacular effects of *Sacrosanctum Concilium* in the Catholic Church during the last forty years places the observer before a sort of tragic destiny of the liturgical constitution. In the history of the hermeneutics of Vatican II, the liturgical reform seems to have a nemesis—a kind of retribution for having overlooked the connections between the liturgical constitution and the overall hermeneutics of Vatican II. This neglect was not shared by Joseph Ratzinger, whose attention

2. See Rita Ferrone, *Liturgy:* Sacrosanctum Concilium (New York: Paulist, 2007), esp. 19–50; Alberto Melloni, "Sacrosanctum Concilium 1963–2003: Lo spessore storico della riforma liturgica e la ricezione del Vaticano II," *Rivista liturgica* 90 (2002): 915–30; Andrea Grillo, *La nascita della liturgia nel XX secolo: Saggio sul rapporto tra movimento liturgico e (post–) modernità* (Assisi: Cittadella, 2003); Massimo Faggioli, *True Reform: Liturgy and Ecclesiology in* Sacrosanctum Concilium (Collegeville, MN: Liturgical, 2012).

3. See Massimo Faggioli, "Concilio Vaticano II: Bollettino bibliografico (2002–2005)," *Cristianesimo nella Storia* 26 (2005): 743–67; "Concilio Vaticano II: Bollettino bibliografico (2005–2007)," *Cristianesimo nella storia* 29 (2008): 567–610; "Council Vatican II: Bibliographical Overview 2007–2010," *Cristianesimo nella Storia* 32 (2011): 755–91; "Council Vatican II: Bibliographical Survey 2010–2013," *Cristianesimo nella Storia* 34 (2013): 927–55.

to the theological and ecclesiological implications of the liturgical reform characterized some of his major works, first as a theologian, then as Roman pontiff.[4]

Theologians and historians have somehow taken for granted the long history of the liturgical movement before Vatican II, the fact that Vatican II was the only council to approve a doctrinal document on liturgy, the undeniable truth that "something happened" for liturgy at Vatican II, the interconnections between the liturgical reform and ecclesiological issues, and the patent fact that the council's liturgical reform is the only major *reform* in the post–Tridentine Catholic Church after the reform of Church discipline between the sixteenth and seventeenth centuries. Theologians and historians seem increasingly inclined to forget the tight associations between the liturgical debate at Vatican II, the reform of the liturgy, the striving for *aggiornamento*, and the updating and reform of the Catholic Church. But most of all, some interpretations of the conciliar documents seem to have forgotten that Vatican II has a deep, internal coherence—as John O'Malley has recently stressed.[5]

No matter what the new generations of deniers of the historical fact of "change" in the history of the Church might say, the Church's liturgical life changed after Vatican II and *Sacrosanctum Concilium*, even if the *Wirkungsgeschichte* (the "history of the effects" of the liturgical reform, in both the local churches and the universal Church) remains to be written.[6]

4. "Als mich nach eigenem Zögern entschlossen hatte, das Projekt einer Ausgabe meiner Gesammelten Schriften anzunehmen, war für mich klar, dass dabei die Prioritätenordnung des Konzils gelten und daher der Band mit meinen Schriften zur Liturgie am Anfang stehen müsse." Joseph Ratzinger, "Zum Eröffnungsband meiner Schriften," in Joseph Ratzinger, *Gesammelte Schriften*, vol. 11, *Theologie der Liturgie*, 2nd ed. (Freiburg i.B.: Herder, 2008), 6.

5. For a thorough appreciation of the intertextual character of the issues at Vatican II, see John W. O'Malley, *What Happened at Vatican II* (Cambridge, MA: Belknap Press of Harvard University Press, 2008), 309–12.

6. For two studies of the reception of the liturgical reform, see Angel Unzueta, "L'action liturgique, expression de la Pentecôte," (about the liturgical reform in the Basque region of

The sometimes self-referential debate about Vatican II sidesteps and obscures the profound significance of *Sacrosanctum Concilium*. The interconnections between liturgy and the council, seen not as a collection of documents but as a coherent reality, must emerge if we want to understand the council's impact on global Catholicism: "The state of the liturgy is the first and fundamental test of the extent to which the programme, not merely of the decree *Sacrosanctum Concilium*, but of all the council's constitutions and decrees, is being achieved."[7]

What is needed is a reflection on the relationship between *Sacrosanctum Concilium* and the council that seeks to understand *whether* and *how* the liturgical debate and the resulting liturgical constitution were received by the council in its unfolding and final documents. In particular, it will be revealing to see how much of *Sacrosanctum Concilium* is present in Vatican II and how much of Vatican II is present in the first constitution, *Sacrosanctum Concilium*. The real stakes are not the recovery of an aesthetics of the rites under the "reform of the liturgical reform." As John Baldovin observed, "Serious critique of the reform—both in its formulation in the Liturgy Constitution and in the subsequent reformed liturgical books and their implementation—needs to be attended to."[8]

In the fifty years after Vatican II, it has become clear that forgetting the theological and ecclesiological background of the council's liturgical reform condemns *Sacrosanctum Concilium* to be quickly filed away with other documents dealing with some of the practical

Spain), and Rémy Kurowski, "La messe dominicale comme creuset de la réception de la réforme liturgique en Pologne: Le cas de la diocèse de Gniezno," in *Réceptions de Vatican II: Le Concile au risque de l'histoire et des espaces humaines*, ed. Gilles Routhier (Leuven: Peeters, 2004), 91–129.

7. Nicholas Lash, *Theology for Pilgrims* (Notre Dame, IN: University of Notre Dame, 2008), 226–28.

8. John Baldovin, *Reforming the Liturgy: A Response to the Critics* (Collegeville, MN: Liturgical, 2008), 1.

adjustments of the Catholic Church. More gravely, forgetting the relations between liturgy and ecclesiologies (plural) at the council condemns Vatican II to the destiny of a council debated on the basis of a political-ideological bias, which overlooks the basic fact that the liturgical debate at Vatican II was the first and most radical effort of modern Catholicism to cope with the dawn of the "secular age" and the "expanding universe of unbelief."[9]

2. Approaches to the Liturgical Constitution
Sacrosanctum Concilium

The profound ecclesiological meaning of the liturgical movement and liturgical reform has been lost. The transformation—or maybe extinction—of the "reform movements" (biblical, liturgical, patristic, ecumenical) as such within the Catholic Church after Vatican II,[10] the development in theology of single-field-centered theological research, and the fragmentation of theological debate and research on the council documents have all undoubtedly contributed to the disconnect of liturgy from ecclesiology and pastoral theology. The growing lack of trust between theologians and the Church's magisterium has presented the field of research within Catholic theology with a specific and far-reaching task, especially for the relationship between liturgists and the magisterium.[11]

One of the most insightful books on the significance of liturgy was first published in 1957, a few years before the announcement of Vatican II. Dom Cipriano Vagaggini opened his book *Il senso*

9. See the masterful work by Charles Taylor, *A Secular Age* (Cambridge, MA: Belknap Press of Harvard University Press, 2007), 352–418.
10. See Massimo Faggioli, *Breve storia dei movimenti cattolici* (Rome: Carocci, 2008), updated and trans. as *Sorting Out Catholicism: Brief History of the New Ecclesial Movements* (Collegeville, MN: Liturgical, 2014).
11. See André Naud, *Le magistère incertain* (Montreal: Fides, 1987); and Francis A. Sullivan, *Magisterium: Teaching Authority in the Catholic Church* (New York: Paulist, 1983).

teologico della liturgia by underscoring two basic elements in the new understanding of liturgy on the eve of Vatican II: the need to study liturgy against the general background of sacred history and in relation to the concept of *sacramentum*.[12] How Vatican II developed showed the importance of these two ideas for the debates on the Church, *aggiornamento*, and the modern world.

The issue of *Concilium* (no. 2, 1964) devoted to *Sacrosanctum Concilium* was published prior to the fall 1964 ecclesiological debate. In his editorial, Johannes Wagner stressed that "with the discussion of the schema on the liturgy the Council was from the first day dealing with its proper object: *De Ecclesia*."[13] In the opening essay about the bishop and the liturgy, Vagaggini once more demonstrated that the liturgical approach was the fullest way to give "completion and equilibrium" to the ecclesiology of the bishop and of the local church, and to the overall ecclesiology that became prevalent after Vatican I.[14]

Vagaggini's prediction about the Council Fathers' grasp of the profound implications of *Sacrosanctum Concilium* turned out to be overly optimistic. After the council, commentators began reading the relationship between *Sacrosanctum Concilium* and *Lumen Gentium* to reframe an ecclesiological equilibrium centered far more on the outcomes of the main battlegrounds of ecclesiology (chapter 3 of *Lumen Gentium* on the papacy and the episcopate) than on the Eucharistic ecclesiology of *Sacrosanctum Concilium*.

12. See Cipriano Vagaggini, *Theological Dimensions of the Liturgy: A General Treatise on the Theology of the Liturgy* (Collegeville, MN: Liturgical, 1976), esp. 3–32, orig. pub. as *Il senso teologico della liturgia: Saggio di liturgia teologica generale*, 4th ed. (Rome: Paoline, 1957). See also Cipriano Vagaggini, *Liturgia e pensiero teologico recente* (Rome: Sant'Anselmo, 1962).

13. See Johannes Wagner, preface to *The Church and the Liturgy* (*Concilium*, no. 2 [1965]; Glen Rock, NJ: Paulist, 1965), 3. See also Frederick R. McManus, *The Revival of the Liturgy* (New York: Herder & Herder, 1963).

14. See Cipriano Vagaggini, "The Bishop and the Liturgy," in *The Church and the Liturgy*, 7–24, at 11.

In 1967, an important volume dedicated to the liturgy in the Unam Sanctam series made important points on the positioning of the constitution on the liturgy within the corpus of Vatican II. Yves Congar's contribution to the volume emphasized that the ecclesiology of *Sacrosanctum Concilium* had moved forward when compared with Pius XII's encyclical *Mediator Dei* (1947). Congar also noted that a certain amount of time had elapsed between the liturgical and the ecclesiological debates, and that therefore there was a difference—at least a gap in the chronology of the final approvals—between the ecclesiologies of *Sacrosanctum Concilium* and *Lumen Gentium*.[15] Competing ecclesiologies of Vatican II also emerged in Pierre-Marie Gy's essay that stressed the need to read *Sacrosanctum Concilium* in light of the whole corpus of Vatican II documents in order to understand the key issues. More importantly, Gy rightly underscored that "the Constitution did not set a balance, but created a movement."[16] Vagaggini, under the telling heading "Leave the Door Open," expressed the very same idea of the liturgical reform as a spark for the renewal of the Catholic Church and therefore for the interpretation of Vatican II: "The council has wished to affirm a spirit, open a road, and so it was on its guard against an attitude that could have consisted in making a few concessions and then again hermetically sealing all doors."[17]

A similar take, but less rich in direct insights on the hermeneutics of Vatican II, was Jungmann's commentary. Although Jungmann saw *Sacrosanctum Concilium* as a beginning, not a final word, it is

15. See Yves Congar, "L'Ecclesia ou communauté chrétienne, sujet intégral de l'action liturgique," in *La liturgie après Vatican II: Bilans, études, prospective*, ed. Jean-Pierre Jossua and Yves Congar (Paris: Cerf, 1967), 241–82.
16. See Pierre-Marie Gy, "Situation historique de la Constitution," in Jossua and Congar, *La Liturgie après Vatican II*, 111–26, quotation at 122.
17. See Cipriano Vagaggini, "Fundamental Ideas of the Constitution," in *The Liturgy of Vatican II: A Symposium*, ed. Guilherme Baraúna, English edition ed. Jovian Lang (Chicago: Franciscan Herald, 1966), 95–129, quotation at 119.

to be regretted that he did not develop a broader analysis of the importance of *Sacrosanctum Concilium* for what he called the "renewal of the concept of the Church" (Erneuerung des Kirchenbegriffes).[18]

While the liturgists provided contributions about the specific significance of the constitution on the liturgy for the life of the Church, Giuseppe Dossetti, an Italian canon lawyer and private theologian expert at Vatican II, suggested that *Sacrosanctum Concilium* was the real ecclesiological heart of the council. On the basis of the Eucharist as the *norma normans*, the "norm for the other norms" of the Church's life, Dossetti opposed the Eucharistic ecclesiology of *Sacrosanctum Concilium* to the juridical aspects of *Lumen Gentium*. He saw in *Sacrosanctum Concilium* not only a chronologically earlier ecclesiology but also a theological priority of *Sacrosanctum Concilium* in the overall corpus of Vatican II.[19]

The 1970s were the age of the liturgical reform's completion: Paul VI's pontificate is still now much identified—especially by the anti–Vatican II component of Catholicism—with that era of decentralizing, pro-laity, and innovative reforms.[20] The election of John Paul II meant not only a new attitude toward Vatican II, but also the beginning of a new indulgence toward the tiny minority

---

18. See Josef Andreas Jungmann, "Kommentar zur Liturgiekonstitution," in *Das Zweite Vatikanische Konzil: Konstitutionen, Dekrete, und Erklärungen lateinisch und deutsch Kommentare*, vol. 1 of *Lexikon für Theologie und Kirche* (Freiburg i.B.: Herder, 1966), 10–109, quotation at 16, trans. Lalit Adolphus, Kevin Smyth, and Richard Strachan as "Constitution on the Sacred Liturgy," in *Commentary on the Documents of Vatican II*, vol. 1, ed. Herbert Vorgrimler (London: Burns and Oates; New York: Herder & Herder, 1967), 1–87. For a similar approach, see Hermann Schmidt, *La Costituzione sulla Sacra Liturgia: Testo, genesi, commento, documentazione* (Rome: Herder, 1966).

19. See Giuseppe Dossetti, *Per una "chiesa eucaristica": Rilettura della portata dottrinale della Costituzione liturgica del Vaticano I; Lezioni del 1965*, ed. Giuseppe Alberigo and Giuseppe Ruggieri (Bologna: Il Mulino, 2002). Dossetti is still largely unknown to English-speaking theologians, but see Nicholas Lash, *Theology for Pilgrims* (Notre Dame, IN: University of Notre Dame, 2008), 263–67; and Alberto Melloni, ed., *Giuseppe Dossetti: Studies on an Italian Catholic Reformer* (Zürich: LIT, 2008).

20. See Heribert Schmitz, "Tendenzen nachkonziliarer Gesetzgebung: Sichtung und Wertung," *Archiv für katholisches Kirchenrecht* 146 (1977): 381–419.

of Catholic traditionalists who rejected liturgical reform as a device for rejecting Vatican II. The traditionalists grasped better than many advocates of the council's reforms the theological force of *lex orandi, lex credendi* for Vatican II.

This development affected not only the focus of research on liturgical renewal and liturgical reform but also the very reception of *Sacrosanctum Concilium* by the magisterium. The achievement of the codification of canon law in 1983 did not help the constitution on the liturgy consolidate a new role in the life of the Church. If we follow Thomas Stubenrauch's research on the reception of Vatican II in the *Codex Iuris Canonici* of 1983, we must note that, differently from *Sacrosanctum Concilium*, the juridical concept *liturgia ab ecclesia*, "liturgy originating from the Church," in the *Codex* takes the place of the theological rationale *ecclesia a liturgia*, "Church originating from the liturgy." It is clear that the new *Codex* failed to fully receive Vatican II, especially concerning the liturgical ministry of deacons and the laity.[21]

Scholars have been overly confident about the coherence and consistency between the ecclesiology of the liturgical reform and the ecclesiological renewal in post–Vatican II Catholicism. In 1982, Franziskus Eisenbach noted the substantial continuity between the liturgical constitution and *Lumen Gentium*. Moreover, he expressed regret over the lack at the council of a tighter connection between liturgy and ecclesiology, because "the constitution on the liturgy could not take advantage" of the debate on *Lumen Gentium*.[22] Eisenbach's approach to the ecclesiology of the local church according to *Sacrosanctum Concilium* nos. 41–42 did not save him

---

21. See Thomas Stubenrauch, *Wer ist Träger der Liturgie? Zur Rezeption des II. Vatikanischen Konzils im Codex Iuris Canonici von 1983* (Trier: Paulinus, 2003), esp. 343–52.
22. See Franziskus Eisenbach, *Die Gegenwart Jesu Christi im Gottesdienst: Systematische Studien zur Liturgiekonstitution des II. Vatikanischen Konzils* (Mainz: Matthias-Grünewald, 1982), 587.

from a self-reassuring harmonization between the ecclesiologies of *Sacrosanctum Concilium* and *Lumen Gentium.*[23]

Twenty years after the approval of *Sacrosanctum Concilium* and shortly before the Extraordinary Synod of Bishops of 1985, the largely accomplished but still ongoing reform of liturgy contributed to the disappearance of any fruitful debate about the relationship between the liturgy and Vatican II as such.[24] Furthermore, the emphasis on collegiality and Church reform in the theological debate in the 1970s and the 1980s contributed to an increasingly technical-liturgical reading of *Sacrosanctum Concilium.*[25] The indult from the Holy See of 1984 and John Paul II's *motu proprio Ecclesia Dei* of 1988 granted permission to celebrate "the old liturgy," so it could not but weaken the theological impact of *Sacrosanctum Concilium* on the living ecclesiology of Catholicism.

The five-volume *History of Vatican II* edited by Giuseppe Alberigo and Joseph Komonchak provided new information about the key role of the liturgical debate within the council and about the dynamics in the preparatory and conciliar liturgical commissions.[26] Nevertheless, studies on *Sacrosanctum Concilium* published almost concurrently with the *History* focused on an "ideological" continuity between the early-twentieth-century liturgical movement and *Sacrosanctum Concilium,*

23. See Franz Frühmorgen, *Bischof und Bistum—Bischof und Presbyterium: Eine liturgiewissenschaftliche Studie zu den Artikeln 41 und 42 der Liturgiekonstitution des Zweiten Vatikanums* (Regensburg: Pustet, 1994).

24. See Annibale Bugnini, *The Reform of the Liturgy, 1948–1975,* trans. Matthew J. O'Connell (Collegeville, MN: Liturgical, 1990), orig. pub. as *La riforma liturgica, 1948–1975* (Rome: Centro Liturgico Vincenziano-Edizioni Liturgiche, 1983).

25. As can be seen also in Giuseppe Alberigo et al., eds., *The Reception of Vatican II* (Washington: Catholic University of America, 1987).

26. See Mathijs Lamberigts, "The Liturgy Debate," in *History of Vatican II,* vol. 2, *The Formation of the Council's Identity, First Period and Intercession, October 1962–September 1963* (Maryknoll, NY: Orbis, 1997), 107–66; and Reiner Kaczinsky, "Toward the Reform of the Liturgy," in *History of Vatican II,* vol. 3, *The Mature Council, Second Period and Intercession, September 1963–September 1964* (Maryknoll, NY: Orbis, 2000), 192–256.

and thus they overlooked the impact of the constitution on Vatican II as such.[27]

The many studies published for the fortieth anniversary of *Sacrosanctum Concilium* offered nothing really decisive.[28] The Tübingen-based five-volume *Herders theologischer Kommentar zum Zweiten Vatikanischen Konzil*, edited by Peter Hünermann and Hans-Jochen Hilberath, contributed to a new appreciation of *Sacrosanctum Concilium*.[29] In the volume of *Kommentar* devoted to *Sacrosanctum Concilium* and in the *History of Vatican II*, Reiner Kaczinsky stressed the novelty of the constitution in the context of the history of the councils and of the liturgy.[30] More profoundly, he emphasized the function of *Sacrosanctum Concilium* no. 5—the centrality of the paschal *mysterium*—not only as a center of the constitution but also as a "heart-word" (*Herzwort*) for Vatican II.[31]

But it seems that many commentaries on *Sacrosanctum Concilium* are outrun by the haste and aggressiveness—more than by the intellectual command—of the advocates of a revision of the liturgical reform of Vatican II. In the last ten years, the influential calls for

27. See, e.g., Maria Paiano, *Liturgia e società nel Novecento: Percorsi del movimento liturgico di fronte ai processi di secolarizzazione* (Rome: Storia e Letteratura, 2000).

28. See, e.g., in *Liturgisches Jahrbuch* 53 (2003): Joseph Ratzinger, "40 Jahre Konstitution über die Heilige Liturgie: Rückblick und Vorblick," 209–21; Jürgen Bärsch, "'Von Grösstem Gewicht für die Liturgiefeier ist die Heilige Schrift' (SC 24): Zur Bedeutung der Bibel im Kontext des Gottesdienstes," 222–41; and Andreas Odenthal, "Häresie der Formlosigkeit durch ein 'Konzil der Buchhalter': Überlegungen zur Kritik an der Liturgiereform nach 40 Jahren 'Sacrosanctum Concilium,'" 242–57.

29. See Hans Jochen Hilberath and Peter Hünermann, eds., *Herders Theologischer Kommentar zum Zweiten Vatikanischen Konzil*, 5 vols. (Freiburg i.B.: Herder, 2004–05).

30. See Reiner Kaczynski, "Toward the Reform of the Liturgy," in *History of Vatican II*, vol. 3, *The Mature Council, Second Period and Intercession, September 1963–September 1964* (Maryknoll, NY: Orbis, 2000), esp. 220–34.

31. See Reiner Kaczynski, "Theologischer Kommentar zur Konstitution über die Heilige Liturgie Sacrosanctum Concilium," in *Herders Theologischer Kommentar*, 2:9–227, esp. 63, where he quotes Angelus A. Häussling, "Pascha-Mysterium: Kritisches zu einem Beitrag in der dritten Auflage des Lexikon für Theologie und Kirche," *Archiv für Liturgiewissenschaft* 41 (1999): 157–65.

a "reform of the reform" of the liturgy have fueled a political-theological debate about the fortunes and misfortunes of *Sacrosanctum Concilium* and have called forth defenses of the historical memory of that postconciliar period,[32] rather than defenses of the deep theological implications and ecclesiological depth of the constitution. The political-ecclesiological debate on the council has compelled the advocates of Vatican II to defend the liturgy. However, they have failed to emphasize that liturgy was not only the chronological starting point of Vatican II but also the theological starting point. Perhaps more importantly, it was the first and most undisputed common ground of the Council Fathers.

Somewhere between nostalgia for the pre–Vatican II era and the undeniable contribution of *Sacrosanctum Concilium* to the liturgical life of the Catholic Church, some scholars have underscored the continuity between Pius XII's encyclical *Mediator Dei* and Vatican II, and between Pius X's *motu proprio Tra le sollecitudini* (1903) and Vatican II.[33] The bizarre mix of tradition and *ressourcement* in theological discourse has generated ambiguity in the debate on Vatican II that John O'Malley recently analyzed in his *What Happened at Vatican II*.[34]

---

32. See Piero Marini, *A Challenging Reform: Realizing the Vision of the Liturgical Renewal, 1963–1975,* ed. Mark R. Francis, John R. Page, and Keith F. Pecklers (Collegeville, MN: Liturgical, 2007).

33. See Aidan Nichols, *Looking at the Liturgy: A Critical View of Its Contemporary Form* (San Francisco: Ignatius, 1996); Martin Mosebach, *Häresie der Formlosigkeit: Die römische Liturgie und ihr Feind,* new, exp. ed. (Munich: Hanser, 2007); Pamela Jackson, *An Abundance of Graces: Reflections on* Sacrosanctum Concilium (Mundelein, IL: Hillenbrand, 2004); and Pamela Jackson, "Theology of the Liturgy," in *Vatican II: Renewal within Tradition,* ed. Matthew L. Lamb and Matthew Levering (New York: Oxford, 2008), 101–28.

34. See O'Malley, *What Happened at Vatican II,* 300–301.

3. The Agenda of Vatican II and the Liturgical Debate

John XXIII's announcement of Vatican II caught everyone by surprise: on January 25, 1959, less than three months after his election, he symbolically threw open the windows of the Vatican in order to—in his very words—"let in some fresh air." However, the liturgy had been on the agenda of Catholicism for quite some time. The call for liturgical reform was no surprise.[35]

The last years of Pius XII had already seen some decisions made in this direction. The novelty of the council benefited from the riches of the early-twentieth-century liturgical movement, but the liturgical reform could develop its deep theological assumptions only in a council where the issue of change met clearly one of the key points of the liturgical movement: the notion of *ressourcement*.[36]

This is why, far from being an issue of concern only to liturgists, Vatican II's liturgical reform was clearly a path-opening debate. John XXIII's choice to inaugurate the debates with the schema *De Liturgia* was grounded not just on the better shape and reception of this schema compared with the other seven schemata sent to the Council Fathers immediately before the beginning of the first session in the fall of 1962.

Interpretations of John XXIII's decision underscored the propaedeutic function of the liturgical debate for the council as a whole, and commentaries on *Sacrosanctum Concilium* have again ventured interpretations of this decision.[37] Nevertheless, in recent

---

35. See Giuseppe Alberigo and Alberto Melloni, eds., *Verso il concilio Vaticano II, 1960–1962: Passaggi e problemi della preparazione conciliare* (Genoa: Marietti, 1993).

36. See Marie-Anne Vannier, ed., *Les Pères et la naissance de l'ecclésiologie* (Paris: Cerf, 2009); Etienne Fouilloux, *La Collection "Sources chrétiennes": Éditer les Pères de L'Église au XXe siècle* (Paris: Cerf, 1995).

37. "See Piero Marini, introduction to *Concilii Vaticani II synopsis in ordinem redigens schemata cum relationibus necnon patrum orationes atque animadversiones: Constitutio de sacra liturgia Sacrosanctum concilium*, ed. Francisco Gil Hellín (Vatican City: Libreria Editrice Vaticana, 2003, x–xi).

years, Catholic theologians and historians have been much more focused on the "technical" outcomes of the liturgical reform and its direct effects than on its profound meaning for Vatican II and the Church. Benedict XVI's decisions have indeed promoted this feature of the post–Vatican II ecclesiological debate, boosting the impact of a political-aesthetic standpoint on liturgy and making it easier to overlook the ties between the liturgical reform and Vatican II as an agent of change or, as O'Malley insists, Vatican II as a "language event."[38]

The liturgical debate opened Vatican II and became an event within the event, because it ignited a motion stretching beyond the dreams of the "progressive" majority at the council. Starting with the liturgy—with the liturgical debate and with the celebration of liturgy in different rites every morning in Saint Peter—helped bishops rediscover the potential of liturgy as a tool for a Church facing an increasingly secular and globalized world.[39] But this debate also gave voice to the call for Church reform more generally.[40] Even in the preparatory phase, the preparatory commissions and especially the Central Commission for overall coordination of the council discussed the function of the liturgical debate and its scheduling in addressing the main issues on the conciliar agenda. The decision of the Council of Presidents on October 15, 1962, to reschedule the debates and put the liturgical schema before the other schemata highlights the rise of the main division within the council concerning the way of addressing the issue of change: the decision was greeted with John XXIII's positive response.[41] The relationship between *libro e*

38. O'Malley, *What Happened at Vatican II*, 306.

39. See Schmidt, *La Costituzione sulla Sacra Liturgia.*

40. See especially Yves Congar and B.-D. Dupuy, eds., *L'épiscopat et l'Église universelle* (Paris: Cerf, 1962).

41. See Angelo Giuseppe Roncalli - Giovanni XXIII, *Pater amabilis: Agende del pontefice, 1958–1963*, ed. Mauro Velati (Bologna: Istituto per le scienze religiose, 2007), 443.

calice (book and chalice) had emerged as a key element in Roncalli's theology already in his years as apostolic delegate in Bulgaria from 1925 to 1934; it was a salient point of his homily when he took possession of the Lateran Basilica on November 23, 1958.[42]

At the beginning of the preparatory phase of Vatican II, it became clear even to the Roman Curia that the liturgical reform would play a major role, but they hoped it would do it as an "icebreaker" for a quick and smooth council, not as a "path-opener."[43] The history of the council shows that the debates went all but smoothly, and that the debate on the liturgical constitution between October 1962 and November 1963 turned out to be much more than an icebreaker.

The Roman Curia and the so-called minority rejected the comprehensive and programmatic reform of the liturgy laid out in the schema prepared by the liturgical preparatory commission, while the "majority" accepted the reform and long-awaited renewal of liturgy as the best possible interpretation of the pastoral character of the council. The outcomes of the debate and the almost unanimous final vote on the constitution on November 22, 1963, left no doubt as to the step taken in the direction of liturgical renewal.[44]

4. The Liturgical Constitution:
A Forgotten Hermeneutics of Vatican II?

A contribution regarding Vatican II as "constitution" for the Catholic Church came between 2005 and 2006 from Peter Hünermann in the conclusions to the five-volume *Herders theologischer Kommentar zum*

---

42. See Giuseppe Ruggieri, "Appunti per una teologia in papa Roncalli," in *Papa Giovanni*, ed. Giuseppe Alberigo (Rome: Laterza, 1987), 245–71.
43. See Antonino Indelicato, *Difendere la dottrina o annunciare il Vangelo: Il dibattito nella Commissione centrale preparatoria del Vaticano II* (Genoa: Marietti, 1992), 171–98; and Andrea Riccardi, "The Tumultuous Opening Days of the Council," in *History of Vatican II*, 2:1–67.
44. See Lamberigts, "Liturgy Debate," 107–66.

113

Zweiten Vatikanischen Konzil, edited by Hünermann himself and B. J. Hilberath. Hünermann develops aspects of his lecture given at the Bologna Conference in 1996 about the "pragmatics of the conciliar texts,"[45] but also includes and substantially supports Ormond Rush's suggestion about the hermeneutical principles (hermeneutics of the authors, texts, and recipients) of Vatican II.[46]

In a long and boldly reasoned essay,[47] Hünermann designates the corpus of conciliar texts as a "constitution" for the Catholic Church: "As a kind of first approach to the shape of the text of the Second Vatican Council, if one looks for an analogy by which to characterize the council's decisions, one can see a certain similarity to constitutional texts as drawn up by representative constitutional assemblies. This similarity is expressed in a particular way in the texts of Vatican II."[48] For Hünermann, the designation of Vatican II as a "constitution" surely does not mean placing the conciliar texts above the gospel: "The legitimation of a council and its authority

---

45. See Peter Hünermann, "Il concilio Vaticano II come evento," in *L'evento e le decisioni: Studi sulle dinamiche del Concilio Vaticano II,* ed. Maria Teresa Fattori and Alberto Melloni (Bologna: Il Mulino, 1997), 63–92.

46. See Ormond Rush, *Still Interpreting Vatican II: Some Hermeneutical Principles* (New York: Paulist, 2004). For the relationship between "letter" and "spirit" in the interpretation of *Dei Verbum,* see Ormond Rush, *"Dei Verbum* Forty Years On: Revelation, Inspiration, and the Spirit," *Australasian Catholic Record* 83 (2006): 406–14.

47. See Peter Hünermann, "Der Text: Werden—Gestalt—Bedeutung: Eine Hermeneutische Reflexion," in *Herders Theologischer Kommentar* 5:5–101, esp. 11–17, 85–87.

48. "Sucht man im Sinne einer ersten Annäherung an das Profil des Textes des II. Vatikanischen Konzils nach einer Analogie, um die Beschlüsse zu charakterisieren, so ergibt sich eine gewisse Ähnlichkeit mit Verfassungstexten, die von repräsentativen verfassungsgebenden Versammlungen ausgearbeitet werden. Diese Ähnlichkeit ist bei den Texten des II. Vatikanums besonders ausgeprägt und zeigt sich lediglich in stark vermittelter, abgestufter Form auch im Blick auf das Trienter Konzil und das I. Vatikanum." Ibid., 12. Hünermann outlined the analogies between a "constitution" and Vatican II's final documents: (1) the situation of "crisis or historical necessity" (in a state as well as in the Catholic Church), which calls for a constitution; (2) the quality of the final texts as texts discussed and approved by large assemblies, representative of different if not opposite political stands; (3) a similarity in the process (committees, subcommittees, plenary assemblies); (4) the relationship between the issues at hand and the texts describing and influencing the ongoing situation; and (5) the relationship between the final approval of a constitution and the act of reception of Vatican II.

is essentially different from that of a constitutional assembly of a modern state. . . . For this reason the conciliar text possesses an authority essentially different from that of a constitutional text."[49] In his conclusion, Hünermann precisely states the proposal to consider the texts of Vatican II as a "constitutional text for the faith":

> The corpus of texts of this council recalls a similarity to the texts of a constitution. At the same time, there are profound differences between the two beginning with the authority and specificity of the material of conciliar texts. For this reason the text of Vatican II can be prudently defined as a "constitutional text of faith." If this assumption about the text of Vatican II is valid, then what follows is a whole series of problems and questions, criticisms, and, not least of all, unfounded ways of interpreting Vatican II since they do not conform to the literary genre of the text.[50]

This definition of the nature of the texts of Vatican II establishes the council as a corpus of hermeneutical principles for the life of the Church that is capable of establishing what is "constitutional," and hence what is "unconstitutional," in the ecclesiology of the postconciliar Church.[51]

---

49. "Die Legitimation eines Konzils und damit seine autorität eine wesentlich andere ist als die einer verfassungsgegebenden Versammlung in staatlichen Sinne. . . . Der Konziltext besitzt von daher eine wesentlich andere Autorität als ein Verfassungstext." Ibid., 15–16.

50. "Das Textcorpus dieses Konzils weist eine Ähnlichkeit mit den Texten einer verfassunggebenden Versammlung auf. Dabei ergeben sich zugleich tiefgreifende Differenzen aus der anderen Autorität und der Eigentümlichkeit der Sache, die in den Konziltexten zur Sprache kommt. Auf Grund dieses Befund kann der Text des II. Vatikanischen Konzils vorsichtig als 'konstitutioneller Text des Glaubens' bezeichnet werden. Ist dieser *Vorbegriff* vom Text des II. Vatikanischen Konzils triftig, dann ergibt sich daraus, dass eine ganze Reihe von Problemstellungen und Anfragen, Kritiken und nicht zuletzt Auslegungsweisen in unbegründeter, weil dem Textgenus nicht entsprechender Weise an das II. Vatikanische Konzil herangetragen werden." Ibid., 17.

51. "Läßt man sich vom 'konstitutionellen' Charakter dieses Textcorpus überzeugen, so ergeben sich allerdings erhebliche Auswirkungen für die theologische Auslegung und die Rezeption dieser Texte." Peter Hünermann, "Der Text: Eine Ergänzung zur Hermeneutik des II. Vatikanischen Konzils," *Cristianesimo nella storia* 28 (2007): 339–58, quotation at 358. See also Peter Hünermann, "Zur theologischen Arbeit am Beginn der dritten Millenniums," in *Das Zweite Vatikanische Konzil und die Zeichen der Zeit heute: Anstöße aur weiteren Rezeption*, ed. Peter Hünermann with B. J. Hilberath and Lieven Boeve (Freiburg i.B.: Herder, 2006), 569–93.

Sacrosanctum Concilium constitutes one of the pillars of the ecclesiology of Vatican II. The liturgical constitution presents a way to defend the council's ecclesiology on the basis of Eucharistic ecclesiology, thus without making the option between juridical and Eucharistic ecclesiology the first and last word on the Church of Vatican II.

The definition of *Sacrosanctum Concilium* as "le parent pauvre de l'herméneutique conciliaire" (the forgotten element in the hermeneutics of Vatican II) is correct because, as we have seen, its hermeneutical function has been consistently downplayed.[52] The dire need for a hermeneutics of Vatican II once again centered on *Sacrosanctum Concilium* is justified on the basis of a chronologically rooted relationship between the liturgical constitution—the first document approved and voted at the council—and Vatican II as such. The necessity of and opportunity for a hermeneutics of the council based on *Sacrosanctum Concilium* becomes clear if we take into account that it opens the way for a new balance between the "clash of ecclesiologies" at the council and the gravitational center of the Church of Vatican II: Scripture and the Eucharist.

The liturgical constitution has been approached differently by the two hermeneutical and historiographical traditions on Vatican II—the pro-majority (pro-reform) and the pro-minority (nostalgic) traditions. Most pro-majority interpreters of Vatican II have looked at *Sacrosanctum Concilium* as the first reform of Vatican II, the beginning of the event, but seemed to entrust the defense of its profound message and implications to liturgists, who prefer an ecclesiological approach—based on *Lumen Gentium* and the relationship between the papacy and the episcopate—for the implementation of Vatican II.

---

52. See Patrick Prétot, "La Constitution sur la liturgie: Une herméneutique de la tradition liturgique," in *Vatican II et la théologie: Perspectives pour le XXIe siècle*, ed. Philippe Bordeyne and Laurent Villemin (Paris: Cerf, 2006), 17–34.

Surprisingly, pro-minority and essentially anticonciliar interpreters of Vatican II seem to have given up the effort for a direct reinterpretation of the council and its ecclesiology, and moved toward a downgrading of Vatican II through a dismissal of *Sacrosanctum Concilium* and a trivialization of the deep theological meaning of the liturgical reform. Despite the trivialization, some pro-minority interpreters of the council seem to have a grasp of *Sacrosanctum Concilium* that is richer than the grasp of the average defender of Vatican II.

That is why Vatican II interpreters need to attempt a more profound reading of the connections between Vatican II and the liturgical constitution. Only a hermeneutic based on the liturgy and the Eucharist, as developed in the constitution on the liturgy, can preserve the riches of the overall ecclesiology of Vatican II without getting lost in the technicalities of a "theological jurisprudence."

It is time to make the case for a strong relationship between *Sacrosanctum Concilium* and the ultimate meaning of Vatican II. This relationship is not a standard defense of the post–Vatican II liturgical renewal, nor a criticism of the "liberalization" of the Tridentine liturgy. Nonetheless, I assert that a deeper understanding of the new conception of liturgy developed at Vatican II and in the post–Vatican II liturgical renewal is the first step toward seeing the profound implications and the real implementation of Vatican II and of seeing what its implementation means.

It is time to demonstrate that *Sacrosanctum Concilium* represents the early and, at the same time, mature outcome of a council grounded in the four following ideas:

1. *Ressourcement* is the most powerful source of updating and reform for global Catholicism in the modern world. The anti–Vatican II "new liturgical movement" is moved not by

pure nostalgia; its theological and ecclesiological consequences reach far beyond nostalgia. The advocates of the anti–Vatican II "new liturgical movement" are indeed right as they identify in *Sacrosanctum Concilium* the main target, since this constitution is the most radical instance of *ressourcement* and the most obviously nontraditionalist document of the council. The principle of *ressourcement* affected the liturgical constitution like no other conciliar document; it is hard to find in the corpus of the documents of Vatican II passages more expressive of the very essence of the Church and driven by the idea of *ressourcement*.

2. The liturgical reform as intended in *Sacrosanctum Concilium* aimed at the rediscovery of the centrality of Scripture and the Eucharist. *Sacrosanctum Concilium* is a most direct way to grasp Vatican II's ecclesiology. The liturgical constitution is aware that "the life of the Church cannot be reduced to the sole eucharistic moment" (nos. 9–10), and that liturgy has its role in the Church as a "theologia prima" (a primary theology), as "locus theologicus" (a source for doing theology) and as "culmen et fons" (summit and source). The liturgical constitution sponsored a new awareness within the Roman Catholic Church that *things change*. That is why the liturgical reform of Vatican II and the most recent calls for a "reform of the reform" touch the whole essence of Vatican II. Changing worship sets off a rethinking of ecclesiology in a more profound and long-lasting way than the definition of the Church in *Lumen Gentium*.

3. This Eucharistic ecclesiology provides the grounds for the basic direction of Vatican II, that is, *rapprochement* inside and outside the Church. *Rapprochement*—a term used many times by the pioneer of ecumenism and liturgist Lambert Beauduin[53]—is not part of the corpus of Vatican II in a material way, but it belongs

fully to the aims of Vatican II. The council's liturgical reform plays a significant role in developing (during Vatican II) and performing (after Vatican II) this key feature of the council, in a way that is not less important than other, better-known, "*rapprochement* manifestos" of Vatican II, such as the decree on ecumenism *Unitatis Redintegratio*, the declaration *Nostra Aetate*, and the pastoral constitution *Gaudium et Spes*. The main *rapprochement* carried out by *Sacrosanctum Concilium* consists of a reconciled and unifying vision of the Church, of Christian life, and of the existential condition of the faithful in the world.[54] Far from being a purely aesthetic option, the theological starting point of the liturgical reform aimed at resetting the relationship between Christian liturgy, spiritual needs of the faithful, and Catholic theological reading of the modern world in its historical and social dimensions.

4. *Ressourcement,* Eucharistic ecclesiology, and *rapprochement* require a drive for a full implementation of Vatican II and provide an unambiguous appraisal of the issue of Vatican II's continuity and discontinuity and the role of liturgical reform in the Church of the twenty-first century. Any attempt to undermine the liturgical reform of Vatican II reveals a clearly reductionist view of the council and its epoch-making changes.

53. See Raymond Loonbeek and Jacques Mortiau, *Un pionnier, Dom Lambert Beauduin (1873–1960): Liturgie et unité des chrétiens*, 2 vols. (Louvain-la-Neuve: Collège Erasme, 2001), esp. 1:907–9. See also Jacques Mortiau and Raymond Loonbeek, *Dom Lambert Beauduin: Visionnaire et précurseur (1873–1960); un moine au coeur libre* (Paris: Cerf, 2005).

54. See Giuseppe Dossetti, *Per una "chiesa eucaristica": Rilettura della portata dottrinale della Costituzione liturgica del Vaticano II; lezioni del 1965*, ed. Giuseppe Alberigo and Giuseppe Ruggieri (Bologna: Il Mulino, 2002), 41.

6

The Battle over *Gaudium et Spes*
Then and Now

Dialogue with the Modern World after Vatican II

The pastoral constitution *Gaudium et Spes* is the most typical document of Vatican II. But most typical is also the history of its reception, and in this sense recovering this history is essential to understand the complexity of the conciliar reception in its entirety.[1]

1. The Special Role of Gaudium et Spes *at Vatican II*

When we try to contemplate the significance of the pastoral constitution *Gaudium et Spes* fifty years after the beginning of Vatican II, it is difficult not to begin with two definitions given to the pastoral constitution: the *schema vedette*, that is, the "star of

---

1. This chapter was published originally as "The Battle over 'Gaudium et Spes' Then and Now: Dialogue with the Modern World after Vatican II," *Origins* 42, no. 34 (January 31, 2013): 545–51.

Vatican II" (according to the Vatican correspondent for the Paris-based newspaper *Le Monde*, Henri Fesquet) and the "promised land of the council" (in the words of the most important theologian of Vatican II, French Dominican Yves Congar).

These enthusiastic assessments of the pastoral constitution came from two Frenchmen, French theology and French Catholic culture being the main thrust of the theological work behind *Gaudium et Spes* and causing more than a little discomfort to German theologians at Vatican II—and for a long time after. As we will see, this clash of theological cultures within the "progressive" conciliar majority is one of the typical features of the history of *Gaudium et Spes*. Nevertheless, other elements make the pastoral constitution unique among the documents of Vatican II and in the history of the councils of the Catholic Church. *Gaudium et Spes* was and still is the most delicate and crucial text of post–Vatican II Catholic theology, for several reasons:

- The pastoral constitution is the longest document of Vatican II (almost thirty-seven thousand words in its English translation on the website of the Vatican, www.vatican.va).
- *Gaudium et Spes* is a new kind of Church document: new for its subject (Church and modern world) and new for the preparation of Vatican II as well, given that there was no preparatory schema that led to the schema XVII, then schema XIII, and finally *Gaudium et Spes*, in contrast to the other constitutions of Vatican II.
- *Gaudium et Spes* (GS) faced new issues and addressed old issues (already addressed by the recent magisterium of the Church, such as, for example, social and economic justice, peace and war, marriage and family) in light of the "signs of the times" (GS paragraph 4). This makes *Gaudium et Spes* the unavoidable

checkpoint for any debate on social issues facing Catholics today, and for any debate a new or next general council or synod of the Catholic Church (on issues such as, for example, human sexuality and the role of women in the Church).

- The literary genre of *Gaudium et Spes* constitutes an absolute novelty in the history of council documents, and not only because of its length.

- *Gaudium et Spes* was the last document to be approved by Vatican II, acquiring its definitive structure only in January 1965 (the "Ariccia text") and later was redrafted in an important fashion on November 15–17, 1965 (the fifth version or *textus recognitus*), that is, quite late in the history of the council in comparison with other major texts, especially the other three constitutions. ·

- This timing revealed some strains of fragmentation in the "conciliar majority" that led Vatican II to the major reforms passed in the first three sessions. In this way, this was also a preview of the tensions of the postcouncil period. The tension around *Gaudium et Spes* was typical of the last fifty years concerning the anthropological issue and the resulting relationship between Church and the modern world. The divisions in the conciliar majority saw on one side the skeptical front toward *Gaudium et Spes* (Karl Rahner, Joseph Ratzinger, Giuseppe Dossetti, and a small but important group of French, including Henri de Lubac and Jean Danièlou) versus the more enthusiastic supporters of *Gaudium et Spes*: the French, the Dutch (Edward Schillebeeckx), and Latin-American theologians.

2. *Gaudium et Spes* and the Loyal Opposition to Vatican II: Ratzinger and de Lubac

Gaudium et Spes was and still is at the very heart of the two major streams of interpretation of the council. Henri de Lubac and Joseph Ratzinger were the champions of a more Augustinian view of the modern world and therefore were not enthusiastic about *Gaudium et Spes*.

The skepticism of Henri de Lubac (1896-1991) toward the anthropology of Vatican II, and especially *Gaudium et Spes*, was already evident during the council. We see this as we browse through the pages of his "conciliar journal" between 1964 and 1965 and in the debate about the final drafts of the pastoral constitution, in which de Lubac expressed harsh judgments about the fundamental orientations, if not the very basic theological knowledge, of some prominent leaders of the conciliar majority. De Lubac's perception of Vatican II shared nothing with the Lefebvrian rejection of the council, as de Lubac remained always loyal to Vatican II as a legitimate council of the Catholic Church, but his perception of Vatican II as a "surrender" to an excessive optimism about the modern world would only grow in the years to come. In the introduction to *Augustinisme et théologie moderne* (1971), de Lubac wrote, "Today we are witnesses of an endeavor that wants to dissolve the Church into the world . . . the tide of immanentism is growing irresistibly."[2]

De Lubac developed an analysis of the post–Vatican II period as a time in which the theological balance between nature and grace had been disrupted in favor of a naïve confidence in nature and the world, against the need of grace and faith and against the idea of transcendence. But de Lubac also saw a dissonance between "the

2. Henri de Lubac, *Augustinisme et théologie moderne*, Oeuvres complètes XIII (Paris: Cerf, 2008), xxiv.

council" on one side and "the para-council" on the other (a distinction that many others adopted after him): "Just as the Second Vatican Council received from a number of theologians instructions about various points of the task it should assume, under pain of 'disappointing the world,' so too the 'post–conciliar' Church was immediately and from all sides assailed with summons to get in step, not with what the Council had actually said, but with what it should have said."[3] Immediately before the 1985 Extraordinary Synod of Bishops, Henri de Lubac repeated his view of the post–Vatican II situation as an unprecedented crisis in the history of Catholic theology and stressed the need to avoid in the interpretation of Vatican II the "analogical interpretation" of the documents of the council. De Lubac described the relationship between Vatican I and Vatican II in unequivocal terms: "Vatican II completed the work initiated by Vatican I . . . through a solemn teaching that confirms the teaching of the whole Catholic Tradition."[4] For that matter, de Lubac's positive judgment of Karol Wojtyla's interventions in the subcommittee about atheism during the drafting of *Gaudium et Spes* only foreshadowed the influence of de Lubac's views on the future John Paul II.

But Ratzinger's appreciation of Wojtyla's anthropology was even more important than de Lubac's influence on John Paul II's pontificate and on the history of the debate about Vatican II. Ratzinger agreed with much of de Lubac's views about the postconciliar situation, but as a cardinal prefect of the Congregation for the Doctrine of the Faith from 1981 to 2005 and as pope after his election in April 2005, Ratzinger had many more opportunities to enforce his judgment. As a matter of fact, Ratzinger's Augustinianism

---

3. See Henri de Lubac, *A Brief Catechesis on Nature and Grace*, trans. Richard Arnandez (San Francisco: Ignatius, 1984), 235.

4. Henri de Lubac, *Entretien autour de Vatican II: Souvenirs et réflexions* (Paris: France Catholique/ Cerf, 1985), 76.

dates back to his years in high school, in Nazi-ruled Germany, when the idea of a "City of God" worked as an antidote to the political and ethical totalitarianism that was ruling Germany, including Catholic Bavaria. But it is his postdoctoral work on Bonaventure that helps in understanding Ratzinger's future overall assessment of the anthropology and ecclesiology of Vatican II and his evolution from young theologian pushing for renewal (as *peritus* of Cardinal Frings of Cologne during Vatican II) to the pointed reviewer of Vatican II beginning in the early 1970s.

From the very beginning of the post–Vatican II period, Ratzinger stressed the importance of a correct interpretation of the new openness to other Christians and to the problems of humankind. Already in 1968, he criticized the anthropology of *Gaudium et Spes*:

> The way "people of God" is turned into a sort of empirical term, can only be regarded as extremely questionable. We can only agree with Giuseppe Alberigo that this way of speaking of the Church involves no small danger of sinking once more into a purely sociological and even ideological view of the Church through ignoring the essential insights of the Constitution on the liturgy and the Constitution on the Church and by oversimplifying, externalizing and making a catchword of a term which can only keep its meaning if it is used in a genuinely theological context.[5]

Ratzinger's judgment of Vatican II focused on the role of *Gaudium et Spes*, and in particular, it mirrored Ratzinger's proximity to Augustine's pessimism about human *freedom* and, in general, the rejection of a Thomist epistemology in favor of a more kerygmatic vision of Christian faith.

---

5. Joseph Ratzinger, "Introductory Article and Chapter I: The Dignity and the Human Person," in *Commentary on the Documents of Vatican II*, ed. Herbert Vorgrimler, vol. 5, *Pastoral Constitution on the Church in the Modern World* (New York: Herder and Herder, 1969), 118–19 (whole section by Ratzinger, 115–63).

In Ratzinger's *Principles of Catholic Theology*, in the chapters entitled "Review of the Postconciliar Era—Failures, Tasks, Hopes" and "Church and World" (published in German in the mid-1970s), we can read one of the starkest possible assessments of *Gaudium et Spes* and of Vatican II by the future pope Benedict XVI: "Something of the Kennedy era pervaded the Council, something of the naïve optimism of the concept of the great society. It was precisely the break in historical consciousness, the self-tormenting rejection of the past, that produced the concept of a zero hour in which everything would begin again and all those things that had formerly been done badly would now be done well."[6]

Given this view, it is clear why the pastoral constitution *Gaudium et Spes*, concerning the Church and the modern world, is at the center of Ratzinger's critique, as he states, "The lack of clarity that persists even today about the real meaning of Vatican II is closely associated with such diagnosis and, consequently, with this document."[7] Ratzinger followed this by saying that the affirmations in *Gaudium et Spes* "breathe an astonishing optimism," resulting in nothing more than "a revision of the *Syllabus* of Pius IX, a kind of counter-syllabus," which was intended to reverse the negative stance adopted by Pius IX against *the political and doctrinal* "errors" of modernity listed in the *Syllabus* of 1864.[8]

Ratzinger's Augustinianism is at the basis not only of his judgment of *Gaudium et Spes* (a judgment he shared, in 1965, with other German theologians at Vatican II, such as Karl Rahner), but also of his views about theology of liberation and the political theology of

---

6. Joseph Ratzinger, *Principles of Catholic Theology: Building Stones for a Fundamental Theology* (San Francisco: Ignatius, 1987), 372. The first publication of this article, "Der Weltdienst der Kirche: Auswirkungen von "Gaudium et spes" in letzten Jahrzehnt," dates back to issue 4 of the journal *Communio* (1975).

7. Ibid., 378.

8. Ibid., 381.

Jürgen Moltmann and Johann Baptist Metz. Ratzinger's assumption that the dualism between the "kingdom of God" and the "order of history" is essential to the core of Christian faith comes from Ratzinger's postdoctoral work on Bonaventure and shapes much of his overall assessment of Vatican II.

Nevertheless, Ratzinger's view of the theological roots of Vatican II put him at odds with a widespread perception of the "modernity" of the council. Ratzinger fought the assumption of "liberal" theologians about the reconciliation between Catholic theology and modernity by reminding them of the "roots" of the theological reorientation of Vatican II, that is, the fathers of the Church: "Today it is being said with increasing frequency that the Council thereby placed itself under the aegis of the European Enlightenment. But the Council Fathers had a different motive for their orientation; they derived it from the theology of the Fathers of the Church, where St. Augustine, for example, strongly emphasized the difference between Christian simplicity and the empty pomp of pagan liturgies."[9] Ratzinger's defense of Augustinianism was matched, during the years in which he formed a harsh opinion of Vatican II, by the impression that the defenders of Scholastic theology at the council had soon surrendered to a kind of new modernism. Ratzinger saw this new modernism in the adoption of a "utopian interpretation" of Vatican II, tied ultimately to a "theology of the world."[10]

9. Ibid., 376.
10. See Joseph Ratzinger, "Zehn Jahre nach Konzilsbeginn—wo stehen wir?," epilogue to *Dogma und Verkündigung* (Munich-Freiburg i.B.: Wewel, 1973), 439–47, quotation at 443.

3. Other Reformers Critical of *Gaudium et Spes*:
Dossetti and Alberigo

Ratzinger's criticism of *Gaudium et Spes* was the harshest, but he was not the only theologian to criticize it. If we want to give a fair representation of the debate about *Gaudium et Spes* after Vatican II, we should not listen only to the voices of Ratzinger and de Lubac, who have become in these last three or four decades the most important theologians of an easily labeled "conservative Catholic theology." If we did, we would not understand the importance of the role of the pastoral constitution in the last fifty years.

One criticism of *Gaudium et Spes* comes directly from the same "Bologna school" that in recent years has been accused of writing and publishing (and translating into seven languages) an "openly liberal" history of Vatican II. Both the founder of the Bologna institute (founded in 1953 with the name "Centro di documentazione," now "Fondazione Giovanni XXIII per le scienze religiose"—John XXIII Foundation for Religious Studies), the Italian politician, then priest, and conciliar theologian Giuseppe Dossetti, and his successor, Giuseppe Alberigo, who was also the leader of the Bologna institute until his death in 2007, showed concerns about the theological solidity of *Gaudium et Spes* already in 1965.

In a series of lectures given in Bologna in October 1966, Dossetti, who was then the main aide of the archbishop of Bologna, Cardinal Lercaro, assessed the contribution of *Gaudium et Spes* as mainly positive: "The very fact that we have this document is a great, positive element in the life of the Church." But in the unfolding of Dossetti's lecture and of his other lectures given in the immediate postcouncil period, Dossetti expressed concerns that the popularity of *Gaudium et Spes* would come at the expense of the other constitutions, especially of the constitution on the liturgy.[11] Dossetti was and remained one of the most important politicians and intellectuals within Western European "Left Catholicism"; however, for him, this was not inconsistent with his judgment of *Gaudium et Spes*.[12]

In those same years, the Church historian Giuseppe Alberigo (the future editor of the five-volume *History of Vatican II*) underlined the importance of the pastoral constitution; after all, he was a great friend and admirer of Marie-Dominique Chenu. But he also quoted and shared Ratzinger's critique of *Gaudium et Spes* in terms of it lacking a deep anthropology and appreciation of the theology of the cross in the Christian understanding of the announcing of the gospel *ad extra*.[13] Nevertheless, in the conclusion of the five-volume *History of Vatican II*, written in 1999, Alberigo granted the epoch-making importance of the pastoral constitution but repeated his criticism:

> It is no accident that Christian history displays a wealth of ambiguities, both in the sense of deafness and blindness to the major twists of history and in the sense of misinterpretations of the messianic meanings of history itself. In fact, at the concrete level, the Council showed in more than one case that it was applying criteria that it had itself formulated in keeping with a *lectio facilior*. This happened both in dealing with the problems of the influence of the media in modern societies and in the facile historical optimism of "Western" kind that runs through so much of the constitution *Gaudium et Spes*, as well as in the tentativeness with which the same document reads the Gospel background of the cry of the peoples for peace.[14]

11. Giuseppe Dossetti, *Il Vaticano II: Frammenti di una riflessione*, ed. Francesco Margiotta Broglio (Bologna: Il Mulino, 1996), 82–102, quotation at 82; see also Giuseppe Dossetti, *Per una "chiesa eucaristica": Rilettura della portata dottrinale della Costituzione liturgica del Vaticano II. Lezioni del 1965*, ed. Giuseppe Alberigo and Giuseppe Ruggieri (Bologna: Il Mulino, 2002), 33–35.

12. See *Giuseppe Dossetti: Studies on an Italian Catholic Reformer*, ed. Alberto Melloni (Berlin: LIT, 2008); *Left Catholicism, 1943–1955: Catholics and Society in Western Europe at the Point of Liberation*, ed. Emmanuel Gerard and Gerd-Rainer Horn (Leuven: Leuven University Press, 2001).

13. See Giuseppe Alberigo, "Die Konstitution in Beziehung zur gesamten Lehre des Konzils," in *Die Kirche in der Welt von heute: Untersuchungen und Kommentare zur Pastoralkonstitution "Gaudium et spes" des II. Vatikanischen Konzils*, ed. Guilherme Barauna (Salzburg: Otto Müller Verlag, 1967), 49–76.

From the 1980s on, Dossetti and Alberigo became very important leaders not only in the effort to write a history of Vatican II, but also in their hermeneutical approach to Vatican II as a council that needed to be implemented looking not only at the letter of the documents, but also at its spirit. They saw the limits of the pastoral constitution, but they never failed to acknowledge its pivotal role for Vatican II, and not just because of their theological proximity to Congar and Chenu.

4. The Neo-Thomists in Defense of *Gaudium et Spes*

In contrast to Ratzinger and von Balthasar, the "Bolognese" criticisms of *Gaudium et Spes* never became the defining elements of their judgment of the council. The approach to *Gaudium et Spes* of the Bologna school resembled Karl Rahner's view of the pastoral constitution: despite being aware of the weak points of *Gaudium et Spes*, Dossetti, Alberigo, and Rahner saw *Gaudium et Spes* as part of a complex *corpus* of council documents. In his famous comments, "Remarks on the Schema 'De Ecclesia in Mundo Huius Temporis' in the draft of May 28, 1965," Rahner criticizes, among other things, the lack of a theology of sin and an inadequate Christian anthropology.[15] But after Vatican II, Rahner did not blame the weaknesses of *Gaudium et Spes* for the difficulties of the postcouncil period, and he more than once stressed the importance of the pastoral constitution

---

14. Giuseppe Alberigo, "Transition to a New Age," in *History of Vatican II*, ed. Giuseppe Alberigo and Joseph A. Komonchak, vol. 5, *The Council and the Transition: The Fourth Period and the End of the Council, September 1965–December 1965* (Maryknoll, NY: Orbis, 2006), 611.

15. Rahner's unpublished critique, "Anmerkungen zum Schema De Ecclesia in Mundo Hujus Temporis (in der Fassung vom 28.5.65)," is the subject of Thomas O'Meara, O.P., "Karl Rahner's Remarks on the Schema, De Ecclesia in Mundo Hujus Temporis, in the Draft of May 28, 1965," *Philosophy & Theology*, 20.1/2 (2008), 331–39: see Brandon Peterson, "Critical Voices: The Reactions of Rahner and Ratzinger to Schema XIII" (Gaudium et Spes)," *Modern Theology* Volume 31, Issue 1 (January 2015), 1-26, esp. 7.

in the ecclesiology of the post–Vatican II Church.[16] Rahner can be seen as an eminent member of the "neo-Thomist" interpretation of Vatican II, together with other neo-Thomists such as French Dominicans like Marie-Dominique Chenu and Yves Congar.

In the well-known essay by Chenu—whose role in the drafting of *Gaudium et Spes* was different and not as central as Congar's—in the commentary on the pastoral constitution in the collection "Unam Sanctam," Chenu offered a short history of the key expression "signs of the times" (for the first time used by John XXIII in the bull of the convocation of the council, *Humanae Salutis*, December 25, 1961) and emphasized its importance for theology: "Faith finds its nourishment in reading history." Chenu was aware of the issues regarding the "theological diagnosis" of the modern world in *Gaudium et Spes*; nevertheless, he replied to the many criticisms against "a certain optimism" and the ambiguities of *Gaudium et Spes* with "The world is ambiguous." In a remarkable defense of the pastoral constitution, Chenu affirmed, "The expression 'signs of the times' makes sense not just in the literary context of Vatican II, but in the body of Catholic doctrine itself—and its method—where the Church is defined in its consubstantial relationship with the world and with history. This expression is indeed a 'constitutional' category, and in this pastoral constitution *Gaudium et Spes* it is decisive of the laws and conditions of evangelization."[17]

Similarly, Yves Congar, in his essay published in the same commentary on *Gaudium et Spes*, addressed the criticisms by many, included Jacques Maritain, against the optimism expressed by the

---

16. See Karl Rahner, "Basic Theological Interpretation of the Second Vatican Council," in Karl Rahner, *Concern for the Church* (New York: Crossroads, 1981), 77–90.

17. The famous article by Marie-Dominique Chenu, "Les signes des temps: Réflexion théologique," in *L'Église dans le monde de ce temps: Constitution pastorale "Gaudium et Spes,"* ed. Yves Congar and Michel Peuchmard (Paris: Cerf, 1967), 205–25, quotations at 214, 216, and 225.

pastoral constitution. Congar replied by pointing out the differences between Christendom's old approach to the world in its attempt to dominate it, "in the attempt to keep the world a child," and what *Gaudium et Spes* offers as a new approach to the world and to secular realities: "The Church of Vatican II relates to the world and wants to serve. Of course, the first article of the Christian mission in the world talks about conversion to the Gospel, but the mission of the Church entails a second article, service to the world as it is, until, in the eschatological kingdom, Church and world will be one."[18]

5. *Gaudium et Spes* in the Recent Catholic Theological Debate

Gaudium et Spes has played a central role in the debate about Church and modernity in the last five decades.[19] It is a council document that stirs emotions and does not leave theologians indifferent—even the ones who have not read it. In these last fifty years, *Gaudium et Spes* has served as a marker of the new globalized identity of Catholicism, and I would like to offer here just a few examples of its renewed importance.

First, *Gaudium et Spes* works as the major evidence of the multiculturalism of globalized Catholicism, given the different receptions of *Gaudium et Spes* depending on the geographical and cultural setting of the receivers. In the churches of Latin America, Africa, and Asia, we do not find the polarizing views on *Gaudium et Spes* that have become typical of American Catholicism. In Europe, the reception of *Gaudium et Spes* has not been intercepted by debates

18. Yves Congar, "Église et monde dans la perspective de Vatican II," in Congar and Peuchmard, *L'Église dans le monde de ce temps*, 32–33.

19. See Guy Jobin, "*Gaudium et Spes* dans le monde vécu de ce temps: Réflexions épistémologiques sur l'herméneutique de la constitution pastorale," in *Vatican II et la théologie: Perspectives pour le XXIe siècle*, ed. Philippe Bordeyne and Laurent Villemin (Paris: Cerf, 2006), 177–201.

34

on socioeconomic justice and "life issues" that now are the major part of the debate on the role of Catholicism in public life in America. This is a new development since the years of Vatican II: we now see the importance of studying the reception of Vatican II locally and globally, given that *Gaudium et Spes* is one of the examples of a "diversified reception" of the council according to the culture of the local church.[20]

Second, despite the persisting criticisms of neo-Augustinians (and despite the creation of a "Ratzinger brand" that is perceived on both sides of the cultural spectrum of Catholicism as defining for the fate of Vatican II),[21] *Gaudium et Spes* has become an integral part of the message of Vatican II. In his thousand-page interpretation of Vatican II, French-German Jesuit Christoph Theobald has recently inserted *Gaudium et Spes* in the ecclesiological architecture of Vatican II built around two dimensions, horizontal-communional and vertical-hierarchical. The horizontal dimension of the Church (*ad intra* and *ad extra*) must be balanced with the vertical dimension by giving priority to the idea of revelation expressed in the constitution *Dei Verbum* (and in the declaration on religious liberty *Dignitatis Humanae*). In Theobald's dynamic hermeneutics of conciliar texts, through a crossing of horizontal (*Lumen Gentium, Unitatis Redintegratio, Nostra Aetate, Gaudium et Spes*) and vertical (*Dei Verbum, Dignitatis Humanae, Lumen Gentium, Sacrosanctum Concilium*) dimensions in the conciliar texts and a profound consideration of

20. See, for example, Gustavo Gutierrez, "The Church and the Poor: A Latin American Perspective," in *The Reception of Vatican II*, ed. Giuseppe Alberigo, Jean-Pierre Jossua, and Joseph Komonchak (Washington, DC: Catholic University of America Press, 1985) 171–93; Peter Phan, "Reception of Vatican II in Asia: Historical and Theological Analysis," in *Greogorianum* 83, no. 2 (2002): 269–85.

21. For the characterization of Joseph Ratzinger as a "neo-conservative" see Lieven Boeve, "*Gaudium et Spes* and the Crisis of Modernity: The End of the Dialogue with the World?," in *Vatican II and Its Legacy*, ed. Mathijs Lamberigts and Leo Kenis (Leuven: Leuven University Press, 2002), 83–94.

the historical nature of the texts, *Gaudium et Spes* plays a key role in the horizontal axis. Theobald does not deny the ingenuities and the "utopical character" (Theobald quotes here the French historian of modernism, Émile Poulat) of that idea of Catholicism: "If we consider the 'reframing' operated by *GS*, we perceive the limits of the pastoral constitution. The idea of 'integral vocation of the human being,' that in *GS* 11 anticipates the interpretation of the Gospel, is part of the 'integralist' tradition of Pius IX, Leo XIII, Pius X, and Pius XI—*Omnia instaurare in Christo*."[22] But *Gaudium et Spes* is an integral part of that "reframing" (in French, *recadrage*) that is the major accomplishment of Vatican II: a theology that tries to be more faithful to the gospel than to a culture, a sociology, or an ideology.

Nevertheless, in a very deep book published ten years ago, the French theologian Pierre Bordeyne has successfully recovered the original driving forces in the drafting of the pastoral constitution, emphasizing its key role in the formation of Catholic moral theology in modernity. Bordeyne names two forces: (1) the *déplacement*, the shift in the way Catholic theology approaches moral issues, that is, the role of human experience, and (2) the drive of *Gaudium et Spes* to address the needs of contemporary humanity. The pastoral constitution is not about optimism—its original title was *Gaudium et Luctus, Spes et Angor* (Joy and grief, hope and anguish)—but it is about hope as an answer for "anguish for justice as the initial spark for moral reasoning."[23] Bordeyne sees correctly *Gaudium et Spes* as the document through which "Vatican II fulfills its responsibility of issuing a moral judgment on modern society."[24]

---

22. Christoph Theobald, *La réception du concile Vatican II: Vol. I. Accéder à la source* (Paris: Cerf, 2009), 771–93, quotation at 788–89.
23. Philippe Bordeyne, *L'homme et son angoisse: La théologie morale de Gaudium et spes* (Paris: Cerf, 2004), 21 ("le texte conciliaire s'est davantage preoccupé de l'angoisse existentielle et de l'angoisse de la justice en tant qu'initiatrices du questionnement moral").

A few years ago, the Leuven-based theologian Joseph Selling affirmed that *Gaudium et Spes* and *Nostra Aetate* are "two of the most significant documents that were produced at Vatican II."[25] He is sure that *Gaudium et Spes* played a significant role in the development of Catholic moral theology in a "world-Church" globalized and aware of the complexities of religious "otherness" and its consequences on our theological ethics. The work of moral theologians like James Keenan, among others, constitutes a witness of the legacy of *Gaudium et Spes* in contemporary moral theology, especially beyond the boundaries of North Atlantic Catholicism.[26]

My third and final example is that in looking at the "theological geography" of Catholicism, it is interesting to investigate the permanence of a divide between French and German Catholic theologians around the pastoral constitution. French conciliar theology still claims *Gaudium et Spes* as the fruit of the work of its most important theologians at Vatican II. On the other bank of the French-German border, Johann Baptist Metz and Hermann Pottmeyer have not softened their cautious assessment of *Gaudium et*

---

24. Bordeyne, *L'homme et son angoisse*, 342 ("le concile exerce enfin sa responsabilité de critique sociale"). In another recent work, Bordeyne reminded us of the great importance of *Gaudium et Spes* in reshaping modern Catholic moral theology and "public theology," especially in the Southern Hemisphere: Africa, Latin America, and Asia. But Bordeyne was also right when he identified the "paradox" of *Gaudium et Spes*: "On one side, *Gaudium et Spes* revives an interest [in Vatican II] as a source of inspiration for moral theology, but, on the other side, the research on Vatican II has disappeared from the horizons of many moral theologians, so that what is lacking today is the *habitus* to go into action." Pierre Bordeyne, "La réappropriation de *Gaudium et Spes* en théologie morale: Une redécouverte de la particularité chrétienne," in *Vatican II et la théologie*, ed. Philippe Bordeyne and Laurent Villemin (Paris: Cerf, 2006), 153–76, quotation at 161.

25. Joseph A. Selling, "Gaudium et Spes: A Manifesto for Contemporary Moral Theology," in Lamberigts and Kenis, *Vatican II and Its Legacy*, 149.

26. See James Keenan, *A History of Catholic Moral Theology in the Twentieth Century: From Confessing Sins to Liberating Consciences* (New York: Continuum, 2010); *Catholic Theological Ethics in the World Church* (Padua Conference), ed. James Keenan (New York: Continuum, 2007); *Catholic Theological Ethics: Past, Present, and Future*, Trento Conference (Maryknoll, NY: Orbis, 2011).

Spes. But Karl Rahner's students—Karl Lehmann among others—have shown a more positive approach to the constitution. Recently, the younger generations of German Catholic theologians has shown more nuance in their approach to the heavily French-influenced anthropology of *Gaudium et Spes*. In the recently published five-volume *Kommentar* of Vatican II, Hans-Joachim Sander still reminds the reader of the weaknesses of the anthropology and sociology of *Gaudium et Spes*, but he identifies Vatican II as "the introductory moment of a *change of venue* of Christian faith becoming a world Church" (in German, *Ortswechsel*) as a consequence of the pastoral constitution.[27] In the conclusion of the five-volume *Kommentar* of Vatican II, the dogmatician from Tübingen Peter Hünermann clearly affirms the path-opening role of *Gaudium et Spes* in the dialogue between Church and modern world.[28]

6. Dialogue between Church and Modern World: Perspectives on Ecclesiological Issues

It is common language, especially in some Catholic quarters, to see in *Gaudium et Spes* an outdated document. But usually in those Catholic quarters, the history of the debate on *Gaudium et Spes* is forgotten, if not completely unknown. Here the ideological divide between different "camps" of Catholic culture is much stronger than the generational divide. For me as a teacher, there is no doubt that

27. Hans-Joachim Sander, "Theologischer Kommentar zur Pastoralkonstitution über die Kirche in der Welt von heute," in *Herders Theologischer Kommentar zum Zweiten Vatikanischen Konzil*, ed. Bernd Jochen Hilberath and Peter Hünermann (Freiburg i.B.: Herder, 2005), 5:831–32 and 585 (whole commentary at 5:581–886).

28. Peter Hünermann, "Die Gestalt des Textes: Einheit—Strukturen—Grundzüge," in Hilberath and Hünermann, *Herders Theologischer Kommentar zum Zweiten Vatikanischen Konzil*, (Freiburg i.B.: Herder, 2005), 5:72. See also Peter Hünermann, "Kriterien für die Rezeption des II. Vatikanischen Konzils," *Theologische Quartalschrift* 191, no. 2 (2011): 126–47.

the pastoral constitution (just as *Nostra Aetate*) speaks volume to the younger generation of Catholics.

What is forgotten is the fact that the fundamental insights of *Gaudium et Spes* in terms of theological method are still valid, if not prophetic in light of the signs of our time. The future and the significance of *Gaudium et Spes* is connected to the future of dialogue between the Church and the modern world, and in general to the future of Catholic ecclesiology—I would say to the future of the "practical ecclesiology" of Catholicism. I will try here to share a few thoughts on several issues:

- First is the ecclesiological issue of the relationship between universal and local dimensions in Catholic ecclesiology, probably the most riveting debate that ever happened (in public) between two cardinals, then Cardinal Ratzinger and Cardinal Kasper in 2002). *Gaudium et Spes* is part of the picture of Catholic ecclesiology, clearly balancing universal and local not on the basis of an idealized historical or philosophical model, but through the lens of ecclesial experience. The pastoral constitution takes into account "the world" both in its local and universal dimension, thus bypassing a Platonic worldview and assuming a deep historical awareness of the Christian experience.
- Another important issue is the relationship between Church and the world as it was reshaped by the new translation of the Eucharistic prayer and the change from "for all" to "for many." This change is clearly a step back from the deepest yearnings of *Gaudium et Spes* and of one of its theological prophets, Teilhard de Chardin, when he defined the liturgical celebration as "the Mass on the world": "I, your priest, will make the whole earth my altar and on it will offer you all the labours and sufferings of the world."[29] The calls for a "reform of the liturgical reform"

distorts the theology contained by the liturgical constitution also because it extracts and isolates the liturgical constitution from the context of Vatican II as a whole, but it also presupposes a silent abrogation of *Gaudium et Spes.*

• *Gaudium et Spes,* in its contribution to the formation of Catholic postconciliar moral theology, reshapes the relationship between the role of the magisterium, the role of theologians, and the primacy of the conscience in modernity. *Gaudium et Spes* paragraph 16—"Conscience is the most secret core and sanctuary of a man. There he is alone with God, Whose voice echoes in his depths" —is one of the most forgotten (but not yet abrogated) texts of Vatican II.

• *Gaudium et Spes* still plays a critical role for our current ecclesial issues, particularly for the ability of the Church to "discern" the "signs of the times" (*GS* 4). In the Catholic Church of today, it seems very easy to make a judgment on the signs of our times in secular culture, but *Gaudium et Spes* can and must play a role also in the discernment of the signs of our times *in the Church.* One of the basic teachings of the pastoral constitution is that the Church lives in history, and we cannot live out of the simplistic assumption that the institutional Church is an island of grace surrounded by evil. *Gaudium et Spes* is a critical tool for a moral judgment on the worldly matters, but also for our way to be a Church. The anti–*Gaudium et Spes* sentiment implies the inability to accept this coming to terms with the human and visible side of the Church.

• A healthy approach to Vatican II implies not asking everything from that council and those texts. But *Gaudium et Spes* is key

---

29. Teilhard de Chardin, "The Offering," in *The Mass on the World,* in Thomas M. King, *Teilhard's Mass. Approaches to "The Mass on the World"* (New York/Mahwah, NJ: Paulist, 2005), 145.

for the approach of Catholicism to current cultural-theological issues, and in particular, *Gaudium et Spes* is the key document to penetrate the "shifting meanings" of the secular age and its new "social imaginary"[30]: *Gaudium et Spes* is the most important moment of awareness of change and dynamism in history and in the world in modern Catholicism, and this is a point of no return.

• In this moment in time in our culture, the encounter between "radical orthodoxy" and a new form of "Catholic communitarianism," especially in the Anglo-Saxon world, represents a very delicate moment—not just for the survival of the legacy of *Gaudium et Spes*, but for the survival of a Catholicism able to interact with modern social imaginary.

• It is therefore clear that the neoliberal and neoconservative attacks on *Gaudium et Spes* in these last twenty years (at least) have so far paid off. But the price tag of this battle is also clear: "common good" and "universal common good" are extremely difficult cases to make in absentia of an ecclesial and magisterial reception of *Gaudium et Spes*. The crisis of the idea of common good in some Catholic quarters is a product of the cynicism against Vatican II and of the dismissal of *Gaudium et Spes* in particular.

• Finally, in a world where in many countries religious freedom is a day-by-day life-and-death issue, in order to defend this fundamental human right, we need to read *Gaudium et Spes* intertextually together with the declaration on religious freedom *Dignitatis Humanae*. In that latter document, religious freedom is part of freedom of conscience and not, as it was in the Middle

---

30. See Charles Taylor, *A Secular Age* (Cambridge, MA: Belknap Press of Harvard University Press, 2007).

Ages, part of the *libertas Ecclesiae*—the freedom of a purely monarchical Church vis-à-vis the empire. *Gaudium et Spes* is part of that effort to subtract from Catholicism its "imperial" features in order to make it more obedient to the gospel.

Remembering Vatican II is the statement of a hermeneutical intention, the will to approach Vatican II and to make it relevant for the Church and the world of today. Remembering makes a statement of an intention, the will to approach Vatican II. The hermeneutics of Vatican II are also the reflection of a case for or against public theology and a case for a particular kind of public theology. In the case of *Gaudium et Spes*, the immediate cultural and social ramifications of its reception are evident today maybe more than they were in 1965.

7

The Political Significance of Vatican II
and Its "Constitutional" Value

Vatican II was not a political event and does not convey a political message. But the event, the way it unfolded, and the final documents contain a political culture that is necessary to understand in order to understand the value of Vatican II in the world of today.[1]

1. The Anniversaries of Vatican II
and Anticonciliar Traditionalism

Celebrating anniversaries is a special kind of "public liturgy," often used to remember facts and events that are relevant only for specific persons but totally irrelevant or even annoying for all others. This phenomenon of modern life strikes a note of caution, if we consider that the years 2012–2015 mark the fiftieth anniversary of Vatican

1. This chapter was published originally in Italian as "Il Vaticano II come 'Costituzione' e la 'recezione politica' del concilio," *Rassegna di Teologia* 50 (2009): 107–22.

II (1962–1965). Nevertheless, anniversaries have been, in the last decades, important occasions for the Church to remember and re-understand the council. The twentieth anniversary saw the celebration of a decisive moment in the history of the reception of the council with the Extraordinary Synod of the Bishops celebrated in Rome in 1985. The fortieth anniversary of the conclusion of the Council left significant traces in the Church in 2005, a year marked by the passing of John Paul II, the conclave that swiftly elected Cardinal Joseph Ratzinger, and the beginning of the pontificate of Pope Benedict XVI. Much less significant to the debate about the reception of Vatican II was the Great Jubilee of 2000, whose legacy was largely celebratory, if not for the reflexes of the dispute between Ratzinger and Kasper on the relationship between an ecclesiology of the local and universal Church.[2]

But there are also other anniversaries tied to the event of Vatican II. The fortieth anniversary of the liturgical constitution *Sacrosanctum Concilium* in 2003 saw the first signs of the resurgence for a kind of nostalgia of the Tridentine liturgy and the first signs of the current "uprising" against the liturgical reform of Vatican II.[3] Not long after the beginning of the debate on the liturgical reform of Vatican II, the election of Benedict XVI in 2005 brought about a visible change in the approach to the liturgical debate in the Church, and not only for the direct statements, decisions, and the liturgical style of the new pontiff, successor of John Paul II.[4]

---

2. See Walter Kasper, "Zur Theologie und Praxis des bischöflichen Amtes," in *Auf Eine neue Art Kirche sein: Festschrift J. Homeyer*, ed. Werner Schreer and Georg Steins (Munich: Don Bosco, 1999), 32–48; Joseph Ratzinger, "L'ecclesiologia della Costituzione Lumen Gentium," in *Il Concilio Vaticano II: Recezione e attualità alla luce del Giubileo*, ed. Rino Fisichella (Cinisello Balsamo: San Paolo, 2000), 66–81; Kilian McDonnell, "The Ratzinger/Kasper Debate: The Universal Church and Local Churches," *Theological Studies* 63 (June 2002): 222–50.
3. See Piero Marini, "Sacrosanctum Concilium 40 anni dopo: Tra consegne e impegni permanenti," *Rivista Liturgica* 91, no. 5 (2004): 771–80. About the anticonciliar "reform the liturgical reform," see John Baldovin, *Reforming the Liturgy: A Response to the Critics* (Collegeville, MN: Liturgical, 2009).

The chance to reappraise things forgotten or past sometimes takes the appearance of "incidents." When these incidents are public and given to the public through the media, the cost of re-appreciating things that we should not have forgotten is much higher. In early 2009, the fiftieth anniversary of the announcement of the council (January 25, 1959) could have passed as an innocuous anniversary among so many others that crowd the calendar. Unexpectedly, the fiftieth anniversary instead took on the tones of an international incident and a call to reflection of the whole Catholic Church, showing a freedom of speech at all levels: bishops and episcopal conferences, the cardinals of the Curia, theological faculties, the Catholic press, Catholic and non-Catholic political leaders, and Catholic and non-Catholic opinion makers. The decision by Benedict XVI on January 21, 2009, to lift the excommunication imposed by John Paul II in 1988 on the four bishops ordained by Monsignor Marcel Lefebvre went right back to the center of the discussion of the relationship between contemporary Catholicism and Vatican II; the council that this small schismatic sect created in the 1970s has always been accused of heresy and of being the cause of all evil for the Church.[5] This decision of Benedict XVI moved the Catholic Church—along with other Christian churches, Jewish communities, and the public—to reflect on Vatican II far deeper than they could have done any formal study or conference speech. The debate confirmed (if proof were needed) that "something happened" at Vatican II.[6]

---

4. See Neil J. Roy and Janet E. Rutherford, eds., *Benedict XVI and the Sacred Liturgy* (Dublin: Four Courts, 2010).

5. See Peter Hünermann, "Excommunicatio—Communicatio: Versuch einer Schichtenanalyse," in *Herder Korrespondenz* 3 (2009), 119–25.

6. See David G. Schultenonver, ed., *Vatican II: Did Anything Happen?* (New York: Continuum, 2007); John W. O'Malley, *What Happened at Vatican II* (Cambridge, MA: Belknap Press of Harvard University Press, 2008).

Felix culpa, "o happy fault," one is tempted to say. But the reactions to the lifting of the excommunication of the Lefebvrians were not exhausted in damage control, which has become a special kind of communication in the "liturgies" of the social and political communication of the global era. The case has been much more of an international diplomatic incident, or a miscommunication, or mismanagement from the operatives of the political-administrative machine also called the Roman Curia. The timely publication on the Internet of the statements of one of the followers of the bishops of Marcel Lefebvre, Richard Williamson, denying the historical fact of the Holocaust (statements that could be a surprise only to those who completely ignore the roots of Lefebvre's political and cultural worldview), triggered a public reaction that has reached previously unheard tones, especially in Europe and in the Americas.[7]

Reactions to Benedict XVI's decision, expressed by representatives of national bishops' conferences and individual bishops, as well as world and political leaders and parliamentary groups of Catholics, led the Holy See to numerous and repeated explanations. Eventually, all recognized the object of contention: Vatican II, or rather, several declarations by Lefebvre and his followers that they could not recognize Vatican II and, in particular, some elements of the whole theological balance of Vatican II, especially the document *Nostra Aetate* on relations with other religions and the deploration of anti-Semitism expressed therein.[8]

---

7. See Peter Hünermann, ed., *Exkommunikation oder Kommunikation? Der Weg der Kirche nach dem II. Vatikanum und die Pius-Brüder* (Freiburg i.B.: Herder, 2009).

8. About Lefebvrism and the tradition of Catholic anti-Judaism fully visible in its theology during Vatican II, see Nicla Buonasorte, *Tra Roma e Lefebvre: Il tradizionalismo cattolico italiano e il Concilio Vaticano II* (Rome: Studium, 2003); Giovanni Miccoli, "Two Sensitive Issues: Religious Freedom and the Jews," *History of Vatican II*, ed. Giuseppe Alberigo, English version ed. Joseph A. Komonchak, trans. Matthew J. O'Connell (Maryknoll, NY: Orbis; Leuven: Peeters, 2003), 4:95–193.

All these reactions notwithstanding, Benedict XVI's attempt to absorb the Lefebvrian schism, created by the refusal of a small group to accept Vatican II, made clear that, beyond the insignificant number of the schism created by Archbishop Marcel Lefebvre, the council represents for the Church of the twenty-first century an element of internal debate, not only a "compass" for the Church, as John Paul II called it in his testament.[9] This says something to scholars and observers of the Catholic Church's role on the world stage. But of course, it also speaks to historians of the hermeneutics of Vatican II, the greatest religious event of the twentieth century.

Among the many possible reasons for our interest in this "political-theological" case, three are of interest to scholars of Vatican II. The first is that, in the eyes of contemporary Catholicism, international politics, and world public opinion, Vatican II has undoubtedly a role as a "guarantee," as "condition of citizenship" of the Catholic Church in the modern world. The second reason is the fact that this "guarantee" has been identified, especially by international politics and public opinion worldwide, with the final rejection of anti-Semitism as an element of premodern and antidemocratic social and political culture, and with some specific elements of the theology of Vatican II, particularly those that constitute the break from those theological ideas that were traditional before the council. Among the newer ideas associated with Vatican II in this context were freedom of conscience and religious freedom, ecumenism, dialogue with Judaism, dialogue with other religions, collegiality, and shared responsibility in the government of the Church. The third reason, which is the most relevant point for this chapter, is that the elements central to public reception of the council are essential to the content

9. John Paul II, apostolic letter *Novo millennio ineunte* (January 6, 2001), par. 57.

of the liturgy of Vatican II and are the ones that the Lefebvrian schism always declined to accept, as the result of "heresy" of Vatican II.[10]

2. The Idea of Constitution in the Debate on Vatican II

The dogmatician emeritus of Tübingen Peter Hünermann proposed a few years ago the use (under certain conditions) of the concept of "constitution" for Vatican II. The use of this term should not be confused with the term *constitution* referring to the four constitutions of Vatican II. In Hünermann's proposal, "constitution" incorporates the idea of a fundamental law in the Western legal and political experience.

In the fifth and final volume of the *Herders Theologischer Kommentar zum Zweiten Vatikanischen Konzil*,[11] Hünermann developed some aspects of his lecture at the 1996 Bologna conference on Vatican II on the "pragmatic of the conciliar texts" and included some important contributions coming from Ormond Rush's *Hermeneutical Principles*.[12] In his conclusions to the *Theologischer Kommentar*, Hünermann emphasized the particular feature of the corpus of the conciliar texts for the Catholic Church:[13] "If we look for an analogy to the profile of the text of the Second Vatican Council in order to better characterize its decisions, then there is a certain similarity with the constitutional texts elaborated by constitutional assemblies of representatives. This similarity characterized particularly the texts

10. See Nicolas Senèze, *La crise intégriste: Vingt ans après le schisme de Mgr Lefebvre* (Paris: Bayard, 2008).
11. See Peter Hünermann and Hans Jochen Hilberath, eds., *Herders Theologischer Kommentar zum Zweiten Vatikanischen Konzil*, 5 vols. (Freiburg i.B.: Herder, 2004–05).
12. See Ormond Rush, *Still interpreting Vatican II: Some Hermeneutical Principles* (New York: Paulist, 2004).
13. See Peter Hünermann, "Der Text: Werden—Gestalt—Bedeutung; Eine Hermeneutische Reflexion," in Hünermann and Hilberath, *Herders Theologischer Kommentar zum Zweiten Vatikanischen Konzil*, 5:5–101, esp. 11–17 and 85–87.

of Vatican II and also shows up in the texts of the Council of Trent and Vatican I, but only in a much less mediated and minor way."[14]

Hünermann pointed out that the legitimacy of a council and its authority are essentially different from those of a constituent assembly and that the conciliar text possesses an authority essentially different from that of a constitutional text. However, he also pointed out some similarities between a constitution and Vatican II:

- The situation of "crisis or historical necessity" that requires (in a state as in the Church) a constitution;

- The quality of the final texts as texts discussed and approved by "representatives" representing different if not opposing positions;

- A similarity in the proceedings (commissions, subcommissions, plenary sessions);

- The relationship between the issues on the table and the texts that describe and influence the situation;

- The relationship between the final approval of a constitution and the act of theological reception of Vatican II.

In fact, writes Hünermann, "the corpus of the texts of Vatican II resembles the texts drawn up by a constituent assembly. . . . For this reason the texts of Vatican II can prudently be described as a 'constitutional text of the faith.' If this pre-understanding of the conciliar texts is correct, then it follows that a number of problems and questions, criticism and interpretations are unfounded, because they are addressed to a kind of text which is not that of Vatican II."[15]

In emphasizing the differences in the type of texts of Vatican II vis-à-vis the texts of Vatican I or the Council of Trent, Hünermann

14. Ibid., 12.
15. Ibid., 17.

made another reference to the *Regula Benedicti*, to the Rule of St. Benedict, in order to outline a correct interpretation of the final documents of Vatican II. In so doing, he eliminated unequivocally any misunderstanding that this concept of Vatican II as a constitution could lead to a possible return to the hypothesis of a *Lex Ecclesiae Fundamentalis* (a Fundamental Law of the Church), which Pope Paul VI had tried unsuccessfully to have approved in the early 1970s.[16]

Having said that, in identifying Vatican II as a "constitution," Hünermann did not mean to put the texts of the council over the gospel: "The legitimacy of a council and its authority is essentially different from that of a constitutional assembly of a modern state. . . . For this reason, the Council text has authority essentially different from that of a constitutional text."[17] Nevertheless, "if one is convinced of the 'constitutional' character of this corpus of texts, then this entails significant effect on the theological interpretation and reception of these texts."[18]

Although Hünermann's attempt to preserve and revitalize the Church at a time with the council through the concept of Vatican II as a constitution is new, the idea of a particular nucleus inside Vatican II is not.[19] However, this proposal has attracted objections from some scholars participating (like Hünermann) in the international team

16. See also Peter Hünermann, "Der Text: Eine Ergänzung zur Hermeneutik des II. Vatikanischen Konzils," *Cristianesimo nella Storia* 28, no. 2 (2007): 339–58. For the *Lex Ecclesiae Fundamentalis*, see *Legge e vangelo: Discussione su una legge fondamentale per la Chiesa* (Brescia: Paideia, 1972), with writings of Giuseppe Alberigo et al., edited by the Fondazione per le scienze religiose di Bologna; Daniel Cenalmor Palanca, *La ley fundamental de la iglesia: Historia y analisis de un proyecto legislativo* (Pamplona: Eunsa, 1991).

17. Hünermann, "Der Text: Werden—Gestalt—Bedeutung," 15–16.

18. Hünermann, "Der Text: Eine Ergänzung," 358. See also Peter Hünermann, "Zur theologischen Arbeit am Beginn der dritten Millenniums," in *Das Zweite Vatikanische Konzil und die Zeichen der Zeit heute*, ed. Peter Hünermann (Freiburg i.B.: Herder, 2006), 569–93.

19. See Giuseppe Dossetti, *Il Vaticano II: Frammenti di una riflessione*, ed. Francesco Margiotta Broglio (Bologna: Il Mulino, 1996); Giuseppe Dossetti, *Per una "chiesa eucaristica": Rilettura della portata dottrinale della Costituzione liturgica del Vaticano II. Lezioni del 1965*, ed. Giuseppe Alberigo and Giuseppe Ruggieri (Bologna: Il Mulino, 2002), 35.

involved in the project of the *History of Vatican II*, directed by Giuseppe Alberigo. In particular, the Franco-German Jesuit Christoph Theobald has criticized the idea of the council as constitution, based on a complex hermeneutics of the conciliar texts and the primacy of Scripture.[20] Theobald's major objection was that the "constitutionalization" of Vatican II could reopen the issue of the relationship between Vatican I and Vatican II and thus recenter Vatican II on the Church.[21] Finally, Theobald criticized the proposal because the idea of Vatican II as constitutional texts would undermine the possibility of interpreting those texts as "compromise texts."[22]

But the timeliest objections to Vatican II as a constitution came from Benedict XVI, who had addressed the issue in a passage of his now-famous speech to the Roman Curia on December 22, 2005.[23] During that speech, the pope, after stating that "the hermeneutic of discontinuity risks ending in a split between the pre- and post–conciliar Church," attacked the idea of a hermeneutic of the council in accordance with the "spirit," and not according to the texts:

> In this way, obviously, a vast margin was left open for the question on how this spirit should subsequently be defined and room was consequently made for every whim. The nature of a Council as such is therefore basically misunderstood. In this way, it is considered as a sort of constituent that eliminates an old constitution and creates a new one. However, the Constituent Assembly needs a mandator and then confirmation by the mandator, in other words, the people the

20. Christoph Theobald, "Mise en perspective," in *Vatican II sous le regard des historiens*, ed. Christoph Theobald (Paris: *Médiasèvres*, 2006), 3–23, esp. 12–13.

21. Ibid., 15. See Hervé-Marie Legrand, "Relecture et évaluation de l'Histoire du Concile Vatican II d'un point de vue ecclésiologique," in Theobald, *Vatican II sous le regard des historiens*, 49–82.

22. See Christoph Theobald, "Enjeux herméneutiques des débats sur l'histoire du Concile Vatican II," *Cristianesimo nella Storia* 28, no. 2 (2007): 359–80.

23. Benedict XVI's implicit but clear criticism of the five-volume *Kommentar* in the speech of December 22, 2005, has been confirmed by Peter Hünermann himself in *"In der Freiheit des Geistes leben": Peter Hünermann im Gespräch*, ed. Margit Eckholt and Regina Heyder (Ostfildern: Matthias-Grünewald, 2010).

constitution must serve. The Fathers had no such mandate and no one had ever given them one; nor could anyone have given them one because the essential constitution of the Church comes from the Lord and was given to us so that we might attain eternal life and, starting from this perspective, be able to illuminate life in time and time itself.[24]

For Pope Benedict XVI, the criticism of the idea of the council as constitution was based on the fact that the only constitution was given to the Church by the Lord, that the constitutional process is equivalent to a "rupture," and not to "reform," and that the idea of a "discontinuity" in the Catholic Church between a before and an after Vatican II must be rejected. Similarly to Christoph Theobald, who rejected the plausibility of the term *constitution* because of its ecclesiocentrism, Benedict XVI criticized this term and its inadequacy to understand the council from an ecclesiological perspective: the inability to enforce the continuity of the tradition of the Church in the transition from an old to a new constitution and the difference on the role of "mandator," that is, the sovereign, between the Church led by the Lord and the popular will that is expressed (but limited) by the constitutions of modern states.[25]

3. Vatican II and the "Constitutional Character" of the Postconciliar Church

The late American neoconservative Richard John Neuhaus famously quoted George Lindbeck's quip about the alignment between

24. Benedict XVI, speech to the Roman Curia, December 22, 2005, in *Insegnamenti di Benedetto XVI* (Vatican City: Libreria Editrice Vaticana, 2006), vol. 1, 1018–32, also available at "Address Of His Holiness Benedict XVI to the Roman Curia Offering Them His Christmas Greetings," The Holy Fathers: Benedictus XVI, The Holy See website, http://www.vatican.va/holy_father/benedict_xvi/speeches/2005/december/documents/hf_ben_xvi_spe_20051222_roman-curia_en.html.
25. The German version of Pope Benedict XVI's speech has *Auftraggeber* for "sovereign" and *Verfassung* (not *Konstitution*, nor *Grundgesetz*) for "Constitution."

Vatican II Catholicism and world politics: "The Roman Catholic Church has now joined what might be called the 'Western liberal consensus.'" Neuhaus saw in this development the "new ecclesiocentrism" of Vatican II, wrapped in the idea of "this-worldly fulfillment" and "otherworldly hope." In the late 1960s and early 1970s, one could say that "the views expressed [at Vatican II] are consistently progressive."[26] In the twenty-first century, fifty years after Vatican II, all that needs a reassessment, and there is no doubt that there is a "constitutional" content of Vatican II that has survived the huge changes in the political cultures of the globalized world.

Taking note of the excommunication *latae sententiae* against bishop Marcel Lefebvre and his followers, John Paul II's *motu proprio Ecclesia Dei* of 1988 had already made of the Lefebvrian schism an opportunity to reflect on the Second Vatican Council:

> The outcome of the movement promoted by Mons. Lefebvre can and must be, for all the Catholic faithful, a motive for sincere reflection concerning their own fidelity to the Church's Tradition, authentically interpreted by the ecclesiastical Magisterium, ordinary and extraordinary, especially in the Ecumenical Councils from Nicaea to Vatican II. From this reflection all should draw a renewed and efficacious conviction of the necessity of strengthening still more their fidelity by rejecting erroneous interpretations and arbitrary and unauthorized applications in matters of doctrine, liturgy and discipline. . . . Moreover, I should like to remind theologians and other experts in the ecclesiastical sciences that they should feel themselves called upon to answer in the present circumstances. Indeed, the extent and depth of the teaching of the Second Vatican Council call for a renewed commitment to deeper study in order to reveal clearly the Council's continuity with Tradition, especially in points of doctrine which, perhaps because they are new, have not yet been well understood by some sections of the Church.[27]

26. See Richard John Neuhaus, *The Catholic Moment* (San Francisco: Harper and Row, 1987), 37–69, quotation at 53.
27. John Paul II, *motu proprio Ecclesia Dei*, July 2, 1988, n. 5.

In lifting the excommunication of the Lefebvrian bishops in coincidence with the fiftieth anniversary of the convocation of the council, Pope Benedict XVI indirectly raised again that issue that John Paul II had dealt with twenty years before. But the debate on Vatican II at the beginning of 2009 shed new light on the process of reception of the council and its "constitutionality," and allowed us to better understand the proposed interpretation of the council as "a Constitution" as part of a lifelong reflection by Hünermann on the role of *loci theologici* and of culture for theological hermeneutics in the postconciliar Church.[28]

Hünermann's proposal deserves to be taken up and analyzed from a theological and non-ecclesiocentric perspective. In the light of the legacy of the global pontificate of John Paul II and of the theological-political contribution of Benedict XVI to the reception of the council, it is necessary that we first reflect on the reception of Vatican II: a reflection that embraces a "political-cultural" perspective able to take into account the specific characteristics of how various areas of the world received a constitutional core of Vatican II. From the debate concerning the lifting of the excommunications of the four bishops of the Society of Saint Pius X (SSPX), founded by Monsignor Lefebvre in 1970, it emerged clearly that the problem was not only the anti-Semitic statements of SSPX bishop Richard Williamson, but the whole position of the Lefebvrite schism about the Second Vatican Council and, in particular, its core elements of novelty and discontinuity within the recent tradition of the Church.

To this nucleus of "constitutional contents" of Vatican II belong evidently the recognition of religious freedom and freedom of conscience, as well as the commitment to ecumenical dialogue and interreligious dialogue. However, other elements also belong to this

---

28. See Peter Hünermann, *Dogmatische Prinzipienlehre: Glaube, Überlieferung, Theologie als Sprach- und Wahrheitsgeschehen* (Münster: Aschendorff, 2003).

nucleus: the liturgical reform and its theological content (being the liturgical constitution the first fruits of Vatican II), the position of Scripture in the Church, and the existence and role of bishops' conferences and episcopal collegiality (rejected by Lefebvrians as in discontinuity with the tradition of monarchical government of the Church). This group of new elements can be described not just as "constitutive" of the corpus of Vatican II, but also as "constitutional," because those statements of Vatican II configure the new face of the Catholic Church not only *ad intra* and *ad extra* but also in the "public ecclesiology" of the Catholic Church. There is a core of contents that is essential to the Church in the global world not just in terms of image and public relations, or (in the case of anti-Semitic Holocaust denial) in terms of respect of the law, or because the rejection of anti-Semitism belongs to the "global civil religion" that has sacralized some of the values inherited from the Enlightenment.[29] This core is a *development of the tradition* of the Church also thanks to a political-cultural exchange between a centuries-long universal claim by the Catholic Church and its ability to articulate this claim in the global world. The gap between the Church and the world was dramatically evident at the moment of the 1948 Universal Declaration of Human Rights; at the time of Vatican II and in the years after, that gap is substantially different.

Here we have for historians and the interpreters of Vatican II an interesting element of the most recent episode of the incident with the Lefebvrite bishop Richard Williamson, who denied the holocaust in an interview published shortly before the decision of Benedict XVI to lift the excommunication for the Lefebvrites in January 2009. That episode made clear Vatican II's constitutional core, which exists independently of the formal, traditional hierarchies of the texts of

29. About this, see Enzo Traverso, *Fin de la modernité juive: Histoire d'un tournant conservateur* (Paris: La Découverte, 2013).

the council (constitutions, decrees, and declarations) and that has more to do with the history of the conciliar event, the postconciliar period, and the Church's position on international affairs than with the technicalities of the theological hermeneutics of the final texts of Vatican II. All of this can be understood not only through a study of the theological culture of Vatican II, but also in light of a reflection on the political culture of Vatican II and of the political perception of the *aggiornamento* of Vatican II and its consequences on the international position of the Catholic Church during Vatican II and after.[30]

When, in the days of the Williamson scandal in early 2009, German Chancellor Angela Merkel stated that the repudiation of anti-Semitism is a mainstay of the Federal Republic of Germany, she was also addressing to contemporary Catholicism a reminder about the cultural and political responsibility of the Church not only in Germany, but on the global stage. The German chancellor was acting as an indirect interpreter of Vatican II and of its discontinuity in the relationship between the Church and Judaism after World War II and the Holocaust. From a Church history standpoint, if for the history of the ecclesiological hermeneutics of Vatican I (1869–1870), we must read the exchange of letters of 1875 between Chancellor Bismarck, the German bishops, and Pope Pius IX,[31] so also, in order to assess the moment of the reception of Vatican II during the pontificate of Benedict XVI, it was equally indicative to consider, together with the reactions of the bishops, episcopal conferences, and Catholic faculties of theology, also the reaction of the Jewish communities and the initiative of the German chancellor and member of the Lutheran

---

30. See Alberto Melloni, ed., *Vatican II in Moscow (1959–1965)* (Leuven: Bibliotheek van de Faculteit Godgeleerdheid, 1997); Alberto Melloni, *L'altra Roma: Politica e S. Sede durante il Concilio Vaticano II (1959–1965)* (Bologna: Il Mulino, 2000).

31. See Heinrich Denzinger, *Enchiridion symbolorum, definitionum et declarationum de rebus fidei et morum*, 38th ed., ed. Peter Hünermann (Freiburg i.B.: Herder, 2000), 3112–17.

Church in Germany Angela Merkel. The statements by the German chancellor, along with those of large sectors of the Church as well as world public opinion, have contributed—side by side with the voice of theology and historiography on Vatican II—to get rid of a sometimes self-referential and anesthetic kind to implement the council over the past two decades.

The particular moment of political reception of Vatican II at the beginning of 2009 reminded the Catholic Church of an essential element for understanding the council: that Vatican II came *after* the Second World War and the Holocaust (and not before the Great Jubilee of 2000 or before the Catechism of 1992). The deeper issues of Vatican II cannot be understood if it is approached surreptitiously in light of ecclesiastical-political agendas of various kinds, especially if these agendas are disconnected from a deep understanding of the historical, political, and cultural as well as theological depth of the transition from the Catholicism of the "long nineteenth century" to the era of conciliar Catholicism.

4. Vatican II and the Globalization of the Catholic Claim

The interpretation of Vatican II is faced with two options not rarely used by Catholic theologians: on the one hand, an ideological interpretation of Vatican II, and on the other hand, the illusion of being able to assess the council without considering the enormous consequences of that event and of those texts to the standing of contemporary Catholicism. If the consequences of a neoconservative ideologization of Vatican II are evident in the debate about the hermeneutics of the council,[32] no less obvious are the temptations to look at the council apart from an awareness of the long-term

---

32. See Massimo Faggioli, *Vatican II: The Battle for Meaning* (Mahwah, NJ: Paulist, 2012).

consequences on the political-cultural dimensions of Vatican II, in a minimizing interpretation of Vatican II.

The political culture of the Holy See led by Pope Benedict XVI seemed to have left behind the Wojtylian activism in world politics, but also the awareness of the existence of a global political culture of the Second Vatican Council. The lifting of the excommunication of the Lefebvrian bishops is another confirmation of the discontinuity of the pontificate of Benedict XVI compared with that of John Paul II regarding a certain political sensibility of the papacy.

At the end of the fifties, the choice of putting behind the "age of Constantine" was a turning point germinated in the biography of Angelo Giuseppe Roncalli (Pope John XXIII), and this shift was brought to maturity in the years of the Second Vatican Council. During Vatican II, the universal, or catholic, identity of the Church was a prerequisite to the culture of dialogue and dialogue between cultures and political ideologies. It was a theological choice acquired at the center of the Catholic Church in Rome, which found, in its political and diplomatic dimensions, some clear limits (like in the council debates dealing with Communism) due to the tensions of the Cold War. But this new global political awareness sometimes also needed to "convince" the beneficiaries of the dialogue with the Communist sphere, including Catholic nations (such as the Polish and German, for reasons opposite to each other) that resisted the idea of putting some distance between the Catholic and national identities.[33]

Looking at the fifty years of the postconciliar period, it is difficult to doubt the actual novelty of the gestures and symbols, as well as the words of the Holy See, concerning the perception of the relevance

---

33. See Karl-Joseph Hummel, ed., *Vatikanische Ostpolitik unter Johannes XXIII. und Paul VI., 1958–1978* (Paderborn: Ferdinand Schöningh, 1999); Alberto Melloni, ed., *Il filo sottile: L'Ostpolitik vaticana di Agostino Casaroli* (Bologna: Il Mulino, 2006).

of religions and of the Catholic Church for world peace. It was a turning point, first culturally and theologically and later politically and diplomatically. But during Vatican II, some of the world political powers (in the Western world, in the Communist sphere, and in the Middle East) did not take long to grasp the epochal changes happening less than a century after the loss of the temporal power of the pope.

Some interpretations of Vatican II and of these last fifty years of life of the Church—interpretations that are theologically radical as much as historically uninformed—do not seem to take into account the costs of a withdrawal of the Catholic Church from the international scene of dialogue between Churches and religions. These last five decades the Roman papacy and the Catholic Church shaped by Vatican II have created in their audience (even in the most paranoid quarters) expectations and habits that are directly connected to the conciliar identity of Catholicism.

In other words, the "discontinuity of the council" from the previous period (for the relationship between Church and democracy, collegiality, religious freedom, ecumenism, and interreligious dialogue) and the kind of interpretations of the novelties of Vatican II (from the large and sometimes nominalist vision of Vatican II by John Paul II to the more restrictive of Benedict XVI) have political effects, because these novelties are part of the undeniable existence of a constitutional core in Vatican II. Political actors (political leaders, parliaments, public opinion, and religious and cultural communities active inside and outside Catholicism) are aware of this constitutional core, and they interact with the Church as they believe this core has been acquired permanently and irrevocably. The elements of this core are, for example, the discovery of democracy, individual rights, and the value of human conscience; the value of participation and co-decision, even within the Church; the appreciation of freedom, a century after the *Syllabus* of Pius IX; the comprehension of the relationship between Church and its historical nature; an assimilation at a deep level of the lesson of the tragic experience of the Second World War; a serious commitment for the assessment of the links between anti-Jewish culture of the Christian theological tradition, racist anti-Semitism, and the Holocaust in Europe.

If we examine the recent debates on the role of Vatican II in the Catholic Church, it is undeniable that the declaration *Nostra Aetate* on relations of the Church with non-Christian religions,[34] the declaration on religious freedom *Dignitatis Humanae*, and the constitution *Gaudium et Spes* on the Church in the modern world represent Vatican II in a special way. Nevertheless, it is impossible to deny that the three "issues under the issues"—namely, the basic issues of the council identified by John O'Malley: the change in the Church, relations between center and periphery of the Church, the council as a linguistic event and the "style" of Catholicism—are closely interrelated, and that the denial of one of them involves immediately a "sterilization" of the other two issues.[35]

Among the elements of the transition of Vatican II, there is definitely a change of the categories of thought that presuppose a modern exegetical-critical approach for the interpretation of the Scriptures and a relationship between the pope, bishops, clergy, and laity that must be shaped, from the point of view of institutional practices, by freedom, responsibility, and accountability. From this epochal transition, it follows that the form of the faith must be communicable and able to bear witness in the world not less than

---

34. See Alberto Melloni, "Da *Nostra aetate* ad Assisi '86: Cornici e fatti di una ricezione creativa del concilio Vaticano II," *Convivium Assisiense* 9, no. 1 (2007): 63–89.
35. See O'Malley, *What Happened at Vatican II*, 309–11.

in the "world Church" that Karl Rahner talked about at the end of Vatican II.[36]

It is evident that the epochal changes of Vatican II have an impact that is not exclusively internal to the Church. This impact is directly related to the political-cultural discontinuities of Vatican II and to the constitutional core of Vatican II, which coincide with what is rejected by the schismatic culture of Marcel Lefebvre and its followers.

Now, the acknowledgment of the relationship between the interpretation of Vatican II and the "politics" of its recipients means recognizing first of all the need for a study on the political cultures of Vatican II and, secondly, the need for a reflection on the impossibility of going back from the essential elements of the political and constitutional culture of Vatican II. This does not mean making a new "Constantinian age" or surrendering to the temptations of turning Catholicism into a civil religion (even in parts of the world where this idea is not and never has been part of the social and cultural landscape). Rather, it means being able to notice the complexity of the relationship between Catholicism and contemporary society around and thanks to the Second Vatican Council, especially around its constitutional core of discontinuity with the past tradition.

Vatican II has emerged openly as the driving force for the chances of Roman Catholicism in the political and social culture of the contemporary world: in the Western culture, but also and especially—at a time when some still think that it is possible to "re-Europeanize" Catholicism—for its chances of interaction with non-European and non-Western cultures. Even if Vatican II does

---

36. See Giuseppe Alberigo, *Transizione epocale. Studi sul Concilio Vaticano II* (Bologna: Il Mulino, 2009), 765–859; Karl Rahner, "Basic Theological Interpretation of the Second Vatican Council," in Karl Rahner, *Concern for the Church* (New York: Crossroads, 1981), 77–90.

not have the role of a constitution for the Church in the legal, classic sense of the word, those who reject Vatican II put themselves automatically in "extra-parliamentary" sectors of the Church, also but not only in the eyes of those who observe Catholicism from the outside. In this regard, the Second Vatican Council certainly works as a constitution for the Church of Vatican II, and in a particularly visible way as a guarantee of its commitment to basic conditions of existence in a plural world: interfaith dialogue with Judaism and Islam especially; recognition of freedom of conscience; protection of religious freedom; and commitment to ecumenism and peace among peoples.

Vatican II has become a "guarantee of constitutionality" of contemporary Catholicism. The continuist-revisionist interpretations of the most important religious event of the twentieth century are powered by a theo-conservative ideological vision that sees in the "golden age" of the pre–Vatican II period the solution for an identitarian Christianity, the just social-political "order" to be restored—the only way out for a Western civilization in crisis. Notwithstanding the political agenda of the neo-cons, theo-cons, and radical orthodox, for the Catholic Church to get rid of Vatican II or even just minimize the extent of its epochal discontinuity would have immediate political and cultural consequences. Nearly twenty-five years ago, Samuel Huntington pointed out that the process of democratization in the twentieth century is likely to have more to do with the Second Vatican Council than with the spread of the free market in the vast world beyond the Western European and North American sphere.[37]

Recognizing the influence of external agents (non-ecclesiastical and non-theological) in the debate on the role of the Second Vatican

---

37. See Samuel P. Huntington, *The Third Wave: Democratization in the Late Twentieth Century* (Norman: University of Oklahoma Press, 1991).

Council leads to a comprehension of the existence of the elements of novelty in the Catholic tradition. This comprehension entails going beyond the sterile debate between "letter" and "spirit" of the council, and it can open a third phase in the studies on Vatican II. After the first round of commentaries on the final texts (1960s–1980s) and the second phase of historical reconstruction of the event (1985–2000), it is necessary now to begin a new phase of reflection on the long-term relationship between Vatican II and the historical, political, and cultural movements of the post–World War II period.

8

Vatican II and the Church of the Margins

The ecclesiology of "the peripheries" is one of the many cases when, in order to understand the impact of pope Francis, it is necessary to look at Vatican II and its trajectories, which are still active and visible in the Church of today.[1]

1. Nostalgia and the Legacy of Vatican II

On October 22, 1965, when Vatican II was in its final weeks, Yves Congar received a phone call from the dean of the Faculty of Theology in Fribourg (Switzerland), informing him that the faculty had decided unanimously to give him a doctorate *honoris causa*. Congar was not persuaded by the invitation, as he reported in his journal of the council: "I replied that I was very sensible of the honour . . . etc., but that I was opposed in principle to exercises of this kind. I do not see St. Dominic or St. Thomas as doctors *honoris causa*. . . .

---

1. This chapter was published originally as "Vatican II and the Church of the Margins," *Theological Studies* 74, no. 3 (September 2013): 808–18.

For me it is the office that counts, not the honour. And, if I accepted one offer of this kind I would be obliged to accept others (for there will be others). Better not to START on this road, WHICH IS NOT MINE."[2]

This passage is indicative of Congar's pragmatic view not only of his contribution as a theologian, but also of the role of Vatican II in the life of the Church. Congar was against clerical triumphalism, because he knew that in the two decades before Vatican II, a very high price had been paid to this posture of superiority (a price paid by himself, among other theologians, especially in the aftermath of the encyclical *Humani Generis* of 1950).[3] Congar's approach to Vatican II—during the council and in the decades after—was never empty celebration but always stewardship of that event and of its meaning for the Church.

Always wary of the nostalgia that the "long 19th century," as John O'Malley called it,[4] felt for baroque Catholicism, Congar was also aware of the risks of wistfulness for the period of Vatican II: "The 'recovery' [*relance*] of Vatican II asks that we continue to explain its contributions and riches, but such a project also requires that we attend to its directional inspirations. Our efforts cannot be purely commemorative, retrospective, or repetitive. Tradition is as much creation as transmission and reference."[5] For Congar, just as for many other theologians of the council, Vatican II was not a memory to be cherished, but a work to begin; it was not the battering ram for our impatience with Church reform, but an example of "reform in the

---

2. Yves Congar, *My Journal of the Council*, trans. Mary John Ronayne and Mary Cecily Boulding, ed. Denis Minns (Collegeville, MN: Liturgical, 2012), 821, entry of October 22, 1965, emphasis in original.

3. See Yves Congar, *Journal d'un théologien (1946–1956)*, ed. Étienne Fouilloux (Paris: Cerf, 2001).

4. John W. O'Malley, *What Happened at Vatican II* (Cambridge, MA: Belknap Press of Harvard University Press, 2008), esp. ch. 2.

5. See Yves Congar, *Le Concile de Vatican II: Son Église, Peuple de Dieu, et Corps du Christ* (Paris: Beauchesne, 1984), 107. Translations throughout are mine, unless otherwise indicated.

Church" (*réforme dans l'Église*)—the kind of reform that lasts, a reform from the inside.[6]

This problem is also our problem today. For some, Vatican II is the epitome of what possibly can go wrong in Catholic theology. For others, the council is the equivalent of the "golden sixties": an age of unfettered freedom, unleashed creativity, and great expectations. And according to the latter group, all of these expectations were betrayed by what happened after the council.

Therefore, for our time, in this "year of faith" (2012–2013) proclaimed by Pope Benedict XVI on the fiftieth anniversary of the council's opening,[7] the question is pressed all the more: Does a Church that is "catholic" need Vatican II to be "universal"? Are we perhaps scrutinizing Vatican II because it has diluted the Catholic faith's dogmatic content from the metaphysical to a too-cultural and too-sociological self-understanding? Is Vatican II the source of the "busyness" of the Catholic Church today in its administrative life—committee meetings, reports, dossiers, and pastoral plans?

Blaming the Second Vatican Council is a great temptation indeed. The Church has changed in these last fifty years since the celebration of the council. Things happened not always in the way that we expected. For some, history with its often unpredictable changes is never supposed to happen. But history *does* happen; so does Church history, sometimes in totally unexpected ways—the resignation of Pope Benedict XVI on February 11, 2013, for example. This awareness is part of the legacy of Vatican II for Catholic theology. The inclusion of "historicity" in Catholic theology is one of the most important elements of the new awareness of the council. As Marie-Dominique Chenu wrote in his commentary on council's pastoral

---

6. See Yves Congar, *Vraie et fausse réforme dans l'Église* (Paris: Cerf, 1950; 1969, 2nd edition).

7. Pope Benedict XVI, apostolic letter *Porta fidei* for the Indiction of the Year of Faith, October 11, 2011, http://www.vatican.va/holy_father/benedict_xvi/motu_proprio/documents/hf_ben-xvi_motu-proprio_20111011_porta-fidei_en.html.

constitution, *Gaudium et Spes*: "The expression 'signs of the times' makes sense not just in the literary context of Vatican II, but in the body of Catholic doctrine itself—and its method—where the Church is defined in its consubstantial relationship with the world and with history. This expression is indeed a 'constitutional' category, and in this pastoral constitution 'Gaudium et Spes' it is decisive of the laws and conditions of evangelization."[8]

2. Vatican II Theology, Ecclesiology, and Anthropology

This new theological understanding of history in Catholicism has changed our approach to all the major issues debated at Vatican II, but especially to ecclesiology. The importance of Vatican II for theology and ministry and for the formation of theologians and ministers is therefore closely connected to the council's major ecclesiological insights.

The first theme we need to recover from Vatican II is an "ecclesiological emphasis" on the Catholic form of Christianity. The debate on Vatican II in the last fifty years has run through different phases and trends: for example, ecclesiologists heard of the Church as "the people of God" before the idea of *communio* became dominant in the 1980s and 1990s. But the retrieval of the idea of the Church as a "people of God" remains a fundamental intuition of Vatican II. According to an Italian saying, *il tempo è galantuomo* (time is a gentleman)—that is, time knows how and when to render justice—and this is true also for the history of theology. Both "people of God" and *communio* will always be part of the Church's self-understanding, despite the theological fashions of this or that decade.

---

8. Marie-Dominique Chenu, "Les signes des temps: Réflexion théologique," in *L'Église dans le monde de ce temps: Constitution pastorale "Gaudium et spes,"* ed. Yves Congar and Michel Peuchmaurd (Paris: Cerf, 1967), 205–25, quotation at 225.

Once the dust of the contemporary theological *Zeitgeist* has settled, it is clear that Vatican II was a great moment of "synthesis" of Catholic theology, taking stock of modernity, at least the modernity of the eighteenth, nineteenth, and early twentieth centuries. If we had to describe Vatican II in the language of motion, we would say that the council initiated a movement *in depth*, taking a closer look at the sources of theology and of Catholic theology, and a movement *ad extra*, outside the Church, in a cosmic assumption of responsibility for humankind and the whole of creation, in terms similar to the theological recentering of Teilhard de Chardin. I need to use two French words here to describe this movement of Catholic theology at Vatican II. It was a movement of *ressourcement*, that is, of "theological deepening" (on the vertical axis), and a movement of *rapprochement*, that is, of "reconciliation by proximity" (on the horizontal axis).

Vatican II, and especially some of its principal figures, understood that the condition to proceed in this *ressourcement* and *rapprochement* was the idea of the "poor Church": a Church shaped by poverty in the sense not of material deprivation, but of deprivation of unnecessary cultural and ideological baggage, which is a real burden for a pilgrim community. This is what Cardinal Giacomo Lercaro meant in his November 4, 1964, intervention on the floor of the council during the debate on the schema XIII (future *Gaudium et Spes*), about the need for the Church "to be 'culturally poor,'" meaning that the glorious traditions, the cultural *organon* of Catholicism, should not limit the universality of the Church's language, should not divide but should unite, should not repel many more men and women but should attract and convince. In that speech, Lercaro said that the most authentic and radical demands of the present time would not be met, but would be avoided, if the council tackled the problem of evangelization of the poor as just one theme added to all the others, and from a sociological perspective. There is a very profound link between the presence of Christ in the poor and the other two profound elements in the mystery of Christ in the Church, namely, the Eucharist and the hierarchy; and Lercaro gave also some examples of the practical consequences of his idea for the life of the Church: a limitation in the commitment of material means for Church organization, a general description of a new style and a new conception of the dignity of ecclesiastical authorities, and a fidelity of religious orders to poverty.[9]

Was this speech received by Vatican II? Only partially, especially from the point of view of the institutional reforms of the Catholic Church after the council. But something changed, also thanks to Vatican II and to that speech. In his first speech to the press, Pope Francis gave the authentic exegesis of the name Francesco, mentioning explicitly the very conciliar idea of the "poor Church, a Church for the poor."[10] Poverty of the Church is the Catholic conciliar translation of what Charles Taylor described in his *A Secular Age* as typical of modern mentality, that is, the value of "authenticity."[11] In the eyes of all of us, whether Catholic or non-Catholic, an authentic Church is a poor Church and a Church for the poor.

The second theme that needs to be recovered from Vatican II, in order to draw implications for the rediscovery of the council for theological and ministerial formation, is the pastoral concern at the

9. See Lercaro's speech in *Acta synodalia Sacrosancti Concilii Oecumenici Vaticani II* (Vatican City: Typis polyglottis Vaticanis, 1970–) vol. III n. 6, 249–53; for Lercaro's other speech on poverty, December 6, 1962, see *Acta synodalia* vol. I n. 4, 327–30; and Giuseppe Ruggieri, "Beyond an Ecclesiology of Polemics," in *History of Vatican II*, vol. 2, *The Formation of the Council's Identity, First Period and Intercession, October 1962–September 1963*, ed. Giuseppe Alberigo, English ed. Joseph A. Komonchak (Maryknoll, NY: Orbis, 1997), 345–47.

10. This statement, widely reported in the press, was made off the cuff in an audience for journalists on March 16, 2013, three days after his election.

11. Charles Taylor, *A Secular Age* (Cambridge, MA: Belknap Press of Harvard University Press, 2007), esp. ch. 11, "The Age of Authenticity."

anthropological basis of conciliar theology. *Gaudium et Spes* (GS), the most pastoral of all the conciliar documents, addresses the issue of the anguish of modern human beings facing the fundamental questions: "The joys and the hopes, the griefs and the anxieties of the men of this age, especially those who are poor or in any way afflicted, these are the joys and hopes, the grieves and anxieties of the followers of Christ. Indeed, nothing genuinely human fails to raise an echo in their hearts" (*GS* no. 1).[12]

3. *Gaudium et Spes* and the *Déplacement* of the Church

Gaudium et Spes is one of the most original and characteristic documents of Vatican II—and a unique document from the point of view of its genesis, drafting history, and literary genre.[13] The final vote on the text on December 7, 1965 (2,309 *placet*—yes versus 75 *non placet*—no), gave the Church a document that even from its external features represented something new. It is a constitution on the Church *in* the modern world (*in mundo huius temporis*), and more precisely on the condition of the human person in the modern world (*conditio hominis in mundo moderno*).[14] It is a document on the *habitudo* of the Church with modern world, where *habitudo* does not mean "relationship" or "connection," but suggests that the Church finds its fulfillment in the world: there is an *intima coniunctio*, "intimate

12. Throughout this article, I use the official English translation of documents posted on the Vatican website: http://www.vatican.va/archive/hist_councils/ii_vatican_council/documents/vat-ii_cons_19651207_gaudium-et-spes_en.html.
13. See Roberto Tucci, "Introduction historique et doctrinale," in Congar and Peuchmaurd, *L'Église dans le monde de ce temps*, 33–127; Giovanni Turbanti, *Un concilio per il mondo moderno: La redazione della costituzione pastorale Gaudium et spes del Vaticano II* (Bologna: Il Mulino, 2000); Hans-Joachim Sander, "Theologischer Kommentar zur Pastoralkonstitution über die Kirche in der Welt von heute," in *Herders Theologischer Kommentar zum Zweiten Vatikanischen Konzil*, ed. Peter Hünermann and Bernd Jochen Hilberath (Freiburg i.B.: Herder, 2005), 5:616–703.
14. *Gaudium et Spes*, nos. 4–10.

relationship" between the Church and the world.[15] The constitution, therefore, after its introduction on "the condition of humanity in today's world" (nos. 4–10), gives a theological interpretation of "the church and the vocation of humanity" (part 1, nos. 11–45), followed by a long section on "some urgent problems" (part 2, nos. 46–90): marriage and family, modern culture, socioeconomic life, life in the political community, and peace and the community of nations.

Since 1965, much has changed in "modern culture" and the features of these "urgent problems," but this is not why the legacy of *Gaudium et Spes* in the post–Vatican II Church has been very complex and mixed. The main reason is that *Gaudium et Spes* is the real test for the council's impact on the Church's theological tradition; its text reveals more and more of its prophetic insights as time goes by—as is appropriate for a conciliar document centered around the idea of the "signs of the times," thanks especially to Chenu and John XXIII.[16] The Church's historicity is not about looking back but about moving forward and *ad extra*, about going forth. In other words, as a consequence of the pastoral constitution, Vatican II is "the introductory moment of a *change of venue* [*Ortswechsel* in German] of Christian faith becoming a world church."[17]

Contemporary Catholic theology never lost sight of the fundamental role of the pastoral constitution. In his conclusion to the five-volume commentary on Vatican II, Hünermann clearly affirmed the path-opening role of *Gaudium et Spes* in the dialogue between the Church and the modern world.[18] In a profound book published in

---

15. Ibid., no. 1. On this, see Peter Hünermann, "Die theologische Grundlegung der christlichen Sozialethik in Gaudium et Spes," in *Theologie der Sozialethik*, ed. Markus Vogt (Freiburg i.B.: Herder, 2013), 23–62.

16. See Chenu, "Les signes des temps," 205–25. For the history of this expression at Vatican II, see Marie-Dominique Chenu, *Notes quotidiennes au Concile: Journal de Vatican II, 1962–1963*, ed. Alberto Melloni (Paris: Cerf, 1995); and Giuseppe Ruggieri, "Appunti per una teologia in papa Roncalli," in *Papa Giovanni*, ed. Giuseppe Alberigo (Rome-Bari: Laterza, 1987), 245–71.

17. Sander, "Theologischer Kommentar zur Pastoralkonstitution," 585.

France almost ten years ago, Pierre Bordeyne successfully recovered the original driving forces in the drafting of the constitution, emphasizing its key role in the formation of Catholic moral theology in modernity: (1) the *déplacement*, displacement in the sense of change of point of view in the way Catholic theology approaches moral issues, that is, the decentering of the Church as an institution from moral theology as a consequence of the biblical *ressourcement* of Christian morality; and (2) the drive of *Gaudium et Spes* to address the needs of contemporary humanity. On this second point, the constitution is not about optimism—the original title was *Gaudium et Luctus, Spes et Angor* (Joy and grief, hope and anguish)—but about hope as an answer to the "anguish for justice as the initial spark for moral reasoning."[19] In my view, Bordeyne correctly sees *Gaudium et Spes* as the document through which "Vatican II fulfills its responsibility of issuing a moral judgment on modern society."[20]

Despite the persistent criticisms of neo-Augustinians,[21] *Gaudium et Spes* has become an integral part of the message of Vatican II. It is undoubtedly true that *Gaudium et Spes* is "linked like no other document of Vatican II to the key perspective of the council, which John XXIII had called 'pastoral.'"[22] Theobald has recently inserted *Gaudium et Spes* into the ecclesiological architecture of Vatican II

18. Peter Hünermann, "Die Gestalt des Textes: Einheit—Strukturen—Grundzüge," in Hünermann and Hilberath, *Herders Theologischer Kommentar*, 5:56–75, at 72. See also Peter Hünermann, "Kriterien für die Rezeption des II. Vatikanischen Konzils," *Theologische Quartalschrift* 191 (2011): 126–47.
19. Philippe Bordeyne, *L'homme et son angoisse: La théologie morale de "Gaudium et spes"* (Paris: Cerf, 2004), 21 ("le texte conciliaire s'est davantage preoccupé de l'angoisse existentielle et de l'angoisse de la justice en tant qu'initiatrices du questionnement moral").
20. Ibid., 342. See also Pierre Bordeyne, "La réappropriation de *Gaudium et spes* en théologie morale: Une redécouverte de la particularité chrétienne," in *Vatican II et la théologie*, ed. Philippe Bordeyne and Laurent Villemin (Paris: Cerf, 2006) 153–76.
21. See Lieven Boeve, "*Gaudium et Spes* and the Crisis of Modernity: The End of the Dialogue with the World?," in *Vatican II and Its Legacy*, ed. Mathijs Lamberigts and Leo Kenis (Leuven: Leuven University Press, 2002), 83–94.
22. See Hans-Joachim Sander, "Theologischer Kommentar zur Pastoralkonstitution," 691.

built around two dimensions, horizontal and vertical. The horizontal dimension of the Church (*ad intra* and *ad extra*) must be balanced with the vertical dimension by giving priority to the idea of revelation expressed in the constitution *Dei Verbum* (and in the declaration on religious liberty *Dignitatis Humanae*). In Theobald's dynamic hermeneutics of the conciliar texts, *Gaudium et Spes* plays a key role in the horizontal axis. Theobald shows this by crossing the "horizontal" texts (*Lumen Gentium, Unitatis Redintegratio, Nostra Aetate, Gaudium et Spes*) with the "vertical" texts (*Dei Verbum, Dignitatis Humanae, Lumen Gentium, Sacrosanctum Concilium*) by a profound consideration of their historical natures.[23] This role is an integral part of the "reframing" (in French, *recadrage*) that is the major accomplishment of Vatican II—resulting in a theology that tries to be more faithful to the gospel than to culture, sociology, or ideology:

> The pastoral constitution, therefore, follows an extremely firm structure, founded both on the inductive schema of apostolic pedagogy of Catholic Action and on a precise perception of modern culture and its internal differentiation and a redefinition of the prophetic role of the Church in this culture. The text leads the reader to a reframing [*recadrage*] of the classical doctrine on the human being, society, and human action in the universe—grounded in a rediscovery of the "biblical economy." It is on this point that *Gaudium et spes* joins *Dei verbum*.[24]

4. Rereading Vatican II for Theological and Ministerial Formation

At fifty years from the last great moment of consultation in the Catholic Church, an interesting paradox has become part of our theological landscape: On the one hand, the immersive historical approach taken by *Gaudium et Spes* is more and more important

---

23. Theobald, *La réception du concile Vatican II: I. Accéder à la source* (Paris: Cerf, 2009), 771–93.
24. Ibid., 778.

for facing the challenges to moral theology that come from modern culture, modern science, modern economy, modern warfare—in short, the challenges of modernity. On the other hand, research on Vatican II seems to be no longer part of the professional métier of many theologians. The result of this paradox is that even when the intent of *Gaudium et Spes* is correctly grasped by theologians and ministers, their lack of commerce with conciliar theology makes their engagement with Vatican II less fruitful than what it could be. And the usual shortcut is an appeal to an ecclesiology of Vatican II—horizontal, ministerial, and ecumenical—that is painfully deprived of its most pastoral document.[25]

In other words, one of the forgotten lessons of Vatican II is the necessity of a synergy between ecclesiology and moral theology, because each discipline contributes to the formation of a *habitus*, a disposition toward the particular and the universal. It is in the particular, concrete, real situations that we are most challenged as moral individuals. It is the universal that is typical of the Catholic understanding of the Church.[26]

From the point of view of theological and ministerial formation, what is the use of the council and of this synergy between different conciliar documents in an intertextual approach to them: moral theology and ecclesiology, liturgy and ecclesiology, Word of God and ecclesiology? Some might think that this intertextual approach is too abstract, too sophisticated, too out of touch. I would argue,

---

25. But on this, see James Keenan, "Vatican II and Theological Ethics," *Theological Studies* 74 (2013): 162–90; Lisa Cahill, "Moral Theology after Vatican II," in *The Crisis of Authority in Catholic Modernity*, ed. Michael J. Lacey and Francis Oakley (New York: Oxford University Press, 2011), 193–224; Darlene Fozard Weaver, "Vatican II and Moral Theology," in *After Vatican II: Trajectories and Hermeneutics*, ed. James L. Heft with John O'Malley (Grand Rapids, MI: Eerdmans, 2012), 23–42; and M. Cathleen Kaveny, "The Spirit of Vatican II and Moral Theology: *Evangelium Vitae* as a Case Study," in Heft with O'Malley, *After Vatican II*, 43–67.

26. See Philippe Bordeyne, "La réappropriation de *Gaudium et spes* en théologie morale: Une redécouverte de la particularité chrétienne," in *Vatican II et la théologie*, ed. Philippe Bordeyne and Laurent Villemin (Paris: Cerf, 2006), 153–76, esp. 164.

however, that it is exactly the opposite. One of the ever-growing and important elements of Vatican II is the practical implications of *ressourcement* and *rapprochement*—"deepening" and "reaching out," "reconciliation by proximity." Vatican II teaches us to look at the global and cosmic *katholon*, the universality, but especially to understand the global and the cosmic through the poor, through the margins.

Vatican II looks at the whole of the great tradition (in order not to become "traditionalists"), and orients itself by looking at the margins and outside the margins of the Catholic *communio*: *ad extra*, the poor, the "separated brothers and sisters," the non-Christian religions, the atheists. The margins, the edges are essential for avoiding the temptation to become slaves of the *Zeitgeist*, of the cultural menu of the day, and of the many religious and political establishments that always threaten Christian freedom.

The word *margin* comes from the Latin noun *margo* and has many meanings. It means the edge or border of a surface, and the edge of the paper that remains blank; but it also means the edge defining inclusion or exclusion from a set or group; it indicates a permissible difference, the room that allows some freedom to move within limits. More figuratively, *margin* means also a position on the border, in a situation that is no longer (or not yet) the reference or the "normal" one. The Italian *margine* is very close in meaning to the original Latin *margo*; it means also the scar of a wound inflicted on a body (as seen, for example, in the writings of Boccaccio and Manzoni). If we apply all these meanings of *margin* to the Church, we will see that they characterize the Church of Vatican II: a Church that redefined the boundaries of inclusion/exclusion; a Church that is less institution and more movement because its margins are moving; a Church that reaches out; a Church that sees the margins, the wounds, and tries to heal them with the "medicine of mercy," as John XXIII said in his address opening the council.

Vatican II happened in Rome, at the historical, geographical, and political center of the Roman Catholic Church. But the council was transacted—between 1959 and 1965, and after 1965—largely by the Church's margins; in Congar's words, Vatican II was "a recentering of the *Urbs* [Rome] on the *Orbis* [the world], because the *Orbis* almost took possession of the *Urbs*."[27] Vatican II is a theological event that took off from a Church that fifty years ago was still very much at the center of the public scene; Catholicism was still very popular because it was inoffensive and in line with the cultural mainstream of the Western world. Times have changed, but Vatican II still indicates the path for a more "marginal" Church—marginal in the sense of being closer to the margins of our world because it is closer to the example given by Jesus Christ.

In the Chrism Mass of March 28, 2013, Pope Francis spoke about the ecclesiological relevance of these "edges," drawing on Psalm 133:2: "It is like the precious oil on the head, running down upon the beard, on the beard of Aaron, running down over the collar of his robes." In this Chrism Mass homily, Pope Francis gave an ecclesiological meaning of this anointing: "The precious oil which anoints the head of Aaron does more than simply lend fragrance to his person; it overflows down to 'the edges.' The Lord will say this clearly: his anointing is meant for the poor, prisoners and the sick, for those who are sorrowing and alone. My dear brothers, the ointment is not intended just to make us fragrant, much less to be kept in a jar, for then it would become rancid . . . and the heart bitter."[28]

---

27. Congar, *Le Concile de Vatican II*, 54.
28. See Pope Francis, homily, Saint Peter's Basilica, March 28, 2013, available at http://www.vatican.va/holy_father/francesco/homilies/2013/documents/papa-francesco_20130328_messa-crismale_en.html.

This homily by the newly elected pope came just two weeks after the preconclave congregations of the cardinals, where he said that the Church should reconsider evangelization in light of the "existential peripheries" and avoid the danger of becoming "a self-referential church."[29] The notion of "peripheries" in relation to the mission of the Church has become one of the key ideas by which to understand the pontificate of Pope Francis. The "change of pace" of this pope has very little to do with the simplistic notion of a "pope of humility," just as "the good pope" is a simplistic characterization of John XXIII. From the theological point of view, conceptual incorporation of marginality is a step in the slow acceptance of the institution of an ecclesiology that came to maturity in the twentieth century. This ecclesiology realizes that the Church serves much better when its ministers of the gospel follow the "marginal Jew,"[30] Jesus Christ, who went to the social and religious peripheries, the edges of Second Temple Judaism, rather than follow the Emperor Charlemagne, who civilized medieval Europe. The ministerial style inspired by Jesus requires an abandonment of the symbols of power. But from the ecclesiological point of view, the challenge is even greater: this challenge brought by biblical theology to ecclesiology implies a *déplacement*, a recentering of the Church from the center to the "peripheries,"[31] to the edges. The Church lives in a world in which it is assumed that all of us are now—thanks to the Internet—at the center, online, connected, free, and in control of ourselves. This is not so, and the Catholic Church knows that, perhaps better than anybody else.

29. The text of cardinal Bergoglio's speech at the pre-conclave session of March 7, 2013 in "Cardenal Ortega Revela Palabras del Cardenal Bergoglio," in www.palabranueva.net (March 25, 2013).

30. See John P. Meier, *A Marginal Jew: Rethinking the Historical Jesus*, 4 vols. (New York: Doubleday, 2001–09).

31. In the United States, the word *suburb* connotes wealth; in Europe, it tends to connote poverty.

Today, sometimes we are led to believe that we live in a world without barriers, without borders, or with borders that we can cross if we have the financial means. But our borders have changed: we do not have three different kinds of worlds as it was in the 1970s and 1980s, but one world with less visible borders, less visible barriers, but perhaps barriers that are actually higher and more difficult to cross.

It is no accident that inclusion and exclusion have become two key ideas in our ecclesiological debate. Their meaning becomes clear if we go back to the peripheries of our world—social-cultural peripheries—and connect *ressourcement* and *rapprochement* to them.[32] Usually the "marginality" of the Church in secular society is taken as a sociological fact and, sadly, as a symptom of the irrelevance of Christianity today. However, in these last few decades, the "option for the poor" and for people at the margins of society has provided major new impulses for biblical studies, systematic theology, Church history, ecclesial practice, and the academic study of religion. Sometimes the "option for the poor" has been reduced to the need to show mercy for the poor as a minority group. But the idea of the "margins" expressed by Vatican II pushes us much further.

Vatican II offers a view that calls us today to a new sense of unity. "Marginality" need not be a choice imposed from the outside, and should not be identified with irrelevance. Marginality can be an opportunity to rediscover the real boundaries of the Church.

---

32. See Dennis Doyle, Timothy J. Furry, and Pascal D. Bazzell, eds., *Ecclesiology and Exclusion: Boundaries of Being and Belonging in Postmodern Times* (Maryknoll, NY: Orbis, 2012).

PART III

Vatican II and the Agenda of the Church

9

The Relevance of Vatican II after Fifty Years

"Is Vatican II still relevant after fifty years?" This is not a rhetorical question. The Church and the world have changed since the opening of the council on October 12, 1962. For many other councils in the history of the Catholic Church, that same question—"Is the ecumenical council of fifty years ago still relevant?"—would have received a negative answer (to put it mildly). Let us imagine a gathering of theologians in 1562 (during the Council of Trent!) trying to understand the relevance of the Fifth Lateran Council (1512–1517), which had ended in Rome in the same year as the ninety-five theses of Martin Luther: an ecumenical council that never detected the evident signs of corruption within the Church and of the "theological unrest" from Northern Europe that later become known as "the Reformation."

In contrast, other councils proved, fifty years after their completion, their relevance and their role in the life of the Church and of theology.[1] Not only the ecumenical councils of the fourth and fifth centuries, but also the Council of Trent itself, proved their importance in the decades and generations following their conclusions.

This tells us that—first fact—*there are different kinds of councils*, even among ecumenical councils. There are councils with a lasting impact and councils with an ephemeral life (or, as then-Cardinal Ratzinger put it a few years ago, "failed councils").[2] Vatican II clearly does not belong in the category of the failed councils. Whereas no one in 1562 was talking about the Fifth Lateran Council that had begun fifty years before, the role of Vatican II in today's Catholicism is completely different. Not only is Vatican II remembered and studied, but it has become part of Catholics' everyday life and a compass for the Church and for Catholic theology.[3]

A second fact is that *Vatican II had, in its first fifty years of life, a quite interesting and complex history of reception*, always rooted in a theological debate that encompassed all cultural and geographical latitudes of world Catholicism. The debate on the reception of Vatican II survived not only the generation of bishops and theologians who were at Vatican II, but also the most difficult and important moments in the relationship between magisterium, theologians, people of God, and the outer world. These moments

1. See Massimo Faggioli, *Vatican II: The Battle for Meaning* (Mahwah, NJ: Paulist, 2012); Giuseppe Alberigo, ed., *History of Vatican II*, vols. 1–5, English version ed. Joseph A. Komonchak (Maryknoll, NY: Orbis, 1995–2006).
2. See Joseph Ratzinger, "A Review of the Post-Conciliar Era," in *Principles of Catholic Theology* (San Francisco: Ignatius, 1987), 367–93.
3. See the flow of literature about Vatican II: Massimo Faggioli, "Concilio Vaticano II: Bollettino bibliografico (2000–2002)," *Cristianesimo nella Storia* 24, no. 2 (2003): 335–60; "Concilio Vaticano II: Bollettino bibliografico (2002–2005)," *Cristianesimo nella Storia* 26, no. 3 (2005): 743–67; "Council Vatican II: Bibliographical Overview 2005–2007," *Cristianesimo nella Storia* 29, no. 2 (2008): 567–610; "Council Vatican II: Bibliographical Overview 2007–2010," *Cristianesimo nella Storia* 32, no. 2 (2011): 755–91; "Council Vatican II: Bibliographical Survey 2010–2013," *Cristianesimo nella Storia* 24, no. 3 (2013): 927–55.

include the encyclical *Humanae Vitae* in 1968, Paul VI's disappointments of the mid-1970s, the new Code of Canon Law in 1983, the Extraordinary Synod of 1985, the Great Jubilee of the year 2000, and the election of the first pope who was not a council father, Pope Benedict XVI, in April 2005. All these eventful and consequential moments never managed to overshadow the council or put it in the broader context of the theological zeitgeist of the "sixties." The message of Vatican II has not become tame or a distant reference, at least for theologians.

Third fact: *all the most important events in the history of Catholic theology in the last fifty years are firmly rooted in the council's message.* The new push for evangelization in the 1970s, the ecumenical and interreligious outreach of John Paul II, the new protagonism of lay theologians, the vitality of Catholic theology facing new challenges—all this would be unthinkable without Vatican II: the final documents and the event, the letter and the spirit of the council.

Vatican II is still relevant because it has produced a change that is now clearly, in its fundamental core, irreversible—or reversible only at an unimaginable cost. The amount and the quality of change have now gone beyond anyone's ability to turn back the clock. Much still needs to be accomplished. But even those who try to appeal to nostalgia of various kinds know that too much has already been accomplished. To use a metaphor taken from the world of aviation, Catholicism is today at a point of no return; the Church is no longer capable of returning to the airfield it took off from, that is, the "long nineteenth century" of Catholicism.[4]

The Church of Vatican II is surely not immune to infidelity to the message of the council, or to attacks trying to make of Catholicism a kind of natural refuge for conservative ideologies of different kinds.

4. See John W. O'Malley, *What Happened at Vatican II* (Cambridge MA: Belknap Press of Harvard University Press, 2008), 53–92.

This is clearly a very delicate moment. We are not sure of what kind of Catholicism we will have in fifty years. But we are sure it will not look like the Catholicism of fifty years ago.

1. Vatican II: *Ad intra* and *ad extra*

Vatican II is a special kind of ecumenical council because it started, from the very beginning, as a council aimed at dealing with ecclesiology, and in particular with ecclesiological issues both *ad intra* and *ad extra*—for the inner life of the Church and its relationship with the outside.[5] Some of the core issues of Vatican II—liturgy and ecclesiology—are part of both the *ad intra* and the *ad extra* dimensions of the council. The impossibility of turning back is clear if we examine the closely connected theological dimensions of *ad intra* and *ad extra*, especially in the field of liturgy and ecclesiology and for their impact on the rest of the conciliar teaching.

1.1. Liturgy *ad intra* and *ad extra*

The liturgical reform is the most visible and important fruit of Vatican II—no wonder the liturgical reform has been under attack from various fronts in these last ten years at least. The connection between theological *ressourcement* and liturgical reform is one of the keys to understanding the liturgical reform and its importance for the life of Vatican II.

The anti–Vatican II "new liturgical movement" (very active on the Web and not only) is nostalgic but not moved by pure nostalgia;

5. For Cardinal Suenens's formulation of the ecclesiological dimension *ad intra–ad extra*, see Alberto Melloni, "Ecclesiologie al Vaticano II (autunno 1962–estate 1963)," in *Les commissions conciliaires à Vatican II*, ed. Mathijs Lamberigts, Claude Soetens, and Jan Grootaers (Leuven: Peeters, 1996), 91–179; Alberigo, ed., *History of Vatican II*, 2:281–357.

its theological and ecclesiological consequences reach far beyond nostalgia. The advocates of the anti–Vatican II "new liturgical movement" are indeed right as they identify in *Sacrosanctum Concilium* the main target, since the liturgical constitution of Vatican II is a powerful moment of *ressourcement* in the theology of the council and the most antitraditionalist document of the council. The principle of *ressourcement* affected *Sacrosanctum Concilium* like no other conciliar document; it is hard to find in the corpus of the documents passages more expressive of the very essence of the Church and more driven by the idea of *ressourcement*.[6]

For the dimension *ad intra*, the liturgical reform as intended in *Sacrosanctum Concilium* aimed at the rediscovery of the centrality of Scripture and the Eucharist. It is the most direct way to grasp Vatican II's ecclesiology. *Sacrosanctum Concilium* (SC) is aware that "the life of the Church cannot be reduced to the sole eucharistic moment" (*SC* 9–10) and that liturgy has its role in the Church as a *theologia prima* (generative, original theology), as *locus theologicus* (a theological source), and as *culmen et fons*, as summit and source. The liturgical constitution sponsored a new awareness within the Roman Catholic Church that things change. That is why both the liturgical reform of Vatican II and the most recent calls for a "reform of the reform" touch the whole essence of Vatican II. Changing worship sets off a rethinking of ecclesiology in a more profound and long-lasting way than the definition of the Church in *Lumen Gentium*. Liturgy is not worship of a dominating power, but the celebration of the grace of God, of God's free given gift to us in Jesus Christ.

In its dimension *ad extra*, the Eucharistic ecclesiology of *Sacrosanctum Concilium* provides the grounds for the basic direction

---

6. See Massimo Faggioli, *True Reform: Liturgy and Ecclesiology in* Sacrosanctum Concilium (Collegeville, MN: Liturgical, 2012).

of Vatican II, that is, *rapprochement* inside and outside the Church. *Rapprochement*—a term used many times by the pioneer of ecumenism and liturgist Lambert Beauduin[7]—is not part of the corpus of Vatican II in a material way, but it belongs fully to the aims of Vatican II. The council's liturgical reform plays a significant role in developing (during Vatican II) and performing (after Vatican II) this key feature of the council, in a way that is not less important than the other "*rapprochement* manifestos" of Vatican II, such as the decree on ecumenism *Unitatis Redintegratio*, the declaration *Nostra Aetate*, and the pastoral constitution *Gaudium et Spes*. The main *rapprochement* carried out by *Sacrosanctum Concilium* consists of a reconciled and unifying vision of the Church, of Christian life, and of the existential condition of the faithful in the world.[8] Far from being a purely aesthetic option, the theological starting point of the liturgical reform aimed at resetting the relationship between Christian liturgy, the spiritual needs of the faithful, and Catholic theological reading of the modern world in its historical and social dimensions.

Ressourcement, Eucharistic ecclesiology, and *rapprochement* require a drive for a full implementation of Vatican II and provide an unambiguous appraisal of the issue of Vatican II's continuity *and* discontinuity and the role of liturgical reform in the Church of the twenty-first century. Any attempt to undermine the liturgical reform of Vatican II reveals a clearly reductionist view of the council and its epoch-making changes.

---

7. See Raymond Loonbeek and Jacques Mortiau, *Un pionnier, Dom Lambert Beauduin (1873–1960): Liturgie et unité des chrétiens*, 2 vols. (Louvain-la-Neuve: Collège Erasme, 2001), esp. 1:907–9. See also Jacques Mortiau and Raymond Loonbeek, *Dom Lambert Beauduin: Visionnaire et précurseur (1873–1960): Un moine au coeur libre* (Paris: Cerf, 2005).

8. See Giuseppe Dossetti, *Per una "chiesa eucaristica": Rilettura della portata dottrinale della Costituzione liturgica del Vaticano II; lezioni del 1965*, ed. Giuseppe Alberigo and Giuseppe Ruggieri (Bologna: Il Mulino, 2002), 41.

1.2. Ecclesiology *ad intra* and *ad extra*

Liturgy and ecclesiology are closely connected in the theological balance of Vatican II. The liturgical reform anticipated and called for a Church reform that was centered more on the Eucharist and ministry than on an understanding of the institution that was based more on the juridical structure of the Roman Empire than on the gospel of Jesus Christ. The ecclesiological constitution *Lumen Gentium* did not receive fully the ecclesiology of the liturgical constitution, and its most delicate focus is in the third chapter about the bishops and the papacy—a section that has very few connections with a Eucharistic ecclesiology.

In this sense, the *ad intra* dimension of the ecclesiology of Vatican II is still a building site. There have been failed attempts of Vatican II to reform the institution *ad intra*: the rejection between 1963 and 1965 of the proposal of a Central Board of Bishops (Consilium Centrale Episcoporum) acting with the pope in Rome; the rejection of the proposals for a reform of the appointment of the bishops; the controversial reform of the retirement age for bishops at seventy-five; the creation of Paul VI's "Synod of Bishops" in the summer of 1965, in order to prevent the council from proposing its own design for a "bishops' synod" in the last session of the council; the restrictions imposed on the new forms of collegiality and synodality in the local church (the role of the priests) and at the universal level (the role of the bishops).[9]

But *Lumen Gentium*, together with *Christus Dominus*, the decree on the bishops, restored a fundamental balance within Catholic ecclesiology: between the juridical and communional dimensions of the Church; between the idea of *societas* (which in Latin is much

---

9. For all this, see Massimo Faggioli, *Il vescovo e il concilio: Modello episcopale e aggiornamento al Vaticano II* (Bologna: Il Mulino, 2005).

closer to "institution" than "society") and the idea of "people of God." The new balance between universal ecclesiology and ecclesiology of the local church also opened a path toward new ways to live out communion and collegiality in the Church, and reframed the debate on ministry in light of the gospel, rather than in light of the social functions performed by the Church in medieval and early modern history.[10]

The new ecclesiological self-understanding of the Catholic Church is inextricably connected to the relationship of the Church *ad extra*. The fundamental passage of the *subsistit in* (*Lumen Gentium* 8) about the relationship between the Catholic Church and the Church of Christ gives new shape to the debate about the "members" of the Church and to the historical fact of the fragmentation of Christianity in different churches since the very beginning of Christianity, thus calling Christians to a new unity.[11] The same ecclesiological constitution reframed the issue of the relationship with non-Christians and nonbelievers, in *Lumen Gentium* 15–16 emphasizing new (and now even more visible) forms of communion besides the criteria listed by Cardinal Robert Bellarmin after the Council of Trent: communion in prayer and communion in martyrdom.

The decree on ecumenism, *Unitatis Redintegratio*, built new bridges with other churches, at the same time achieving very important theological results, such as the "hierarchy of truths," now a fundamental and essential tool for the self-understanding of Catholicism. The pastoral constitution *Gaudium et Spes* put an end to the long history of mutual mistrust between the Church and the

10. See Richard Gaillardetz, *Ecclesiology for a Global Church: A People Called and Sent* (Maryknoll, NY: Orbis, 2008); Peter Hünermann, "Theologischer Kommentar zur dogmatischen Konstitution über die Kirche," in *Herders Theologischer Kommentar zum Zweiten Vatikanischen Konzil*, ed. Hans Jochen Hilberath and Peter Hünermann, vol. 2 (Freiburg i.B.: Herder, 2004).

11. See Mauro Velati, *Dialogo e rinnovamento: Verbali e testi del Segretariato per l'unità dei cristiani nella preparazione del concilio Vaticano II (1960–1962)* (Bologna: Il Mulino, 2011).

modern world, and moved the Church toward the ability to assess the "signs of our times," thanks to a new aptitude to understand herself historically, a Church born and developed and living in human history, affected by historical change in her human features not less than other human institutions. The declaration *Nostra Aetate* represented just the first step in knowing and understanding the "religious other," starting from the very source of otherness, the relationship between Judaism and Christianity.

All of these teachings *ad extra* have now become integral parts of the theological identity of Catholicism. The "magisterium through gestures" of John XXIII, Paul VI, and John Paul II still needs a proper theological and magisterial reception. Theology needs to be written in order to preserve the meaning of those gestures and to show that these gestures were interpreting the *sensus fidei*, the "sense of the faith" that the whole Church has. But these gestures would never have been possible without the seeds planted by the council.[12]

2. The Fundamental Changes: From *ad extra* to *ad intra*

A few key examples of liturgy and ecclesiology show the intimate relationship between *ad intra* and *ad extra* in the teaching of the council. Liturgy and ecclesiology represent two major fields of debate in the history of the interpretation of Vatican II. Their relevance is in the fact that the contents of the documents on liturgy and ecclesiology are inextricably connected, the one to the other, but also to the rest of the message of Vatican II. Understanding or misunderstanding the liturgical and ecclesiological content of

---

12. We are still waiting for a study of the "gestures" of the popes of Vatican II and of post–Vatican II and of their meaning for the teaching of the council: John XXIII's "Moonlight Speech" of October 11, 1962; Paul VI's journey to Jerusalem in 1964 and to the United Nations in 1965; John Paul II's journey to Israel and Syria in 2000–2001; Pope Francis's trip to the island of Lampedusa on July 8, 2013, just to mention a few examples.

Vatican II implies understanding or misunderstanding Vatican II as such. Much of what the final texts of Vatican II have in common—and much of their relevance—goes beyond the technical labeling of the different council documents: they express the fundamental fact that Vatican II talks not only to the Church, but also to humanity and humankind as such.

This is the real meaning of a "pastoral council."[13] The value of Vatican II is in the first steps in removing barriers and boundaries between the Catholic Church as a culture, as a theology, as a system and the world.

1. *Sacrosanctum Concilium* reframed Catholicism not around its historically determined social and political patterns, but around the Eucharist; *Lumen Gentium* unlocked the juridical and theological identification between "Church of Christ" and "Catholic Church" in *LG* 8. On this basis, the declaration of religious liberty *Dignitatis Humanae* was the beginning of the end of fifteen hundred years of *Staatskirchentum*—national religion, established church according to the European ideal of medieval "Christendom." With regard to the reason, the council fathers based their argument on personal dignity and human freedom. This principle of reason has been formulated and recognized only in modern times. It is the result of an epochal shift in thinking about Catholic theology and faith.

2. *Sacrosanctum Concilium* rephrased the importance of liturgy under the emphasis of liturgical pluralism; *Lumen Gentium* acknowledged the constraints of history and of canon law on the Catholic self-understanding of the Church. On this very basis, the decrees on ecumenism and on the Eastern Catholic

13. A very important article is Peter Hünermann, "Kriterien für die Rezeption des II. Vatikanischen Konzils," *Theologische Quartalschrift* 191, no. 2 (2011): 126–47.

Churches meant the beginning of the end of a thousand years of division between Western and Eastern Christianity (*Orientalium Ecclesiarum* 14–18; *Unitatis Redintegratio* 13–17). This meant not only the end of theological hatred or enmity, but also the end of a monocultural Church, a Church whose European culture had become a hypostasis for the self-understanding of Catholicism. In *Unitatis Redintegratio*, we have the importance of the positive significance of different liturgical traditions. The riches of the Eastern spiritual traditions, the different religious orders, customs, and traditions, do not preclude the "unity of the church," but rather enrich the Church. Vatican II put an end to "confessionalization" as a way to enforce socially different and competing theological views based on the clashes sparked by the Reformation, four centuries before. One example of these types of issues of faith as the primary vision of the Church is the Bellarminian idea of the Church as a "perfect society." Vatican II rejected a "confessionalized" understanding of faith. In *Dei Verbum*, there is a post–Tridentine explanation of the importance of Scripture and tradition in the definition of the faith; the Old and the New Testament are the soul of theology and of preaching.

3. Following John XXIII's opening speech of the council, *Gaudet Mater Ecclesia*, the liturgical constitution *Sacrosanctum Concilium (SC)* argued in the very beginning of the constitution for a new unity between Church and humanity (*SC* 1); *Lumen Gentium* developed an ecclesiology in light not only of the gospel of Jesus Christ, but also in light of the new needs of a Church evolving in history. The pastoral constitution *Gaudium et Spes* signaled the end of almost two hundred years of hatred of modernity and modern culture. The ecclesiology of *Lumen Gentium* and

the pastoral constitution open a new understanding not only of the Church itself, but also of the role of its members and of ministry in the Church. In *Gaudium et Spes*, we have the dignity of human persons in the context of today's situation, the community of humankind and their activities, their work. It shows these basic themes of modern anthropology in the light of faith. Faith contributes to their understanding and to a corresponding orientation in life. It is spoken in a two-way learning process: the society on one side and the church on the other side. Given the changes reflected in human development in recent decades, in view of the globalization of social and economic conditions, Vatican II made the necessary choices to engage the church in this unfolding modernity.

4. *Sacrosanctum Concilium* recentered Catholic worship around Jesus Christ and the Eucharist (*SC* 7); *Lumen Gentium* argued for a new understanding of non-Catholics and nonbelievers (*LG* 15–16). *Nostra Aetate* showed the key role of Judaism for a deeper understanding of non-Christian religions for what they are—that is, not an accident of history, but a fundamental fact of the human condition. Vatican II discarded the juridical language for the definition of "faith" in the form of a denial of other religions' right to exist. In its place, we have a differentiating affirmation about the distinctions worthy of consideration and about the differences that should be taken into account.

3. The Relevance of Vatican II in the Church of Today

All these changes in Catholic theology—we can call them discontinuities—showed that there is an intimate connection between changes *ad extra* and *ad intra*. As a whole, these changes represent—no less than the moments of continuities of Vatican II with the great tradition of the Church—moments of conversion of Catholic theology in a fundamental reorientation of the Church around the gospel.[14]

A possible difference in their appreciation, between 1962 and now at the beginning of the twenty-first century, is about the value of the *ad extra* dimension for the understanding of the *ad intra* of Vatican II. What the Church says *ad extra*—about non-Catholics, about Jews, about non-Christians, about modernity—has now become impossible to separate from the Church's core identity *ad intra*, that is, from what the Church believes and proclaims about itself. This intimate connection becomes more evident if we consider that one of the visions of hope of Vatican II comes from the fact that the council does not have in mind a determined social or political or cultural or ideological definition of Catholicism. That was key to making the Church able to receive and absorb the huge changes occurring in our world in these last fifty years.

In the relationship between the *ad intra* and *ad extra* dimensions of Catholic theology, these last fifty years have been almost divided in two parts by the interreligious gathering of Assisi in 1986: almost twenty-five years after the opening of Vatican II, and twenty-five years between Assisi 1986 and today. In the almost thirty years between Assisi 1986 and now (with September 11, 2001, in between), we now understand better the signs of hope coming from Vatican II. Only the Church of *Nostra Aetate*, of *Dignitatis Humanae*, of *Gaudium et Spes*, of *Lumen Gentium* can make theological sense of these last fifty years.

The theological unfeasibility of going back cannot reassure us about the inevitability of conciliar theology. On the contrary, the

---

14. See Christoph Theobald, *La réception du concile Vatican II: vol. I. Accéder à la source* (Paris: Cerf, 2009).

hopes of Vatican II need to be cultivated, developed, and transmitted to the next generation of Christians, theologians, clergy, and to each and every person in contact with Catholicism today.

Fifty years after the event of Vatican II, we find ourselves in that crucial moment of passage between the short run and the long run: the "clash of narratives" about Vatican II encounters here the perennial law of the reception of the councils of the Church. Giuseppe Alberigo, recalling the worrisome memorandum sent between 1600 and 1612 by Robert Bellarmine to Pope Clement VIII on the progress of the reforms decided by the Council of Trent (between 1545 and 1563), had estimated that it took at least fifty years for the beginning of the reception of Trent.[15]

The current underestimation of Vatican II in many circles is no different from the underestimation of the consequences of the discovery of vaccines against smallpox and polio. In the last few years, younger generations of Catholic theologians have been credited by theological pundits with a detached or even skeptical view of Vatican II that symbolizes polarization, culture wars, and division in the Church—something they allegedly feel the need to take distance from, as if the common ground they seek could only be a ground as distant as possible from Vatican II.

My experience could not be more different from this misperception. Whether liberal or conservative, Catholic and non-Catholic students of every theological and spiritual orientation know well that longing for and aspiring to revive the period before Vatican II is a dream nourished only by people who do not live the real, day-to-day reality of the Church. Ecumenism, religious freedom, and the rejection of anti-Semitism cannot be reduced to partisan issues: the post–9/11 world has revealed the prophetic value of documents like

15. Giuseppe Alberigo, *La chiesa nella storia* (Brescia: Paideia, 1988), 218–39.

Nostra Aetate, whose theological necessity had vastly outgrown the narrow boundaries of its short text.

To belittle Vatican II is to belittle these achievements as well, while disparaging these achievements means disparaging the very theology of Vatican II that brought about this opening of the Church *ad extra*, but also the reflection of the Church *ad intra*.

The election of Pope Benedict XVI in 2005 and the reopening of the debate about Vatican II are two "signs of the times" for the Church of the early twenty-first century—a time that for the Church is simultaneously a time of progress and regress. For Catholics, the council is not a foil in the self-identification of their ways of being Catholic, but a real reference and a given condition of existence, especially for Catholicism outside the geopolitical and cultural boundaries of the North-Atlantic region.

In 1987, Richard John Neuhaus said this about Vatican II: "The contest over the interpretations of Vatican II constitutes a critical battlefront in our society's continuing cultural wars."[16] That statement must also be read in reverse: the substantial and undeniable ability of the Catholic Church to remain together in the Western Hemisphere and in the rest of the world—despite the wars (cultural and otherwise)—owes much to Vatican II and its interpretations. Behind the very identity of the Church and its relationship with the modern world, there is a specific (if sometimes unconscious or indirect) interpretation of Vatican II.

In the first decades of the post–Vatican II period, the debate on Vatican II lived through major moments of discussion and dispute.[17]

---

16. Richard John Neuhaus, "The Councils Called Vatican II," in *The Catholic Moment: The Paradox of the Church in the Postmodern World* (San Francisco: Harper and Row, 1987), 61.

17. Concerning the almost classical division of the first decades of the post–Vatican II years into three different periods (1965–1975, 1975–1985, and 1985–), see Hermann Josef Pottmeyer, "A New Phase in the Reception of Vatican II: Twenty Years of Interpretation of Vatican II," in *The Reception of Vatican II*, ed. Giuseppe Alberigo, Jean-Pierre Jossua, and Joseph Komonchak (Washington, DC: Catholic University of America Press, 1985), 27–43; Walter

The 1970s saw the beginning of the entrenching of different positions along a fault line in the interpretation of Vatican II within Catholic theology, and the birth of a schismatic group (the Lefebvrites) whose existence found motivation only in their rejection of Vatican II and, in particular, new orientations of the Church *ad extra*. The Code of Canon Law of 1983 and the final results of the Extraordinary Synod of Bishops of 1985 steered the hermeneutics of Vatican II toward a more cautious interpretation of the relationship between letter and spirit of the council and inaugurated John Paul II's complex reception of Vatican II.

A few months after the election of John Paul II's successor, Benedict XVI, the new pope's speech of December 22, 2005, conveyed a clear message about the much-anticipated shift in the doctrinal policy about Vatican II of the former Cardinal Prefect of the Congregation for the Doctrine of Faith. That speech celebrated the passage of Joseph Ratzinger's take on Vatican II from the level of an individual theologian, if not a powerful cardinal, to the level of the Roman pontiff's official interpretation of the council.

The everlasting political and institutional constraints of the "office of Peter" clearly showed Benedict XVI the difficulty of turning back from the language and orientation of Vatican II. Not for the first time in history, the unintended consequences of a major historical event had an effect outside the boundaries of the institution as well, thus creating an external framework for the interpretation of Vatican II that is not less visible and tangible than the hermeneutical balance struck by the Church as a whole—popes, bishops, clergy, monks,

---

Kasper, "Die bleibende Herausforderung durch das II. Vatikanische Konzil: Zur Hermeneutik der Konzilsaussagen," in *Die Kirche Jesu Christi: Schriften zur Ekklesiologie, I*, Walter Kasper Gesammelte Schriften 11 (Freiburg i.B.: Herder, 2008), 1:200–211, esp. 200–201; Karl Lehmann, "Das II. Vatikanum—Ein Wegweiser: Verständnis—Rezeption—Bedeutung," in ed., *Das Zweite Vatikanische Konzil und die Zeichen der Zeit heute*, ed. Peter Hünermann (Freiburg i.B.: Herder, 2006), 11–28, esp. 22–24.

theologians, families, lay men and women, pastoral ministers, and missionaries.

The debate about Vatican II undoubtedly feels outside pressure from that world to which Vatican II sent its message for the entire duration of Vatican II, from the opening speech of Pope John XXIII (*Gaudet Mater Ecclesia*, October 11, 1962) to the pastoral constitution *Gaudium et Spes* (December 7, 1965).

The "incident" of January 2009 in which Benedict XVI decided to lift the excommunication of the Lefebvrian bishops of the Priestly Fraternity of Saint Pius X revealed how profoundly the culture of Vatican II has penetrated the modern world, and that the modern world is now begging the Church to be faithful to those teachings *ad extra*.[18]

The complexity of the debate has also to do with the fact that the history of the post–Vatican II Church intertwines with the growth in knowledge and awareness of Catholic theology about Vatican II. It is a remarkable fact that during the first decades of the debate about Vatican II, the historical and theological research on the council has acquired information and developed approaches to the "thing" (the Second Vatican Council) that were only imaginable in the 1970s or 1980s. Scholars of very different theological affiliations now know much more about Vatican II, both its day-by-day unfolding and its overall and epoch-making dimension as an event of Church history, of the history of theology, of the history of ideas, and of political and social history. The Catholic Church now knows a significant amount of information about Vatican II, from different cultural approaches and geographical points of view. The amount of information about

---

18. See Massimo Faggioli, "Die kulturelle und politische Relevanz des II. Vatikanischen Konzils als konstitutiver Faktor der Interpretation," in *Exkommunikation oder Kommunikation? Der Weg der Kirche nach dem II. Vatikanum und die Pius-Brüder*, ed. Peter Hünermann (Freiburg i.B.: Herder, 2009), 153–74; and Massimo Faggioli, "Vatican II Comes of Age," *Tablet*, April 11, 2009, pp. 16–17.

the change that happened at Vatican II is probably more than Catholic theology expected, and maybe more than the Church as an institution was ready to handle.

But the communion of the Church is much better equipped to handle the rediscovery of its past than the intellectuals on the payroll of the Communist Party of the Soviet Union were, when faced with the permanent, ideological manipulation of recent history. They were mocked with this popular Soviet-era joke: "We know exactly what the future will be. Our problem is with the past: that keeps changing."

The past has not been changed by the lively historical and theological debate about Vatican II—a comforting sign of the vitality of the Church in a world where the so-called neo-atheism takes pride in seeing faith and debate as opposite terms.

The historicization of Vatican II starting in the late 1980s has clearly introduced a hermeneutical shift in the theology of Vatican II. One of the key principles of that hermeneutical shift was the new understanding of modernity and the modern world with the expression of "joy and hope." Undermining that message of joy and hope coming from Vatican II is nothing less than undermining the intention of the council itself.

10

The Role of Episcopal Conferences since Vatican II

A Test Case for Collegiality in the Church

In the fifty years since the close of Vatican II, the issue of the theological status and role of episcopal conferences in the government of the Catholic Church has been a fraught one.[1] This was illustrated afresh when Pope Francis cited the episcopal conferences of Asia, Africa, Latin America, the United States, and France in his apostolic exhortation *Evangelii Gaudium* (November 24, 2013), as if to bolster their magisterial authority. Cardinal Gerhard Müller, prefect of the Congregation for the Doctrine of the Faith, was quick to point out, a few days later, that while papacy and episcopacy are of divine law, episcopal conferences are merely of human law.[2]

---

1. This chapter was published originally as "The Regulation of Episcopal Conferences since Vatican II," *Japan Mission Journal* 68, no. 2 (Summer 2014): 82–96.
2. See http://www.kathweb.at/site/nachrichten/archiv/archive/59657.html (December 27, 2013).

Can episcopal conferences be seen as a necessary and effective expression of the collegiality of bishops stressed by Vatican II? And as such, do they not enjoy, like the synods held every three years in Rome, a high theological status? In this chapter, I shall trace how their status was undercut in a process going through several phases in the postconciliar period.

1. Vatican II on Episcopal Conferences

The debate on the episcopal conferences today, before considering possible solutions to the theological and canonical impasse of the post–Vatican II Church on the relationship between Rome and the world episcopate, must be aware of the debate that took place at Vatican II, in the preparation and in the celebration of the council.

1.1. The Schema *on Episcopal Conferences in the Preparatory Phase*

In 1959, at the beginning of the conciliar process, there were forty episcopal conferences, both national and supranational. Originating in the midnineteenth century, they had been promoted by Pius XII, but the *Annuario Pontificio* began to cite them only in 1959. As often happens, juridical regulation lagged behind reality and experience. The 1917 Code of Canon Law did not even mention episcopal conferences, apart from some canons about the plenary councils in the section about the supreme power in the Church. Yet before the promulgation of the code, episcopal conferences had already made important steps: from the 1840s to the end of the nineteenth century, they had become a characteristic means of intervening in the relationship between Church and society. In 1959, the rules of the existing episcopal conferences were dealt with in connection with the history of the national episcopates and in bilateral agreements with the Apostolic See.[3]

This situation was very clear to the minds of the council fathers from the beginning of the council. An analysis of the *vota* indicates that they sought to revive a nonmonarchical church governance in two different ways: (1) by reanimating traditional assemblies and bodies (primacies and patriarchates, provinces and ecclesiastical regions, provincial and national councils, local synods), and (2) by creating and increasing the activity of new bodies like the regional, national, and continental episcopal conferences.

The issue of episcopal conferences was not included in the list of *quaestiones*, topics given to the preparatory commissions in July 1960, but it became part of the conciliar debate through the activity of the commission on the bishops, chaired by Cardinal Marcello Mimmi and, after his death (March 1961), Cardinal Paolo Marella. The fathers in their *vota* made references to episcopal conferences not only directly, but, due to the differences between local situations and experiences, also indirectly, when they wrote about the relations between local bishops and papal nuncios, and between episcopal conferences and the Roman Curia, and when they proposed new laws about episcopal conferences to be inserted in the Code of Canon Law.[4]

The commission *de episcopis*, after intense debate among its members, especially those from France and Spain, produced the schema *De Episcoporum coetu seu conferentia* ("On the assembly or

3. See Giorgio Feliciani, *Le conferenze episcopali* (Bologna: Il Mulino, 1974), 273–349; Charles Munier, "La coopération des évêques au bien commun de plusieurs églises," in *La charge pastorale des évêques* (Paris: Cerf, 1967) 329–52.

4. See Angel Antón, *Conferencias episcopales: Istancias intermedias?* (Salamanca: Sígueme, 1989), 87–117; François Guillemette, *Théologie des Conférences épiscopales: Une herméneutique de Vatican II* (Montreal: Médiaspaul, 1994), 41–54; Massimo Faggioli, *Il vescovo e il concilio: Modello episcopale e aggiornmento al Vaticano II* (Bologna: Il Mulino, 2005).

conference of bishops") in September 1961. It reflected a pessimistic view of the relations between the Catholic Church and the modern era. In its footnotes and its general spirit, it echoed the 1864 letter of Pius IX to the Bavarian bishops, *Maximae quidem*, which gave papal approval to the Bavarian episcopal conference. It set forth rules for episcopal conferences, which were born *praeter leges canonicas*, in absence of a law, although they had only pastoral functions and could not hinder the celebrations of *Concilia plenaria et provincialia*. Plenary and provincial councils, Part I of the schema, stated that the conferences had to be constituted in every nation, with pastoral functions; if it were not possible to assemble all the bishops due to their number or because of different rites, it would suffice to hold assemblies with some bishops from each province and region together with the metropolitan bishops or with the presidents of the regional episcopal conferences. The conferences had to be ruled by statutes *a Sancta Sede probatis*, approved by the Holy See, which would provide for a permanent council, episcopal commissions, and a general secretary. The force of decisions adopted by the plenary assembly of the conferences could be only a moral obligation, but every bishop who wanted to provide in a different way for his own diocese had to inform the president of the episcopal conference.[5]

Presented on February 20, 1962, at the fourth session of the preparatory central commission, the schema, in the brief version presented by Polish curial bishop Józef Gawlina, was discussed at four meetings. The debate at the central commission focused on the force of the conferences' decision to compel the bishops. It was led by Cardinal Josef Frings of Cologne, representing the traditions of the German episcopal conference, whose president he was from 1945, and by Cardinal Ernesto Ruffini of Palermo. Both proposed

---

5. See *Acta et documenta Concilio Oecumenico Vaticano II apparando*, Series I *Antepraeparatoria*, vol. II no. 3-1, pp. 282–85.

a light model of the national episcopal conference. After that, the subcommission for the emendations accepted the direction espoused by the central commission. The juridical force of the conference's decision for the individual bishop was no longer present (excepting some possible cases in which it was requested by the Holy See), but the obligation for the individual bishop to inform the president about his dissent and his consequent decisions for the diocese was mentioned. The text stated that the agenda had to be sent in advance to the Holy See and the papal nuncio, who were also to receive the proceedings and final decisions.

1.2. The Schemata of 1962–1963 and the Debate in Aula

The first conciliar period showed the importance and the roots of the issue of episcopal conferences, starting from the elections to the conciliar commissions; that was one of the elements that strengthened the importance of the schema about episcopal conferences in the schema *De episcopis*. In October 1962, the schema about episcopal conferences became chapter III of the new schema *De episcopis ac de dioeceseon regimine* (On the bishops and government of dioceses, schema II), which had the rules of the previous schema but nothing about the juridical force of the conferences' decisions or about conference membership. However, it had become obvious that titular bishops, too, should be members.[6]

The 1963 schema (schema III) was a revision that followed the theology of the schema *De ecclesia* and the ideas presented during the debate about the schema *De liturgia*. In November 1963, during the plenary debate in aula about this schema—only a few days after the great ecclesiological debate about *De ecclesia* and collegiality—the

6. See *Acta et Documenta*, vol. II/4-2, pp. 526–36.

third chapter, on the conferences, was discussed. The text envisaged one episcopal conference in every state, as a permanent body, different from plenary and provincial councils (n. 18, 1), its statutes to be approved by the Holy See. It mentioned international episcopal conferences (n. 18, 3) and specified that conference membership should include every ordinary bishop (except for the general vicars) and the coadjutor bishops (n. 19, 1). Rules for the membership of other titular bishops and the nature of their vote were left to the statutes of the individual conferences (n. 19, 2), as were the regulations for the vote of those absent (n. 19, 3). Provision was made for the creation of bodies within the conferences, with criteria for the juridical force of the decisions in each of the following situations (n. 24):

1. In the case of subjects set by the common law or by a mandate from the Holy See;
2. To release statements of great importance in the name of the conference;
3. For subjects to be handled with the civil government for the whole nation;
4. For important subjects that needed to be handled in a uniform way by the bishops.

Juridically binding decisions would need a two-thirds majority of the votes followed by the *recognitio*, the review by the Holy See. Provision was made for appeal to the Holy See against conference decisions (n. 24, 2).

Among the differences from the text of the previous year are a parenthesis stating that coadjutor bishops are *de jure* members of the conference (n. 19, 1), a discussion of regional or ritual conferences for large national episcopates, elimination of the obligation to send the agenda of the meetings to the nuncio, and strengthening of the sentence about the juridical force of decisions (nn. 22-25), now specifying four cases of juridical force for all the bishops.

Episcopal conferences were discussed in aula November 12–13, 1963. One of the most visible members of the conciliar minority, Italian bishop Luigi Carli, stated that episcopal conferences had no foundation in episcopal collegiality *de iure divino*, by divine law (he made reference to Pius VI's bull *Auctorem fidei* against Jansenism), and he called the five votes of October 1963 an *illegitima provocatio*, an illegitimate provocation. He added that collegiality, according to the church fathers, is always horizontal and not vertical. After this "minimalist" relation, supported by Cardinal Giuseppe Siri, the most important interventions came from the German bishops, partly following the light conference model of Cardinal Frings and partly following the request by Cardinal Döpfner that the schema should show the link between episcopal conferences and collegiality. French interventions (Guerry, Garrone, Pailloux, Marty) also stressed collegiality, and Cardinals Wyszynski and Alfrink spoke in favor of episcopal conferences, but with different patterns.

The most complicated issue concerned the "constitutional" pattern for episcopal conferences. On membership, views ranged from full reception of collegiality (with every bishop having the right to membership) to government responsibility criteria (only diocesan bishops being entitled to membership: one diocese, one vote). On the right to vote, positions were divided between deliberative votes for every bishop, for the residential bishops only, and for coadjutors with right of succession as well. On the force of the decisions, the range extended from juridical force for every individual bishop (the majority position among the fathers) to no force, even moral, for the conferences' decisions. There was a similar variety of positions on the Roman *recognitio*, review of the conferences' decisions. There was little time left for treating international conferences and the creation of conferences in the Eastern Catholic churches.

1.3. The 1964 Turning Point and the Final Text of the Decree *Christus Dominus*

In schema IV, approved by the commission *de episcopis* in March–April 1964, the title of the chapter about episcopal conferences was changed to *De Episcopis in commune plurium Ecclesiarum bonum cooperantibus* (On bishops cooperating for the good of a group of Churches). This reflected the experience acquired by the bishops worldwide in the twentieth century. The text stressed the necessity of local councils and synods (n. 34); determined that auxiliary and titular bishops could be conference members, but only if they were charged with national tasks (n. 36, 2); left the question of their voting right to the individual statutes, which now had to be "recognized"—and no longer "approved"—by the Holy See (n. 36, 3); and reduced the cases in which conference decisions had juridical force from four to one, by fusing the "casuistry" of the 1963 text (issues entrusted to the conferences by the common law or by Holy See mandate) and the requirement of a two-thirds majority (but with a higher quorum: a two-thirds majority of all bishops with right of vote, not just of those present).[7]

The second conciliar intersession in the spring of 1964 was the decisive turning point for the schema *De episcopis* as regards the conferences and in particular their link with collegiality and the schema *De ecclesia*. A joint action by the relator Bishop Carli and the general secretary of the council, Monsignor Pericle Felici, who let it be understood that he spoke on behalf of the coordination

7. See *Codex Iuris Canonici* (1917), can. 291 § 1.

commission, led to the elimination of collegiality from the schema *De episcopis.*

The debate in aula in September 1964 did not pay much attention to episcopal conferences, already covered in the 1963 debate. The schema *De pastorali episcoporum munere in Ecclesia* was voted between November 4 and 6, 1964: unlike the first two chapters, the third received the approval of more than two-thirds of the fathers, but it had to be revised according to the *modi,* the requests of amendments. The revised text was postponed to the fourth period and was sent to the fathers on September 16, 1965. During the third intersession, the commission, guided by the prudence especially of Bishop Pierre Veuillot and Belgian canon law expert Willem Onclin, rejected all the *modi* aimed at substantial alteration in the text.

In the final text of *Christus Dominus,* episcopal conferences are simply placed alongside hope for a new life for local synods and councils, the relations between the two kinds of assembly remaining unclarified (n. 36). Each conference had to draw up its own statutes, which needed to be "recognized" by the Holy See. The conferences would have a permanent council, a general secretary, and episcopal commissions. Members would include every ordinary bishop from each rite (except for the vicars), coadjutors, auxiliaries, and other bishops exercising a task committed by the Holy See or by the conference itself. Other titular bishops (retired bishops) and papal diplomats would not be members. The right to vote was confined to ordinary and coadjutor bishops; auxiliaries and other bishops could have a deliberative or consultative vote according to the individual conference's statutes. As to the juridical force of a conference's decisions, the decree *Christus Dominus* gave juridical force to some kinds of decision, much restricted in comparison with the first proposals at the beginning and during the council. Gone is any mention of appeal to the Holy See from bishops dissenting from their own conference's decisions. No juridical force is ascribed to decisions about nonbinding recommendations or ones that fail to win the support of a two-thirds majority. Juridical force is attributed to the decisions adopted with that majority (of all members entitled to vote, not only of those present) and in the cases provided by the common law or upon mandate of the Holy See or upon the conference's demand. In every case, the conference's decisions have to be recognized by the Holy See.

Following the votes of the majority of the fathers, the legislative power of the conferences was confirmed. It would be impossible to erase it after the promulgation of the liturgical constitution and of the *motu proprio Sacram Liturgiam* (January 25, 1964).[8] The final text also dropped all reference to the moral obligation of decisions not juridically binding, and to the obligation for the dissenting bishop to inform the conference's president. The council, during its development, met the desire of many bishops to limit the power of episcopal conferences through raising the quorum and limiting the spheres of intervention. In the end, it showed more interest in the tutelage of diocesan autonomy than in the necessity of uniformity among bishops from the same country. *Christus Dominus* remains very ambiguous and vague about the legislative powers of episcopal conferences, limiting their decisions to a minimum and rejecting the proposal to ascribe to conferences and their decisions some measure of collegiality. *Christus Dominus* offered a framework law for conferences but left their future to their statutes and to the reform of the *Codex Iuris Canonici* that was then beginning.

---

8. About the relationship between liturgical reform and national bishops conferences, see Massimo Faggioli, *True Reform: Liturgy and Ecclesiology in* Sacrosanctum Concilium (Collegeville, MN: Liturgical, 2012).

2. Episcopal Conferences during the 1969 Synod and in the 1970s

In the first postconciliar period (1966–1976), a positive attitude from Rome toward the conferences prevailed. This prompted Heribert Schmitz to remark in 1977 that "one can register in post–conciliar legislation a certain tendency to build up the episcopal conference to a full hierarchical mediatory instance."[9] The trend in this phase was to give episcopal conferences not only individual powers for some subjects, but a general competence for subjects not to be decided by individual bishops. The *motu proprio Sacram Liturgiam* (January 25, 1964) had given the conferences important powers of decision in connection with the liturgical reform. The *motu proprio Apostolica Sollicitudo* (September 15, 1965) constituting the Synod of Bishops assigned a decisive role to the conferences, which had to send their own representatives to the synod.

The *motu proprio Ecclesiae Sanctae* (August 6, 1966) on the application of *Christus Dominus* provided that in every nation, an episcopal conference had to be constituted—thus enforcing what *Christus Dominus* had only recommended—and that the statutes of the conferences had to be compiled and then sent to Rome for the *recognition,* review. The *Archetypon Statuti,* the model of a statute for the bishops conferences, by the Consistorial Congregations, offered as a model for the compiling of the statutes, accepted the rules of *Christus Dominus* n. 38 on the bodies of the conferences (permanent council, episcopal commissions, general secretariat) and strengthened the role of the conference president, but did not impose anything about the content of the statutes.[10] In 1969, the *motu proprio Sollicitudo*

---

9. See Heribert Schmitz, "Tendenzen nachkonziliarer Gesetzgebung: Sichtung und Wertung," *Archiv für katholisches Kirchenrecht* 146 (1977): 381–419, quotation at 390.
10. See the appendix to Marcello Costalunga, "De Episcoporum Conferentiis," *Periodica* 57, no. 2 (1968): 217–80.

omnium Ecclesiarum stated that the agenda of the conferences' meetings had to be sent to the papal nuncio, and it affirmed the right of nuncios to be present at the conference meetings whenever the Holy See requested it. On December 1, 1970, the Apostolic Signature recognized to the conferences the power to make administrative decrees. At this time, continental assemblies were held in Medellín for Latin America (1968), in Kampala for Africa (1969), and in Manila for Asia (1970).

In the first Extraordinary Synod of Bishops, 1969, called in order to study the theological foundations of episcopal conferences and to give solutions in order to support cooperation between Rome and the conferences, the preparatory schema had three parts. The doctrinal introduction reinforced relations between the conferences and the Holy See and relations among episcopal conferences, and it defined the conferences as a "real" but "partial" fulfillment of episcopal collegiality. But in his presentation of part II of the schema, Cardinal François Marty of Paris proposed a major role for episcopal conferences: more power, subsidiarity, participation in doctrinal texts of highest authority, cooperation with the Curia through commissions and meetings, and more power in the choosing of new bishops. The Synod's linguistic groups confirmed what Marty stated: their debate insisted on the relations between episcopal conferences and *collegial* action by the whole episcopal college, and on the necessity to see the conferences as "intermediate bodies" between the pope and the individual bishops. Compared with the preambles, the 1969 Synod had a positive impact on the implementation of the powers of episcopal conferences.[11] The Synod's political constitution exhibited methods (periodicity) and structures (general secretariat, linguistic groups) that could build up collegiality. The Synod fathers

---

11. About this, see Angel Antón, *Primado y colegialidad: Sus relaciones a la luz del primer Sínodo extraordinario* (Madrid: Biblioteca de Autores Cristianos, 1970).

requested a reinforcement of the cooperation between the Holy See and episcopal conferences. There was no new element regarding the theology of episcopal conferences, but a step was taken toward seeing the episcopal conferences as intermediate bodies, something necessary and worth studying in depth, as Paul VI stated in the closing speech.

In the *Directory for the Pastoral Ministry of Bishops*, issued by the Congregation for Bishops (February 22, 1973), part IV, "De Episcopo in Conferentia Episcopali quoad plurium Ecclesiarum particularium necessitates" (On the bishop's role when a bishops conference deals with an issue that concerns many different dioceses) deals with the conferences (nn. 210–13), giving particular force to a conference's decisions:

a) The bishops shall welcome with loyal respect, execute and have executed in his diocese, as having the force of law of the supreme authority of the Church, the decisions legitimately taken by the conferences and recognized by the Apostolic See, even if he should happen to have disapproved of them at first or then felt some discomfort with them.

b) The other decisions and norms of the conferences, not having the force of juridical obligation, the bishop will ordinarily make his own in view of unity with his confreres, unless there are grave considerations against this, of which he is judge before the Lord. These decisions and norms will be promulgated by him in the diocese in his own name and with his own authority, for in these cases the conference cannot limit the power that every bishop maintains personally in the name of Christ. (n. 212)

3. Episcopal Conferences in the 1983
Code of Canon Law

In the same period, in the seventies, the trends in favor of the conferences were counterbalanced by the work on the new Code of Canon Law (*Codex Iuris Canonici*). The handling of the conferences in canons 447–59 of the new code is in a very different style from the texts of the previous period.

In the first (1972–1977) and in the second phase (1977–1980) of composing the new code, the schemata about episcopal conferences underwent many modifications intended to scale down the conferences' powers. The schemata sent to the consultative bodies from 1972 to 1977 attributed to episcopal conferences many competences that disappear in the 1980 schema, in which the idea of an episcopal conference with wide powers is abandoned. This change, affecting the very nature of the conferences, again reflects a concern to protect the autonomy of the individual local churches. Based on observations from the world episcopate, the 1980 schema transfers to the diocesan bishops, not to the Holy See, many of the matters no longer ascribed to episcopal conferences.

The 1977–1980 turning point was important also for other chapters of the schema. The 1977 schema was very close to *Christus Dominus*. A weakening of the text occurred in the chapter stating that bishops exert in the conferences *munera quaedam pastoralia*, some pastoral offices (canon 447), whereas in *Christus Dominus*, they exert *munus suum pastorale*, their own pastoral office. The commission for the new Code of Canon Law canceled the concept of ecclesiastical region (present in *Christus Dominus*) in order to "avoid incorrect or equivocal notions about the nature and purpose of this new juridical body." Instead the conferences, which are not legislative bodies such as the local councils, were defined as instruments of communication and coordination between bishops.[12]

The final text of the 1983 code marked a step forward compared with the 1917 code, but it was a step backward if compared with *Christus Dominus* and the first post–Vatican II laws and praxis. In canon 449.2, the new code recognizes the juridical personality of episcopal conferences, adding something new to what was stated in the *motu proprio Ecclesiae sanctae* (1966), but canon 448.1 states that episcopal conferences have to be national conferences, in accord with the preference expressed by *Christus Dominus*. Moreover the new code canceled the multi-rituality of the conferences, although it remained open to different legislation by individual conferences on this subject.

On membership, canon 450 follows *Christus Dominus* but modifies it by creating three classes of member: members *de jure* (diocesan bishops, coadjutors, auxiliaries, and other titular bishops serving the whole Church in the territory of the conference or at papal behest); persons who can be invited (ordinaries of another rite, an innovation in regard to *Christus Dominus* 36); members not *de jure* (other titular bishops or emeritus bishops, and the representatives of the pope). The Code of Canon Law takes up the principle that for one to be a member of the conference, episcopal character does not suffice, but it is also necessary to share a pastoral responsibility.[13]

Though the Code recognizes the conferences as permanent instruments and juridical personalities, it is very careful to ensure that the conference does not inhibit the powers of individual bishops. The conferences are seen not as organs with legislative power, capable of

12. See Peter Leisching, "Die Bischofskonferenz in der kirchlichen Kodifikation von 1983," in *Die Bischofskonferenz: Theologischer und juridischer Status*, ed. Heribert Müller and Hermann Josef Pottmeyer (Düsseldorf: Patmos, 1989), 158–77.
13. See Winfried Aymans, "Wesenverständnis und Zuständigkeiten der Bischofskonferenz im Codex Iuris Canonici von 1983," *Archiv für katholisches Kirchenrecht* 152 (1983): 46–61.

issuing general decrees with legal effect, but as organs that have *di norma*, normally, only an executive character. On the voting quorum, canon 455 simply follows *Christus Dominus* but specifies that the decision should be made with a two-thirds majority of those entitled to a deliberative vote (whether present at the assembly or not), respecting the conciliar decree but contradicting the code's general principle on elections. Moreover, canon 455 gives more weight than *Christus Dominus* to the *recognition*, the review. As regards the deciding power of conferences, canon 455.4 prescribes that (except in cases of common law or a mandate of the Holy See) unless all members are unanimous, a mandate must be sought from the Holy See, or the individual bishops must be allowed to decide autonomously.

The process of codification leading to the 1983 code brought the first step of the reversal that progressively reduced the legislative competence of the conferences. The new code was a first reaction to the postconciliar trend of assigning ever more competences to episcopal conferences.

4. From the 1985 Synod to the *Motu Proprio Apostolos Suos* (1998)

These steps backward were consolidated in the next fifteen years, between 1985 and 2000. The Extraordinary Synod of Bishops of 1985 was convoked by John Paul II for a reflection on Vatican II after twenty years.[14] A few weeks before its opening, there appeared a conclusive report of the International Theological Commission, produced by the subcommission *De ecclesia* and the October 1985 session of the full commission. In chapter 5, "Particular Churches and

---

14. See Giorgio Feliciani, "Le conferenze episcopali nel magistero di Giovanni Paolo II," *Aggiornamenti sociali* 38 (1987): 141–54.

Universal Church," the text recalls that "the collegial sense that the Council has revived in bishops has subsequently been given concrete embodiment in the important functions conferred on episcopal conferences" and that "the pastoral usefulness, indeed necessity, of episcopal conferences, as well as their grouping on a continental scale, is beyond doubt." But immediately after this comes the affirmation that *Lumen Gentium* 22 and *Christus Dominus* 4–6 "do not permit the qualification of collegial to episcopal conferences or their continental groupings," since collegiality is restricted to ecumenical councils, to the united action of bishops in the various parts of the world, and also in a certain sense to the synod of bishops. The words *college, collegial,* and *collegiality* are used of episcopal conferences only in an analogous and theologically improper sense. These restrictions reflect the guidance of Cardinal Ratzinger, who in the same year expressed his changed view on episcopal conferences in a book-length interview with Vittorio Messori,[15] insisting that episcopal conferences lack a theological basis, are not part of the unalterable structure as willed by Christ, and have only a practical function.[16]

One of the new questions for the synod concerned collegiality and its applications. The relator, Cardinal Godfried Danneels of Mechelen-Brussels, cited three problems that the synod should confront: the relations between universal Church and particular churches, the promotion of collegiality, and the theological status of episcopal conferences. In the synodal debate, episcopal conferences were among the chief topics. Danneels's relation *post disceptationem,* after the first few days of debate, affirmed that there was no doubt about their usefulness and pastoral necessity, but this was based on

15. Josef Ratzinger with Vittorio Messori, *The Ratzinger Report* (1985, translated in several languages, in English: San Francisco: Ignatius Press, 1985).
16. See Hermann Josef Pottmeyer, "Der theologische Status der Bischofskonferenz: Positionen, Klärungen und Prinzipien," in *Die Bischofskonferenz: Theologischer und juridischer Status,* ed. Heribert Müller and Hermann Josef Pottmeyer (Düsseldorf: Patmos, 1989), 44–87.

ecclesiastical law. The results of the discussion in the language groups, all of which addressed episcopal conferences, made clear that the bishops unanimously saw the theme of episcopal conferences as having a greater importance than Danneels's relation had allowed, being "a partial but real form" of the collegial activity of bishops.[17]

The Synod's final report affirmed that there was "a collegial affect that goes beyond effective collegiality understood only juridically," and it defined the conferences as concrete applications in ecclesiastical law of the *affectus collegialis*, the collegial affect or sentiment. The final relation placed the conferences only in terms of collaboration among bishops, avoided qualifying them as "collegial," and so eliminated every link between collegiality and institutions of ecclesiastical law as imperfect realizations of collegiality, seen as deriving from collegiality.

The relation stressed that conferences should be mindful of the good of the Church and the inalienable responsibility of the individual bishop in his relationship with the universal Church and with his particular church. With all this, despite the final wish, also taken up by John Paul II, to explore more amply and deeply the theological status of conferences and especially their teaching authority, the 1985 Synod, paradoxically, was widely judged to be more reserved about episcopal conferences than the 1969 Synod, even if less restrictive than the text of the International Theological Commission in its interpretation of the conciliar texts on episcopal conferences.

---

17. See Giovanni Caprile, *Il Sinodo dei Vescovi: Seconda assemblea generale straordinaria (24 novembre–8 dicembre 1985)* (Roma: La Civiltà Cattolica, 1986), 477–98 and 533–70.

5. The *Instrumentum Laboris* of the Congregation for Bishops (1987–1988)

Some months after the 1985 Synod, in his address of June 28, 1986, to the Curia, John Paul II referred to the letter he had sent to the Congregation of Bishops, asking them to examine the question of the theological status of episcopal conferences, with prior consultation of the local churches. In the course of 1987, the Congregation for Bishops (with the collaboration of the Congregations for the Doctrine of the Faith, for the Oriental Churches, and for the Evangelization of Peoples, and the general secretary of the Synod of Bishops) produced an *instrumentum laboris*, the preliminary text for the preparation of the Synod which was sent to the episcopal conferences in January 1988, with a request to send corrections and emendations by December 31, 1988.

The text of the *instrumentum laboris* was in two parts, dealing respectively with the theological and the juridical status of episcopal conferences. Without intending to be definitive, but rather seeking answers to its inquiries (some of them listed at the end), the text presupposes an "ontological and historical" priority of the universal Church over the local church.[18]

The second paragraph of part I, "Theological Foundation and Actualizations of Collegiality," distinguishes three ways of realizing collegiality. One type involves the college of bishops as a whole, with its head. A second type, including episcopal conferences, reunites bishops for the exercise of their pastoral care; the latter is generated by *affectus collegialis* but is without *effectus collegialis*, whereas for the full

18. About this, see Joseph A. Komonchak, "The Roman Working Paper on Episcopal Conferences," in *Episcopal Conferences: Historical, Canonical and Theological Studies*, ed. Thomas J. Reese (Washington, DC: Georgetown University Press, 1989), 177–204. For the text of the *instrumentum laboris* in Italian, "Status teologico e giuridico delle conferenze episcopali: Instrumentum laboris della Congregazione per i vescovi," *Il Regno: Documenti* 13 (1988): 390–96; in English: "Draft Statement on Episcopal Conferences," *Origins* 17 (1987–88): 731–37.

realization of collegiality both *effectus* (effect) and *affectus* (affect) are requisite. The text speaks of coresponsibility for the conferences but denies that the concept of collegiality properly applies to them: "Real collegiality urges the bishops to express their coresponsibility for the ruling of the universal church via certain organs such as the Synod of Bishops, of which is recognized true, but partial, collegiality."[19]

In part IV, "Deductions to be Applied to the Episcopal Conferences," after distinguishing between membership of episcopal conferences (according to pastoral and governance criteria) and of particular councils (according to a sacramental criterion), the text affirms that "episcopal conferences were not instituted for the pastoral government of a nation nor to substitute the diocesan bishops as a kind of superior and parallel government, but to help them in the fulfillment of some common tasks."[20] The decision mechanisms of conferences are also viewed with reservations: "It should be borne in mind that in the Church and in episcopal assemblies in particular, the criterion of action is not simply one of juridical majority, which is sometimes insufficient, but rather that of *consensus* that is in its turn the fruit of communion. What happened at the Second Vatican Council is, on this point, a paradigm."[21]

The text goes on to signal some dangers facing episcopal conferences: they can become bureaucratic structures that constrict the psychological freedom of bishops and that demand undue autonomy in regard to the Holy See. It denies to episcopal conferences "a generalized competence in legislative material that would be the equivalent of attributing them in principle the same dignity and authoritativeness as particular councils and the oriental synods and could in addition lead to an excessive limitation of the

19. "Draft Statement on Episcopal Conferences," 733.
20. Ibid., 734.
21. Ibid.

authority of individual diocesan bishops."[22] Likewise, the text excludes that the conferences would have a *munus magisterii*, teaching office of their own: the teachings of the episcopal conferences "are proposed, by their own nature, as operative, pastoral and social means, and not directly a doctrinal means."[23] It gives a list of prescriptions, limits, and requirements for documents of doctrinal character.

The responses from the world episcopate to this *instrumentum laboris*, preliminary text, were very critical and negative. Shortly after, Komonchak judged the text "a very reductionistic view of the nature and role of the episcopal conferences. . . . At the end of the document, one is left wondering how it is that the present pope [John Paul II] could have ever called them 'very necessary, useful, and sometimes absolutely indispensable.' The great question remains how could such a document ever have been considered an adequate response to the 1985 Synod's call for a fuller and deeper study of the episcopal conferences."[24] The 1988 *instrumentum laboris* was set aside, and the preparation of a completely new one was begun.

6. The *Motu Proprio Apostolos Suos*

The *motu proprio Apostolos Suos* (May 31, 1998) may be seen as responding, at thirteen years' distance, to the 1985 Synod (for which, incidentally, no postsynodal apostolic exhortation had been envisaged). The failure of the *instrumentum laboris* of the Congregation for Bishops in 1987–1988 did not weaken John Paul II's desire to reply to the questions raised at the conclusion of the 1985 Synod. The text of *Apostolos Suos* was prepared by an international

22. Ibid., 735.
23. Ibid.
24. Komonchak, "The Roman Working Paper on Episcopal Conferences," 201.

commission of bishops and experts in theology and canon law in two sessions in 1990, and then examined between 1991 and 1996 by a group of dicasteries of the Roman Curia guided by the Congregation for Bishops. In 1996, John Paul II handed the text to Congregation for the Doctrine of the Faith for a new and definitive examination.

The intent of the document is to lay down some firm points on the role of episcopal conferences and on the relation between bishop and diocesan church and between bishop, episcopal college, and pope. At the press conference presenting the document, Cardinal Ratzinger repeatedly expressed a negative view of definitions of episcopal conferences as intermediate instances. The theological part, even in the eyes of the most critical theologians, was much improved from the text of 1998, but it brought no marked novelty as regards the theological status of episcopal conferences.

More significant for our concern is what is found in paragraph 22 and the final four "complementary norms," which refer to canon 753, derived from the schemata of the Fundamental Law of the Church (*Lex Ecclesiae Fundamentalis*) and inserted in the code at the last moment. Paragraph 22 prescribes that doctrinal statements of episcopal conferences must be approved unanimously: "If this unanimity is lacking, a majority alone of the Bishops of a Conference cannot issue a declaration as authentic teaching of the Conference to which all the faithful of the territory would have to adhere, unless it obtains the *recognitio* of the Apostolic See, which will not give it if the majority requesting it is not substantial. . . . The *recognitio* of the Holy See serves furthermore to guarantee that, in dealing with new questions posed by the accelerated social and cultural changes characteristic of present times, the doctrinal response will favour communion and not harm it, and will rather prepare an eventual intervention of the universal magisterium."[25]

Even though the *motu proprio* aims to formulate juridical norms and expressly forgoes treatment of the relation between universal church and local church and the theological status of episcopal conferences, it is clear that it proceeds from some quite precise ecclesiological positions, especially the assumption that episcopal conferences are juridical entities created by the Holy See, which are to be sharply differentiated from provincial synods and councils and from the synodal government of the Eastern churches.[26]

Apostolos Suos's handling of the conciliar decree *Christus Dominus* is worthy of notice. It draws several times (nn. 4 and 15) on *Christus Dominus* 37 on the usefulness and potential of episcopal conferences, but it does not recall the affirmation in *Christus Dominus* 38 that bishops exercise *munus suum pastorale*, their own pastoral ministry in the conferences. Also, though the rule of the *recognition*, the review is already found in *Christus Dominus* and holds also for particular councils (canon 446), it is nonetheless striking that in the first of the complementary norms, the *recognitio* is expressly extended from decisions that have binding force of law (*decisiones quae vim habeant iuridice obligandi*) (*Christus Dominus* n. 38) to doctrinal statements: "In order that the doctrinal declarations of the Conference of Bishops . . . may constitute authentic magisterium and be published in the name of the Conference itself, they must be unanimously approved by the Bishops who are members, or receive the *recognitio* of the Apostolic See if approved in plenary assembly by at least two thirds of the Bishops belonging to the Conference and having a deliberative vote." (*Christus Dominus* n. 38). The effect of this extension is that

25. John Paul II, apostolic letter *Apostolos Suos*, May 21, 1998, n. 22, http://www.vatican.va/holy_father/john_paul_ii/motu_proprio/documents/hf_jp-ii_motu-proprio_22071998_apostolos-suos_en.html.

26. See Ladislas Orsy, "Reflections on the Teaching Authority of the Episcopal Conferences," in Reese, *Episcopal Conferences*, 233–52.

the *recognitio* becomes the source of authority whereby the doctrinal statements of the conference become binding also for bishops who voted against them.

The numerical criterion of unanimity means in practice that the totality of doctrinal statements of episcopal conferences (some with more than three hundred members) must be subjected to the judgment of the Holy See, assigned to the Congregation for Bishops or the Congregation for the Evangelization of Peoples depending on the region, after having consulted the Congregation for the Doctrine of the Faith and the Pontifical Council for the interpretation of legislative texts. The consequences for the workload of the curial congregations can easily be appreciated.

If *Apostolos Suos* presents the conferences as organs of the authentic magisterium, their voice is nonetheless subject to the approval of the Holy See, which reduces the participation of the conferences in the formation of the magisterium and allows the Holy See to ensure uniformity in magisterial pronouncements. In recognizing that the conferences have the capacity to produce doctrinal documents, *Apostolos Suos* was not innovating but merely giving new regulations, which in fact by insisting on numerical unanimity and the Roman *recognitio*, impede such doctrinal statements. In fact, the aim of *Apostolos Suos* was not to defend the authority or teaching of the individual dioceses of the episcopal conference (which could have been done by limiting the right to vote to diocesan bishops alone), but rather to impede any members of the conference from taking dissonant doctrinal positions.

Nor does the text confer such a capacity for doctrinal statements on plenary councils (as the *instrumentum laboris*, n. 14, had done). The conferences remain the only assemblies of bishops (apart from fully collegial ones) capable of doctrinal statements, but according to norms such as numerical unanimity that are more restrictive than those that had applied to plenary councils.

Though *Apostolos Suos* does not directly address the theological and juridical status of episcopal conferences, it is the indirect Roman response to the final report of the 1985 Extraordinary Synod of Bishops, which recommended that the question of the magisterial authority of the conferences be deepened and developed. *Apostolos Suos* appeared only a few days after the *motu proprio Ad Tuendam Fidem* of May 18, 1998, and the link between the two is close, especially in the sense of the growing centralization of the magisterial authority in the Vatican and its juridical codification in the Code of Canon Law.[27]

The directory of the curial Congregation for Bishops for the pastoral ministry of the bishops, *Apostolorum Successores* (February 22, 2004), came after the promulgation of the postsynodal exhortation *Pastores Gregis* (October 16, 2003). *Apostolorum Successores* was a revision of the directory of 1973 in light of the more recent directives published under John Paul II and Cardinal Ratzinger in the 1990s. It applied a particular stream of post–Vatican II ecclesiology—the "*communio* ecclesiology"—that at that time was dominating, especially under the influence of the document of the Roman Congregation for the Doctrine of the Faith *Communionis Notio* (1992), the doctrinal policy of the Vatican.

---

27. John Paul II, *motu proprio Ad Tuendam Fidem* (May 18, 1998), by which certain norms are inserted into the Code of Canon Law and into the Code of Canons of the Eastern Churches, http://www.vatican.va/holy_father/john_paul_ii/motu_proprio/documents/hf_jp-ii_motu-proprio_30061998_ad-tuendam-fidem_en.html.

7. Conclusion

During the first decade after Vatican II, episcopal conferences built on the embryonic norms present in *Christus Dominus* and their work were assisted and corroborated by Rome, following an option in regard to *Christus Dominus* 36 that accorded institutional preference to episcopal conferences over plenary or national councils, which in this decade, whether projected or held, met not a few obstacles from Rome. But the advance in the role, authority, and function of the national episcopal conferences was checked by the 1983 Code; the 1985 Synod; the positions taken by the International Theological Commission; a still centripetal ecclesial praxis; and the papal legislative acts of 1998. The result was a clear crisis of synodal and conciliar activity at provincial, regional, and plenary levels—in parallel to the evident crisis of the Synod of Bishops celebrated in Rome.

It was not to shore up the authority of the individual diocesan bishops that the *motu proprio Apostolos Suos* (1998) and *Ad Tuendam Fidem* (1998) thus blocked the evolution of the doctrinal and pastoral function of episcopal conferences, for the diocesan bishops were also more tightly controlled by the Roman instances.[28] From a global systematic point of view, the effort to limit the role of the conferences, especially in areas where Catholicism was developing strongly, connects with a shift in the center of gravity of the Latin Catholic Church in the 1990s from the Euro-Atlantic churches (more

---

28. See the letter of Cardinal Lucas Moreira Neves, prefect of the Congregation for the Bishops, (dated May 13, 1999), "Ai presidenti delle Conferenze episcopali circa le revisione dei loro Statuti," in *Acta Apostolicae Sedis* 91 (1999): 996–99 (also on the Vatican website at http://www.vatican.va/roman_curia/congregations/cbishops/documents/ rc_con_cbishops_doc_19990619_conferenze-episcopali_sp.html). In 1997, the Congregation for the Bishops had already sent a letter with "Instructions on the Diocesan Synods," http://www.vatican.va/roman_curia/congregations/cbishops/documents/ rc_con_cbishops_doc_20041118_diocesan-synods-1997_en.html.

concerned with synodality and collegiality) to the young churches of Africa and Asia. This shift was not regulated through the national or continental conferences but through the continental synods held in Rome.

But national conferences have shown themselves the most competent organs for making decisions and assuming direct responsibility in regard to the faithful and the national community (as seen in the German handling of Catholic counseling of pregnant women or the U.S. handling of clerical child abuse). The silencing of episcopal conferences and the limitation of their capacity to be interpreters, including doctrinally, of the sense of faith of Christians, have been damaging here as well.

This blocking is an attempt to limit the full reception and enactment of Vatican II, and this is clear also to the successor of Benedict XVI.[29] In his apostolic exhortation *Evangelii Gaudium* (really an encyclical, November 24, 2013), Pope Francis has made important statements about the need for a new role for the bishops' conferences:[30] "The Second Vatican Council stated that, like the ancient patriarchal Churches, episcopal conferences are in a position 'to contribute in many and fruitful ways to the concrete realization of the collegial spirit.' Yet this desire has not been fully realized, since a juridical status of episcopal conferences which would see them as subjects of specific attributions, including genuine doctrinal authority, has not yet been sufficiently elaborated. Excessive

---

29. About the relationship between collegiality under John Paul II and Benedict XVI and Francis's exhortation *Evangelii Gaudium*, see Hervé Legrand, "Primato e collegialità per la comunione delle chiese," *Il Regno: Attualità* 12 (2014): 419–28; and Hervé Legrand, "Enjeux ecclésiologiques des réformes institutionelles envisages par le pape François," in *Le grand tournant: L'an I de la revolution du pape François*, ed. Michel Dubost (Paris: Cerf, 2014), 185–210.

30. It is also worth noting that on April 1, 2014, in a message to Cardinal Lorenzo Baldisseri, secretary general of the Synod of Bishops, Pope Francis spoke of the synod as an institution in terms of "affective and effective collegiality," adding a significant *effective* to the more traditional *affective*. See *Bollettino: Sala stampa della Santa Sede*, April 8, 2014, http://press.vatican.va/content/salastampa/en/bollettino/pubblico/2014/04/08/0251/00559.html.

centralization, rather than proving helpful, complicates the Church's life and her missionary outreach" (*Evangelii Gaudium*, 32).

11

Vatican II and the Agenda for Collegiality and Synodality in the Twenty-First Century

Christus Dominus was the decree of Vatican II that was supposed to translate conciliar ecclesiological developments into new government institutions at the episcopal level and in a communional-synodal direction.[1] It was ratified by the conciliar fathers on October 28, 1965, with 2,139 *placet* (yes), 2 *non placet* (no), and 1 invalid vote. Paul VI approved the decree immediately after the vote. The decree, which originated from the integration of the schema *De Cura Animarum* (On the pastoral care of the souls) and the schema *De Episcoporum Munere Pastorali* (On the pastoral ministry of bishops)—which were also the result of the integration of more schemata—reflected a process entailing seven different drafts, forty-

---

1. This chapter was published originally as "Institutions of Episcopal Synodality-Collegiality after Vatican II: The Decree *Christus Dominus* and the Agenda for Synodality-Collegiality in the 21st Century," *Jurist* 64, no. 2 (2004): 224–46.

one votes, and forty-three meetings of the commission *de episcopis*, on the episcopate.[2]

Conceived at the beginning as a decree on the pastoral ministry of bishops, from 1963 the schema *De Episcopis* was envisioned as translating the conciliar teaching on the episcopacy and collegiality into juridical institutions before the reform of the 1917 Code of Canon Law (*Codex Iuris Canonici*) announced by Pope John XXIII. The link with collegiality constitutes the major turning point in the history of *Christus Dominus*: after the debate in the conciliar aula about ecclesiology and collegiality (October 1963), the schema *De Episcopis* acquired a strategic importance as much for the conciliar pro-collegiality majority as for the minority.

Indeed, paragraphs 2 and 8 are a couple of the most important passages of *Christus Dominus* for the fathers and theologians who had followed the history of the *De Episcopis* schemata from the beginning of Vatican II. They attempt to state ecclesiological positions about the episcopacy and bishops, which are hard or actually impossible to find in the constitution *Lumen Gentium*. After the description of the Roman pontiff, the second paragraph reads as follows:

> The bishops also, assigned to their position by the Holy Spirit, take the place of the Apostles as pastors of souls, and together with the supreme pontiff and under his authority are sent to carry on the never-ending work of Christ, the eternal pastor. For Christ gave to the Apostles and their successors the mandate and the power to teach all nations, to sanctify people in truth, and to sustain them spiritually. The bishops,

---

2. For the history of the decree *Christus Dominus*, see *La charge pastorale des évêques: Texte, traduction et commentaires* (Paris: Cerf, 1969); Luigi Maria Carli, "Genesi storico-dottrinale del decreto 'Christus Dominus,'" in *Ufficio pastorale dei Vescovi e Chiese Orientali cattoliche* (Turin: Elle Di Ci, 1967), 11–59; Klaus Mörsdorf, introduction and commentary on the decree *Christus Dominus*, in *Lexikon für Theologie und Kirche: Das Zweite Vatikanische Konzil; Konstitutionen, Dekrete und Erklärungen lateinisch und deutsch Kommentare* (Freiburg i.B..: Herder, 1967), 2:128–247; Massimo Faggioli, *Il vescovo e il concilio: Modello episcopale e aggiornamento al Vaticano II* (Bologna: Il Mulino, 2005).

accordingly, through the Holy Spirit who has been given to them, have been made true and authentic teachers of the faith, pontiffs and pastors.

The statements in paragraph 8 are more precise: "As successors of the Apostles, the bishops in the dioceses entrusted to them possess as of right all the ordinary power necessary for the exercise of their pastoral office. This power belongs to them as bishops and rests in their own hands, always without prejudice to the universal power which, in virtue of his office, the Roman pontiff possesses of reserving cases to himself or to some other authority."

The trend during the last years of the pontificate of John Paul II (1978–2005) and of his successor, Benedict XVI (2005–2013) was to reduce the importance of these results, one of the effects of postconciliar relationships between the bishops and the Roman Curia. The trend has been confirmed by reductionist understandings of *Christus Dominus* compared with *Lumen Gentium*, due to a failure to understand the hierarchy of the final conciliar documents in a theologically adequate fashion.[3] A fresh look at the conciliar decree could help the Church rediscover what Vatican II had to say in favor of a new balance of powers in the Catholic Church, especially between papacy and episcopacy.

With reference to the issues of collegiality-synodality and their development after Vatican II, some specific problems appear in the relationships between the following:

- The expectations and the needs of Vatican II regarding the forms of ecclesiastical government;

---

3. For the dynamic relationship between the conciliar event and the final documents issued by Vatican II, see Peter Hünermann, "Il concilio Vaticano II come evento," in *L'evento e le decisioni: Studi sulle dinamiche del concilio Vaticano II*, ed. Maria Teresa Fattori and Alberto Melloni (Bologna: Il Mulino, 1997), 63–92; and Giuseppe Alberigo, "Criteri ermeneutici per una storia del Concilio Vaticano II," in *Il Vaticano II tra attese e celebrazione*, ed. Giuseppe Alberigo (Bologna: Il Mulino, 1995), 9–26.

- The realization of these expectations in the decree of the *De Episcopis* commission and in the conciliar decree *Christus Dominus*;
- The postconciliar reception of these developments.

In particular, it is necessary to analyze here the following major topics: (1) the Synod of Bishops; (2) the relationship between diocesan bishops and the Roman Curia; (3) the relationship between the diocesan bishop and his diocese; and (4) the creation of new governmental bodies at the crossroads of synods and episcopal conferences, and (5) the role of episcopal conferences.

1. The Synod of Bishops between Paul VI's *Apostolica Sollicitudo* and *Christus Dominus* 5

One of the strongly emerging themes during Vatican II, especially during the preparatory phase and the second session, was the necessity of a reform of the dicasteries of the central government of the Roman Catholic Church.[4] The richness of the proposals on this matter coming from the conciliar fathers and national episcopates can only partially be perceived in the wording of *Christus Dominus* 5.

At first glance, this conciliar text does not suggest many points of interest, if it has been read without an understanding of its historical context. In fact, one of the most unclear and until now obscure passages in the history of Vatican II is the genesis of the institution of the Synod of Bishops by Paul VI in September 1965, and therefore of paragraph 5 of *Christus Dominus*, which depends on that pontifical

---

4. For the change in pontificate in 1963 and the relationship between Paul VI and the Roman Curia, see Giuseppe Alberigo, ed., *History of Vatican II*, English ed. Joseph A. Komonchak, vol. 3 (Maryknoll NY: Orbis, 2000). See Paul VI's address to the cardinals and personnel of the Roman Curia, September 21, 1963, in *Acta Apostolicae Sedis* 55 (1963): 793.

act, although originally the text of the commission on the episcopate was supposed to be the basis for the new synod.

From the beginning of Vatican II during the preparatory phase, but especially during the ecclesiological debate during the second session (October 1963), several conciliar fathers expressed their interest in and made proposals for the creation of a new body at the level of the central Church government. The most interesting among these proposals called for the creation of a core and permanent board of a few bishops who would be in charge of the government of the universal Church, in communion with and in cooperation with the pope and *above* the Roman Curia. These proposals were present in paragraph 5 of the schema prepared for a final vote during the fourth session (1964). Paragraph 5 of *Christus Dominus* should have supported the creation of a "Synod of Bishops," according to the votes of the fathers and the will of the council:

> Given that today the universal ministry of the pope demands major efforts in assistance and support, the Council Fathers earnestly desire that bishops from all the regions of the world help the pope as pastor of the universal Church in ways and forms to be established. The council fathers also express the wish that, if the pope desires [*si Eidem placuerit*], a group or board [*Coetum seu Consilium*] of bishops be established in which bishops from different regions of the world can participate together with the pope in the government [*sollicitudo*] of the universal Church.[5]

It is easy to perceive the difference between this text and the following, *Christus Dominus* paragraph 5, modified by the

---

5. Translation of the draft of *De episcopis*, schema *iuxta modos recognitos*, prepared for a vote during the fourth session, in *Acta Synodalia* vol. IV, no. 2: 510–605. Original quotation at 513: "Cum universale Summi Pontificis munus maiores in dies auxilii et praesidii vires exposcat, Sacrosancti Concilii Patres magnopere exoptant ut aliqui Episcopi diversarum orbis regionum, Supremo Ecclesiae Pastori validiorem praestent adiutricem operam, modis tamen et rationibus ab Ipso opportune statuendis, etiam, si Eidem placuerit, in Coetum seu Consilium quoddam convenientes, quo simul significari possit omnes Episcopos sollicitudinis universae Ecclesiae participes esse."

commission on the episcopate after the *motu proprio* of Paul VI creating the Synod of Bishops:

> Bishops chosen from different parts of the world, in accordance with methods and procedures already established or to be established by the Roman pontiff, will give more effective and helpful service to the supreme pastor of the Church by meeting in a council which shall be called the Synod of Bishops.[6] Acting on behalf of the whole catholic episcopate, it will show that all the bishops in hierarchical communion participate in the care of the whole church.[7]

According to the logic of the conciliar agenda, up to the beginning of the fourth session, the commission on the episcopate did not have the responsibility to support, a posteriori, the Synod of Bishops designed by Paul VI and by some other curial bishops close to the pope, and designed in a different way from the council's proposals for the creation of a synodal board. The timing of the pontifical intervention, in anticipation of the commission's proceedings, was perceived as less scandalous than in other cases. The effect of Paul VI's interventions on the text on ecumenism, on the final text of *Lumen Gentium* with the *Nota Explicativa Praevia*, and on the text on religious freedom during the so-called black week at the end of the third session (November 1964) also plays a significant role in one's understanding of the final text of *Christus Dominus* and the effects of its implementation.

In fact, the first reactions of the conciliar fathers and non-Catholic observers to the new synod after the publication of *Apostolica sollicitudo* (September 15, 1965) were mostly positive. Only a few members, after their initial surprise, perceived that the timing of the *motu proprio* and the synod's structure meant a substantial

---

6. Cf. Paul VI, motu proprio *Apostolica sollicitudo*, September 15, 1965, in *Acta Apostolicae Sedis* 57 (1965): 775–80.

7. *Christus Dominus* 5, in *Acta Apostolicae Sedis* 58 (1966): 675.

undercutting of Vatican II's authority and the conciliar intention to create a new body representing the bishops' will and articulating their voice to the pope.[8]

Actually the Synod of Bishops was an institutional innovation, which originated from the conciliar debate and which could be a turning point from multicentury centralizing tendencies and the Roman practice of church government. But other passages in the text on the new Synod remained undisputed by the conciliar fathers and hidden to the conciliar fathers.

As for Vatican II's other documents, the difference in judging *Christus Dominus* depends on the value that historians and theologians can attribute to the conciliar text. Is the conciliar text a limit—that is, was *Christus Dominus* to be viewed as constituting the final stage of Vatican II's reform of the episcopacy? Or on the contrary, was *Christus Dominus* to be viewed as only the incipit, the beginning of the specific reforms of the episcopacy envisioned by Vatican II?

Forty years after the end of Vatican II, it is possible to identify the real differences between the mind of the conciliar fathers about the problems of church government and the actual solution provided—i.e., the Synod of Bishops—and therefore the decree *Christus Dominus*.

---

8. See Alberigo, *History of Vatican II*, vol. 5. Gilles Routhier here reflects on the actual drafting of the *motu proprio* on the basis of the Belgian theologian Albert Prignon's diary and of Monsignor Vincenzo Carbone's account in 1995. For Routhier, the way chosen to draft the text was to entrust it to the Council for Extraordinary Affairs of the Secretariat of State, which was supervised by Monsignor Samoré. This way of approaching the issue in the schema *De episcopis* differed from the papal *modi* to a conciliar schema (as took place at the end of the third session for other conciliar schemas) and from the *Nota Explicativa Praevia* (which was undisputed by the conciliar fathers and added at the end of *Lumen Gentium*).

First of all, it is worth noting the actual difference between the idea of a "consultative assembly" conceived by the papal *motu proprio* and the idea of a *core, collegial, stable, and permanent* episcopal board involved in universal Church government which was envisioned by a large part of the council fathers. In fact during the conciliar debates, the fathers called for better coordination between the bishops and Rome through the creation of merely "consultative bodies" in terms of relations with the curial congregations, not vis-à-vis the governmental powers of the pope.[9] With respect to the pope's powers, more than once the bishops called for the creation of an *executive, collegial episcopal government body*—a *Consilium episcoporum centrale*, a central board of bishops. During the debate in the second session, similar requests were made not only by the Eastern Catholic bishops (from the *vota* during the preparation of the council and then during the entire duration of Vatican II),[10] but also by other parties. In the conciliar aula, Cardinal Alfrink (Utrecht) and Monsignor Olalia (Lìpa, Philippines) proposed the creation of an episcopal *organum centrale*, central board with the pope for the government of the whole Catholic Church. Outside the conciliar aula, such proposals were elaborated and discussed by bishops and theologians.[11] In 1969, some

9. During the debate in the aula on November 7–8, 1963, some fathers (Gouyon, McCann, Van der Bugt, De Barros Camara, and Rugambwa) sought the creation of an "apostolic council" or a "central congregation" with members elected by the national episcopal conferences. We also must keep in mind the proposal made by Cardinal Lercaro (November 8, 1963) for the creation of a special conciliar commission, which was to reflect Vatican II's desiderata on the new Roman Curia and the bishops' participation in central Church government. Lercaro's proposal never became a reality, and the commission was never created. See Giàcomo Lercaro, *Per la forza dello Spirito* (Bologna: EDB, 1984), 197–205.

10. See Roberto Morozzo della Rocca, "I 'voti' degli orientali nella preparazione del Vaticano II," in *À la veille du Concile Vatican II: Vota et réactions en Europe et dans le catholicisme oriental*, ed. Mathijs Lamberigts and Claude Soetens (Leuven: Peeters, 1992), 119–45.

11. See *Acta Synodalia* vol. II, no. 4: 479–81 and 497–99. In his memoirs, the Tridentine Council historian Hubert Jedin quotes a conference he gave on November 12, 1963, for the German *periti* about the reform of the Roman Curia in light of its history. He says he had long discussions about the subject with Bishop Bengsch of Berlin, whose ideas about the new senate appeared to him more realistic than those of Alfrink (314). Hubert Jedin, *Storia della mia vita,*

Eastern Catholic bishops (Meouchi, Hakim, and the Ukrainian Hermaniuk) proposed the creation of a "permanent synod" with the pope according to the oriental model.[12]

Second, it is clear that there is a real difference between, on the one hand, a core, collegial-synodal, stable, and permanent Church governmental body with the pope and above the Roman Curia, and on the other, an assembly made up of hundreds of bishops called every few years in order to debate some pastoral problem. Here it is not possible to analyze the synod's authority and its capacity to address synod-related problems, but the Synod of Bishops is clearly not able to bring to Rome the voice of the global episcopate and therefore to help the pope in his office.[13] It is also clear that the mind of the conciliar fathers was to diminish the monarchical principle in ordinary universal church government, not to provide for the consultation of the global episcopate about some particular pastoral problems. Moreover, in this choice by Paul VI in reference to the reforms proposed by the conciliar fathers, it is easy to track not only his attempt to soften their more radical reform intentions, but also, after the debate and the shift toward collegiality, his effort to create an institutional barrier between the pope and the episcopate through the Synod of Bishops. This institution presumably could be better controlled by the pope and the Roman Curia than an ecumenical

Italian trans. (Brescia: Morcelliana, 1984). The German Jesuit theologian Otto Semmelroth noted the emergence of new and important issues for the council in the request for a permanent synod with the pope. See *Tagebuch* of Otto Semmelroth, SJ, November 6, 1963 (Archive of Fondazione per le scienze religiose Giovanni XXIII in Bologna). See also Antonino Indelicato, *Il sinodo dei vescovi: La collegialità sospesa (1965–1985)* (Bologna: Il Mulino, 2008).

12. See Andrea Riccardi, *Governo carismatico: 25 anni di pontificato* (Milan: Mondadori, 2003), 197–98; Joseph Famerée, "La fonction du pape: Élements d'une problématique," in *Changer la papauté?*, ed. Paul Tihon (Paris: Cerf, 2000), 63–84.

13. For the development of the *Ordo*, the procedure of the Synod of Bishops from 1967, see *Ordo Synodi*, in Maurizio Bravi, *Il Sinodo dei Vescovi: Istituzione, fini e natura; Indagine teologico-giuridica* (Rome: Pontificia Università Gregoriana, 1995), 337–70; Gian Piero Milano, *Il Sinodo dei Vescovi* (Milan: Giuffré, 1985), 361–92; Patrick Granfield, *The Limits of the Papacy: Authority and Autonomy in the Church* (New York: Crossroad, 1987), 88–97.

council. Such a barrier could be used as a shield for the pope's decisional authority, in order to protect that authority both from the bishops and from the council (the just-concluded Vatican II and the future and hoped for Vatican III).

Thirdly, it is worth noting the relationship between the Synod of Bishops and the Roman Curia, particularly the relationship between the leading bodies of the Synod, the world episcopate, and the Roman Curia. Just as before Vatican II, the post–Vatican II papacy belongs neither to the Curia nor to the synod. The postconciliar papacy is in a peculiar position: exterior to both the Curia and the synod, which have the same status vis-à-vis the pope and are competitors one against the other, not coordinated with each other.[14] Even after the reform of the Roman Curia by Paul VI[15] and by John Paul II,[16] the government practice of the last twenty-five years has showed (1) the greater freedom of the Curia as a stable bureaucratic power with respect to the pope and the synod, a freedom greater than that of the synod; and (2) the celebration of synods as a vehicle supporting John Paul II's guidelines a posteriori and as a purely symbolic tutelage of papal authority by the bishops' representatives in the synod. Contrary to the mind of *Christus Dominus*, the Synod of Bishops remained only a faint shadow of conciliar requests for the bishops' participation in new governmental bodies for the Catholic Church. In these last years, the secretary of the Synod of Bishops gained a sort of curial congregation-type status, and its leaders have been made cardinals, just like the other congregation presidents.

---

14. See Antonio Acerbi, "L'ecclesiologia sottesa alle istituzioni ecclesiali postconciliari," in *L'ecclesiologia del Vaticano II: Dinamismi e prospettive*, ed. Giuseppe Alberigo (Bologna: EDB, 1981), 203–34.

15. Paul VI, apostolic constitution *Regimini Ecclesiae Universae*, August 15, 1967, in *Acta Apostolicae Sedis* 59 (1967): 885–928.

16. John Paul II, apostolic constitution *Pastor bonus*, June 28, 1988, in *Acta Apostolicae Sedis* 80 (1988): 841–930. About this, see Massimo Faggioli, "Riforma della Curia al Vaticano II e dopo il Vaticano II," *Concilium* 5 (2013): 42–52.

2. Relations between Bishops and Roman Curia
(*Christus Dominus* 8–10)

The relations between the bishops and the Roman Curia warrant a detailed examination. The schema *De rationibus Episcopos inter et Sacrae Curiae Romanae Congregationes* (On the relations between bishops and the Roman Curia, 1961) examined the issue of the relations between the diocesan bishops and Rome and proposed the concession of new "powers, privileges, and indults" from the pope and the Curia to the local bishops. It also suggested the co-optation of local bishops from all over the world as new curial congregation members and proposed the creation of an "assembly or conference of bishops in every nation."[17] Even during Vatican II, this chapter on national episcopal conferences did not prompt a broad debate about the balance of powers between the bishops and the Roman Curia. It limited itself to affirming two main principles: local bishops are to possess all the faculties necessary to exercise their pastoral ministry, and there is a need for cooperation between local bishops and the Roman congregations, which must be reorganized. Maximos IV was ignored when he called sharply for a reform of the central government of the Catholic Church, a reform more radical than the easy association of local bishops to the Roman congregations.[18]

Paragraph 8 on the bishops' powers and the relation between them and the pope's power attempted to invert the historical trend of faculties being conceded by Rome to the bishops. Subsequently, there followed paragraphs 9 and 10 of *Christus Dominus*:

9. In the exercise of his supreme, full, and immediate authority over the entire Church, the Roman pontiff makes use of the various departments

---

17. "Episcoporum Coetu, seu Conferentia in unaquaque natione": for the text of the schema *De rationibus Episcopos inter et Sacrae Curiae Romanae Congregationes*, approved on October 1961, see *Acta Synodalia* vol. II, no. 3-1: 286–90.

18. For the speech of Maximos IV, see *Acta Synodalia* vol. II, no. 4: 517.

of the Roman Curia. These departments, accordingly, operate in his name and with his authority for the good of the churches and in the service of the sacred pastors. These departments have unquestionably given outstanding assistance to the Roman pontiff and to the pastors of the Church. Nevertheless it is the express wish of the conciliar fathers that they should be reorganised in a way more appropriate to the needs of our own times and of different regions and rites. What needs particular attention is the number of these departments, their titles, the extent of their authority, the procedure proper to each, and the interdepartmental coordination of their activities. Likewise the fathers strongly desire that the function of the papal legates should be determined in more exact detail in relation to the pastoral office proper to bishops.

10. Further, since these departments have been established for the well-being of the universal Church, it is desirable that their members, officials, and consultors, including papal legates, should as far as possible be drawn more regularly from different regions of the Church, so that the offices or central agencies of the Catholic Church may manifest their truly universal character. It is also desirable that there should be co-opted into the membership of these departments some additional bishops, especially diocesan bishops, who are able to represent more fully to the supreme pontiff the mind, the aspirations and the needs of all the churches. Finally, the fathers of the council judge that it would be of great service for these departments to hear more often the views of lay people distinguished for virtue, knowledge, and experience, in order that they too may plan an appropriate part in the affairs of the church.[19]

On the basis of the decree's history and the final text, we can make three observations. First, the issue of the relationship between the bishops and the Roman Curia, far from being limited to a power struggle within the Church's most significant institutions—between local bishops and curial bishops and monsignors—actually originated as a theological-canonical concern with important pastoral consequences (e.g., pontifical faculties regarding liturgy and

19. *Christus Dominus* 9–10, in *Acta Apostolicae Sedis* 58 (1966): 676–77.

penance). We can see that most of the Vatican II bishops, from all over the world, whether they were part of the "reformist" majority or the "conservative" minority, were convinced of the need for a new balance of powers between the papacy and the episcopacy, between the Roman Curia and the episcopacy.

A second observation is that paragraph 8 of *Christus Dominus* was one of the most difficult and debated texts from the very beginning of the schema's history: the paragraph about the "ordinary, own and immediate power" ("ordinaria, propria ac immediata potestas") of bishops "successors of the Apostles" ("ut Apostolorum successoribus") originated during the debate within the preparatory commission *de episcopis* about the relations between local bishops and Roman congregations. That passage prompted criticism by the leaders of the conciliar minority (especially Bishop Carli) that the conciliar majority's ecclesiology was an attempt to undercut the pope's powers and rights somewhat comparable to the eighteenth-century Synod of Pistoia.[20]

Third and finally, the council got through the problem of the relation between bishops' powers and faculties, providing a new understanding about these faculties. Following the debate on *Christus Dominus*, Vatican II inverted a secular long trend, which had allowed the papacy to "grant" the bishops powers and faculties that were part of their own pastoral office. Such a historical trend had been a

---

20. During the April 26, 1961, meeting of the preparatory commission on the episcopate Pasquazi presented his report, which contained the suggestions on the first two drafts of the schema about the relations between local bishops and the Roman Curia. He underlined the theological issues and noted that the two drafts had some links with the Synod of Pistoia (1786), condemned by Pius VI. The reaction of the commission's members was almost unanimously critical, except for the position of Monsignor Carli, who desired to avoid questioning the relations between the local bishops and the Roman Curia, in order to avoid the risk of echoing the statements from the aforementioned synod. The commission's president, Cardinal Marella, had to close the debate in the commission on this subject. See *Verbale della sessione generale del 25 aprile 1961 (vespere)* and *Verbale della sessione generale del 26 aprile 1961 (mattina)*, in Archivio Segreto Vaticano (ASV), file Conc. Vat. II, 980.

perversion (in Yves Congar's words, "bishops robbed of their rights") with respect to the powers of the *munus episcopale*, episcopal ministry, in light of a correct ecclesiology.[21] But here, too, as in the case of the Synod of Bishops, Paul VI anticipated the wishes of the council and preempted the bishops' action through the *motu proprio Pastorale munus*.[22] But after that turning point, practically speaking, Vatican II could not consider the reform and the powers of the Roman Curia, and had to leave the issue to be handled by Paul VI.[23]

Paul VI, committed to the reform of the Roman Curia, gave a new, more central position to the Secretariat of State and created, beside the post–Tridentine congregations, new institutions, called secretariats and councils.[24] But as regards the reestablishment of equilibrium between the powers of local bishops and those of the Curia, the reform involved only the incorporation of non-Italian personnel (bishops and clergy) in the congregations and in the new institutions. The internationalization of the Roman Curia, despite being a response to proposals supported by most of the fathers, precluded more radical, profound reforms of the structure and the role of the Roman Curia in the Catholic Church.[25]

---

21. See the incisive critique by Congar, who on November 14, 1963, at the end of the debate in the aula, noted: "The Curia people (Ottaviani, Browne, Staffa, Carli, …) are doing EVERYTHING to prevent the episcopate from recovering the rights which have been stolen from it" (Les gens de la Curie (Ottaviani, Browne, Staffa, Carli, . . .) font TOUT pour empêcher que l'épiscopat ne reprenne des droits qui lui ont été derobés."): Yves Congar, *Mon Journal du Concile*, vol. 1, *1960–1963*, présenté et annoté par Èric Mahieu, avant-propos de Dominique Congar, préface de Bernard Dupuy (Paris: Cerf, 2002), 535, English translation Mary John Ronayne–Mary Cecily Boulding, ed. Denis Minns (Collegeville, MN: Liturgical, 2012) 425.

22. See *motu proprio Pastorale munus*, with the significant title *Facultates et privilegia quaedam Episcopis conceduntur*, (Faculties and privileges granted to the bishops) November 30, 1963, in *Acta Apostolicae Sedis* 56 (1964): 5–12.

23. For the recent debate about the reform of the Roman Curia, the role of the papacy, and collegiality-synodality in an ecumenical perspective, see Massimo Faggioli, "Note in margine a recenti contributi per una riforma ecumenica del papato," *Cristianesimo nella Storia* 22, no. 2 (2001): 451–72.

24. As regards the "reform spirit" of Paul VI, see Andrea Riccardi, *Il potere del papa da Pio XII a Giovanni Paolo II* (Rome-Bari: Laterza, 1993), 289–300.

The charisma-based pontificate of John Paul II, who did not act through institutions, was not oriented to Church government concerns as a key priority, and it stressed extraordinary governmental interventions more than ordinary ones.[26] This left most of the problems involving relations between the global and local church untouched, especially those concerning the central government and the centralizing tendencies of Church government. From the point of view of post–Vatican II relations between the bishops and the Roman Curia, the national episcopal conferences' resistance to the purely "administrative" power of the Congregations of the Roman Curia has not proved to be adequate. It also has to be stressed that the freedom of each bishop and each episcopal conference vis-à-vis the Roman Curia also depends on economic relations involving each other: the poorer a local church is, the less independent that church will be of the Roman Curia.

3. The Bishop's Power in His Diocese and The New Ecclesial Movements (*Christus Dominus* 11–18)

From a theological and canonical point of view, *Christus Dominus* served as a turning point with respect to a multicentury trend, i.e., the undercutting of episcopal powers regarding the diocese's spiritual government through the exercise of papal power:

> A diocese is a section of the people of God whose pastoral care is entrusted to a bishop in cooperation with his priests. Thus, in conjunction with their pastor and gathered by him into one flock in

25. See the prophetic words of Hubert Jedin, *peritus* of the *de episcopis* commission. He was convinced that the simple internationalization of the Curia would have led "vom Regen in die Traufe" (into a worse situation). Letter from Hubert Jedin to Ferdinand Klostermann, September 23, 1963, in Archivio Fondazione per le scienze religiose Giovanni XXIII in Bologna, file Jedin G5 a 21. See also John R. Quinn, *The Reform of the Papacy: The Costly Call to Christian Unity* (New York: Crossroad, 2000).

26. See Riccardi, *Governo carismatico*, 198–203.

the Holy Spirit through the Gospel and the Eucharist, they constitute a particular church. In this church, the one, holy, catholic, and apostolic church of Christ is truly present and at work. Individual bishops, to whom the pastoral care of particular churches has been committed, are the proper, official and immediate shepherds of these churches, under the authority of the supreme pontiff. Accordingly, they feed their sheep in the name of the Lord by fulfilling their office of teaching, sanctifying and governing them. At the same time, they themselves must recognise the rights which legitimately belong to patriarchs or to other hierarchic authorities. Bishops should indeed pursue their apostolic work as witness of Christ to all people. Not only should they look after those who already follow the chief shepherd, but they should also give themselves wholeheartedly to those who in one way or another have wandered from the path of truth, or who know nothing of the Gospel of Christ and His saving mercy, so that everyone may eventually walk "in all that is good and right and true" (Eph. 5:9).[27]

Not only theoretically but practically, the conciliar decree restores episcopal authority as primary and original in comparison with other power and decisional centers: coadjutor and auxiliary bishops, diocesan curia and councils, diocesan clergy, parish priests, and members of religious orders.[28]

However, the present situation in the postconciliar Catholic Church is more complex, especially in some European countries. Indeed, the aforementioned development of renewed episcopal authority is actually jeopardized by the presence of a new force in church life: the ecclesial movements (*movimenti ecclesiali*). They are a new, forceful presence and are particularly active in European Catholic churches, yet the conciliar decrees did not consider them because their development was recent, that is, during the last thirty years, particularly during the pontificate of John Paul II.[29]

---

27. *Christus Dominus* 11.
28. See *Christus Dominus* 26–31.
29. As regards the difference between the experience and the concept of church "movements" before and after Vatican II, see Étienne Fouilloux, "'Mouvements' théologico-spirituels et concile (1959–1962)," in *À la veille du Concile Vatican II: Vota et réactions en Europe et dans*

In fact, one of the growing problems for collegiality-synodality in the light of *Christus Dominus* is the struggle between local (and supra-diocesan) episcopal authority and the force of church movements, appointed or self-appointed protagonists of the new evangelization during the pontificate of John Paul II. It is not possible to deny the movements' ascent as one of the main tools of the pontificate of John Paul II. Such "movements" in the Catholic Church constitute a phenomenon whose dynamism is operative at the micro level (within parishes, local communities, and even families) and at the meso level (within dioceses, in relations between local churches, and in the Catholic Church as a whole).

From an ecclesiological point of view in this area, we can identify as a problem the reception of one of the most central aspects of Vatican II—the new role of the diocesan bishop and the understanding of the diocese as the local church.[30] Furthermore, also at stake is the issue of the reception of the new governmental bodies in the local church (diocesan synod, diocesan pastoral council, and parish pastoral council). The possible coexistence between the role of local church and the supra-diocesan dimension of church movements is an open question, which is only partly identified with the broader theological question of the relation between the local church and the "universal Church."[31]

le catholicisme oriental, ed. Matthijs Lamberigts and Claude Soetens (Leuven: Peeters, 1992), 185–99.

30. See Hervé Marie Legrand, "Les évêques, les églises locales et l'Église entière: Évolutions institutionelles depuis Vatican II et chantiers actuels de recherche," *Revue de Sciences philosophiques et théologiques* 85 (2001): 461–509.

31. For the document of the Congregation for the Doctrine of the Faith, *Communionis notio* (May 28, 1992) against the ecclesiological thesis of Christian Duquoc and Jean-Marie R. Tillard, see Heinrich Joseph Dominicus Denzinger, *Kompendium der Glaubensbekenntnisse und kirchlichen Lehrentscheidungen*, 37th ed., ed. Peter Hünermann (Freiburg i.B.: Herder, 1999), nn. 4920–24. For a recent discussion of this issue, see Walter Kasper, "Zur Theologie und Praxis des bischöflichen Amtes," in *Auf Eine neue Art Kirche sein*, Festschrift Joseph Homeyer (Munich: Bernward bei Don Bosco, 1999), 32–48; and the reply of Joseph Ratzinger, "L'ecclesiologia della Costituzione 'Lumen Gentium,'" in *Il Concilio Vaticano II: Recezione e attualità alla luce*

The ascent of church movements, set free from episcopal authority and rooted in a Rome-based, direct fidelity to the official guidelines of the present pontificate, constitutes a reproach to the actual exercise of episcopal governance and its parish-based pastoral focus in the dioceses and in the parishes. But the main problem for the relationship between diocesan bishops and the ecclesial movements lies in the leader-driven and antisynodal culture of the movements and their members, who are used to living the reality of the Church as a *communio* only in the experiential element of the church movement-group-community. It is worth stressing that in the last few years, the new movements' action systematically bypasses the institutions of collegiality-synodality at the diocesan level (diocesan and parish pastoral councils) in the name of an antibureaucratic and antidemocratic animus.[32] One of the main problems is that Vatican II did not address the existence of the movements. This is true for *Christus Dominus*, which was a text conceived at Vatican II during the discussion of episcopal collegiality and which was supposed to provide a new equilibrium between papal and episcopal powers, but not between the bishops and Church movements often acting as an organized ultramontane laity.

---

del Giubileo, ed. Rino Fisichella (Cinisello B.: San Paolo, 2000), 66–81. See the further reply of Walter Kasper in "Das Verhältnis von Universalkirche und Ortskirche: Freundschaftliche Auseinandersetzung mit der Kritik von Joseph Kardinal Ratzinger," *Stimmen der Zeit* 12 (2000): 795–804; also Klaus Ganzer, "Gesamtkirche und Ortskirche auf dem Konzil von Trient," *Römische Quartalschrift* 95, nos. 3-4 (2000): 167–78.

32. See Massimo Faggioli, *Sorting Out Catholicism: Brief History of the New Ecclesial Movements* (Collegeville MN: Liturgical Press, 2014).

4. Synodality beyond the Diocesan Level: National Synods or National Episcopal Conferences? *(Christus Dominus 36–38)*

As we have seen before, the birth of national episcopal conferences as institutions spread throughout the world occurred for many reasons: not only the desire for a better coordination of pastoral activities and guidelines in the exercise of the pastoral ministry within the same region or state, but also the need to protect episcopal power from the powers of the Roman Curia. As regards the former consideration, the decree *Christus Dominus* was impressively effective because collegial-collective episcopal activity within a region or state endured from the midnineteenth century,[33] but the latter issue is still a real problem.

The most important and creative institution from Vatican II for church government at the episcopal level is the national episcopal conference. Operative already before Vatican II, the national episcopal conferences were given a new juridical status by Vatican II, which established them in every country. Different models of episcopal conferences (structure, membership, authority, functions) were operative and debated during Vatican II. The council eventually issued general norms and left to the individual conferences the power to determine the structures and rules in detail:[34]

> 36. From the earliest centuries of the Church, bishops, while in authority over particular churches, have drawn inspiration from the bond of fraternal love and zeal for the mission to all people which was given to the apostles. Accordingly they have pooled their resources and coordinated their plans to promote the common good and also

33. See Giorgio Feliciani, *Le conferenze episcopali* (Bologna: Il Mulino, 1974), 273–349; Alessandra Marani, "Rassegna degli studi più recenti sull'attività collettiva dei vescovi fra Ottocento e Novecento," *Cristianesimo nella Storia* 15 (1994): 71–115; Id., "Tra Sinodi e Conferenze episcopali: La definizione del ruolo degli incontri collettivi dei vescovi tra Gregorio XVI e Pio IX," *Cristianesimo nella Storia* 17 (1996): 47–93.

34. See Paul VI, *motu proprio Ecclesiae Sanctae*, August 6, 1966, in *Acta Apostolicae Sedis* 58 (1966): 758–87, esp. n. 41. For the *Archetypon* for the conferences' statutes, see the appendix in Marcello Costalunga, "De Episcoporum Conferentiis," *Periodica* 57, no. 2 (1968): 217–80.

the good of individual churches. To this end synods, provincial councils and finally plenary councils were established in which the bishops drew up for the different churches a uniform procedure to be followed both in the teaching of the truths of the faith and in the regulation of ecclesiastical discipline. It is the earnest desire of this ecumenical synod that the venerable institutions of synods and councils should flourish with renewed strength, so that by this means more suitable and efficacious provision may be made for the increase of faith and for the maintenance of discipline in the different churches as the circumstances of the times require.

37. At the present time especially, bishops are often unable to discharge their office fittingly and fruitfully unless they do their work in daily closer agreement and collaboration with other bishops. Episcopal conferences have already been established in many nations. Since such conferences have furnished striking evidence of a more fruitful apostolate, in the judgement of this synod it is of the utmost importance that through the whole world bishops of the same nation or region should unite in a single assembly and meet together at regular intervals. The object of these meetings is that, by sharing ideas based on prudence and experience and by exchanging opinions, there may result a holy consortium of resources for the common good of the churches. The synod, therefore, makes the following decrees on episcopal conferences.[35]

What is worth noting here is the difference, which became more evident during the last forty years, between the text of *Christus Dominus* and the history of episcopal conferences in service to the communion of bishops and the local churches, in spite of the centralizing tendencies of John Paul II's pontificate during the last fifteen years.[36] The first seeds of episcopal conferences in *Christus*

---

35. *Christus Dominus* 36–37.
36. As regards the history of episcopal conferences at Vatican II within the commission *de episcopis* and during the years after Vatican II, see Giorgio Feliciani, *Le conferenze episcopali* (Bologna: Il Mulino, 1974); and Massimo Faggioli, "Prassi e norme relative alle conferenze episcopali tra concilio Vaticano II e post–concilio (1959-1998)," in *Synod and Synodality: Theology, History, Canon Law and Ecumenism in New Contact,* ed. Alberto Melloni and Silvia Scatena (Münster: LIT, 2004), 265–96.

Dominus 38, nurtured by Paul VI during the first postconciliar decade, represented a kind of institutional preference given by Rome in favor of episcopal conferences, leaving local-national synods and councils in an uncertain state of health.[37] In that perspective, from Vatican II up to now, national episcopal conferences have gained authority, responsibility, and public importance both within the Church and in their relationship to social and political communities to a degree very different from an initial reading of *Christus Dominus* 36–38: "38. An episcopal conference is a kind of assembly in which the bishops of some nation or region discharge their pastoral office in collaboration, the better to promote the good which the church offers to people, and especially through the forms and methods of apostolate carefully designed to meet contemporary conditions."[38] During the last thirty years, the growing responsibility and competencies of national episcopal conferences led to certain bureaucratic obstacles and doctrinal setbacks from Rome and in many respects a different approach from the pontificate of Paul VI, who gave powers to episcopal conferences in various matters—above all, the liturgy.[39]

The different trend during John Paul II's pontificate can be seen especially if we take a look at the equilibrium between synods and episcopal conferences in *Christus Dominus* 36–38. During Vatican II and the first twenty postconciliar years, the actual disappearance of provincial and national episcopal synods and councils was matched by the strengthening of episcopal conferences as an instrument of

---

37. See Heribert Schmitz, "Tendenzen nachkonziliarer Gesetzgebung. Sichtung und Wertung," *Archiv für katholisches Kirchenrecht* 146 (1977): 381–419. Schmitz saw in the first decade after Vatican II (1966–1976) three tendencies: "pro-episkopale oder restitutive/dezentralisierende Tendenz," "pro-laikale oder innovative Tendenz," and "pro-liberale oder rechtsrezessive Tendenz" (pro-bishops, decentralizing tendency; pro-laity, innovative tendency; liberal, anti-legalistic trend).

38. *Christus Dominus* 38, 1.

39. See John Baldovin, *Reforming the Liturgy: A Response to the Critics* (Collegeville, MN: Liturgical, 2009).

decentralized decision making at the episcopal level (especially for liturgy, pastoral matters, and catechism).[40]

In this present scenario, the still-existing crisis of provincial and national episcopal synods and councils as instruments for decentralization, if joined with the Rome-influenced crisis of national episcopal conferences, could cause a real weakening of collegial-synodal tendencies at the episcopal level after Vatican II. Up to now, patterns of collegiality-synodality at the diocesan level have demonstrated a scant capacity to influence synodal procedures in a globalized Church, which tends to be identified with the positions and "media-friendly style" of John Paul II.[41]

Indeed, despite the theological motivations expressed by those enforcing central authority vis-à-vis the local churches and bishops, the limitations on national episcopal conferences are not envisioned as enabling more vigorous synodal-conciliar activity at the local, regional, or national level, as it is said in the balance articulated by *Christus Dominus*.[42]

Here we cannot find arguments that are, like those expressed by the conciliar majority, opposed to the new postconciliar institutions. Today neither the defense of the power of individual bishops nor the strengthening of particular episcopal assemblies seems to be the

---

40. For the history of recent struggles between Rome and episcopal conferences between 1983 and 1998, particularly the 1983 *Codex Iuris Canonici*, the text of the International Theological Commission of 1985 about episcopal conferences, the 1985 extraordinary synod on Vatican II, and the 1998 document *Apostolos suos*, see, among others, Ladislas Orsy, "Episcopal Conferences: Their Theological Standing and Their Doctrinal Authority," *America* 155 (November 8, 1986): 282–85; Id., "Reflections on the Teaching Authority of the Episcopal Conferences," in *Episcopal Conferences: Historical, Canonical and Theological Studies*, ed. Thomas J. Reese (Washington, DC: Georgetown University Press, 1989), 233–52; Ladislas Orsy, "Episcopal Conferences and the Power of the Spirit," *Jurist* 59 (1999): 409–31; Id., "Die Bischofskonferenz und die Macht des Geistes," *Stimmen der Zeit* 218 (2000): 3–17. By Orsy, see also *Receiving the Council: Theological and Canonical Insights and Debates* (Collegeville, MN: Liturgical, 2009).

41. See *Le gouvernement de l'église catholique: Synodes et exercise du pouvoir*, ed. Jacques Palard (Paris: Cerf, 1997); and John R. Quinn, *The Reform of the Papacy*, passim.

42. See *Christus Dominus* 36.

real object of the new limitations experienced by national episcopal conferences.[43]

Moreover, from a systematic point of view, it is easy to note that the limitation of the role of episcopal conferences is now occurring especially in the geographic areas where Catholicism is experiencing demographic growth. During the nineties, the shift in the center of gravity within the Latin Catholic Church from the Euro-Atlantic churches (more sensitive on historical grounds to issues of collegiality and relations with Rome) to the young churches in Africa and Asia was not determined through the national or continental episcopal conferences, but through continental or national synods convened and celebrated in Rome.

5. Final Considerations

There are major issues underlying the present situation of collegiality-synodality in the Catholic Church, and they have to do with the history, the mind, and the final text of the conciliar decree *Christus Dominus*. An examination of the decree seems inevitable in order to understand some of the main problems of the communion within the Catholic Church and between the churches. In fact, recent proposals for an ecumenical reform of the papacy call for three special collegial-synodal reforms:

1. Self-limitation of the papacy in its titles and in its actual powers;
2. Reform of the Roman Curia and of the central institutions of church government;

43. We note here the 1999–2000 struggle between the episcopal conference of Germany and John Paul II about the participation of Catholics in pre-abortion consulting activities in Germany. See Johannes Reiter, ed., *Der Schein des Anstoßes: Schwangerschaftskonfliktberatung nach dem Papstbrief; Fakten, Dokumente, Perspektiven* (Freiburg i.B.: Herder, 1999); Daniel Deckers, *Der Kardinal Karl Lehmann: Eine Biographie* (Munich: Pattloch-Verlag, 2002), 325–51.

3. Development of a three-level collegiality-synodality ecclesiology, an enhancement of regional episcopal structures and the translation of the theology of collegiality-synodality into canonical structures and actual government praxis.[44]

Points two and three have much to do with the history, the mind, and the final text of *Christus Dominus*. It is true that some of the most important postconciliar governmental institutions (Synod of Bishops, new councils of the Roman Curia, and national episcopal conferences) find a starting point of their recent history in the text of *Christus Dominus*.

During the past fifty years, the potential of *Christus Dominus* as a document pointing to the future has indeed been realized in some cases, such as national episcopal conferences. This has also been true for *Sacrosanctum Concilium* regarding the vernacular languages. The last forty years testify to the potential of collegial-synodal cooperation between bishops, which has experienced Roman opposition only in more recent years.

In other cases, however, disappointments in terms of the reception and "Roman" application of Vatican II (e.g., bishops' synod) are based on a sense of the betrayal of conciliar fathers' expectations. At the very end of Vatican II, the conciliar commission on the episcopate was deprived of the task of drafting a text instituting a *coetum seu*

44. See Paul Tihon, ed., *Changer la papauté?* (Paris: Cerf, 2000); Heinz Schütte, ed., *Im Dienst der einen Kirche: Ökumenische Überlegungen zur Reform des Papstamts* (Paderborn-Frankfurt a.M.: Bonifatius-Lembeck, 2000); Carl E. Braaten and Robert W. Jenson, eds., *Church Unity and the Papal Office: An Ecumenical Dialogue on John Paul II's Encyclical* Ut unum sint *(That All May Be One)* (Cambridge: Eerdmans, 2001); Antonio Acerbi, ed., *Il ministero del papa in prospettiva ecumenica* (Milan: Vita e Pensiero, 1999); Peter Hünermann, ed., *Papstamt und Ökumene: Zum Petrusdienst und der Einheit aller Getauften* (Regensburg: Pustet, 1997); Hermann Josef Pottmeyer, *Towards a Papacy in Communion: Perspectives from Vatican Councils I and II* (New York: Crossroad, 1998); John R. Quinn, *The Reform of the Papacy. The Costly Call to Christian Unity* (New York: Crossroad, 2000).

consilium, a group or board operating together with the pope to foster the *sollicitudo omnium Ecclesiarum*, the care for all Catholic Churches.

In still other cases (e.g., the Roman Curia), continuing difficulties in relations between the center and the local churches in the communion are rooted in the superficial character of the institutional reforms after Vatican II, leaving almost intact a structure lasting from the Tridentine period.[45]

A historically informed reading of *Christus Dominus* suggests the inadequate reception of conciliar expectations by the post–Vatican II church government—that is, an inadequate reception not only of the expectations of the conciliar majority, but also of the conciliar fathers as a whole. We do not mean, however, that the problems of church government are the same today as those during the time of Vatican II or that the solutions proposed by *Christus Dominus* are still entirely valid and applicable without any change.

It is not possible to see the task of *aggiornamento* as regards institutional reform having been achieved once forever with Vatican II. There is no "Vatican II myth" or "reform myth" capable of solving every problem; it would be only a ritualistic and inefficient shortcut. Not following such myths but rather maintaining fidelity to Vatican II's mentality of *aggiornamento* and to the ecumenical destiny of Christians makes the possibility of collegial-synodal reforms in the Catholic Church of the twenty-first century more than a hypothesis; rather, the reforms are a continuing imperative.[46]

---

45. See Giuseppe Alberigo, "Forme storiche di governo nella Chiesa universale," in *Forme storiche di governo nella chiesa universale*, ed. Paolo Prodi (Bologna: CLUEB, 2003), 207–225.
46. See José Oscar Beozzo and Giuseppe Ruggieri, eds., *Per una strutturazione ecumenica delle chiese*, *Concilium* 37, no. 3 (2001).

12

About Vatican II and Women in the Church

Councils and Postconciliar Periods in Modern Catholicism

The way Vatican II dealt (or did not deal) with a given issue and the way the post–Vatican II period dealt with the same issue are relevant to assess the relevance of Vatican II today. But a necessary precedent of Vatican II is Trent: not only for what the council of Trent was, but also for what the post–council of Trent did (or did not do) in comparison to the council.[1]

1. Trent and the Tridentine Era, Vatican II and the Post-Vatican II Era

The "theology of women" and the role of women in the Church are very important topics, if not the most important, on which Vatican

1. This chapter was originally published in Italian as "Concili: Tra testi e contesti," in *Avendo qualcosa da dire: Teologi e teologhe rileggono il Vaticano II*, ed. Marinella Perroni and Hervé Legrand (Milan: San Paolo, 2014), 75–83.

II expressed itself only in an indirect way—that is, not explicitly addressing the issues typical of the intra-Catholic postconciliar debate on the role of women in the Church, both from the theological point of view and from an institutional standpoint. This does not mean Vatican II documents are unusable for the purpose of understanding the relationship between conciliar theology and the theology of women. Indeed, to deny the specificity of Vatican II when it comes to the theology of women vis-à-vis the previous Catholic theological tradition would be tantamount not only to refuting the theological value of the reception of Vatican II, but also to freezing Vatican II in a sort of theological monolith—assigning it a fate that had not even been the one of the Council of Trent.

Those who raise the issue of the relationship between the theology of women and the theology of the Second Vatican Council cannot escape the conviction that an intimate relationship exists between the council as a body of texts and the council as an event, that is, as a time in Church history marked by a ecclesial and theological dynamism with a particular magnitude in relation to the previous councils.[2] But next to the specifics of Vatican II in its role of providing guidance for the life of the Church, there are also similarities with the experience of the ecumenical and general councils before Vatican II. Indeed, the gap between the way Vatican II "did theology" in its documents in the form of words, and the flow and the development of those same instances in the period immediately following the council is not unique to Vatican II. The difference between a council as documents (or the letter of the council) and a council as an event or experience (or the spirit of the council) is particular to the Vatican in size and implications, both within the church and externally, but it is not unique to Vatican II.[3]

---

2. See Serena Noceti, "Un caso serio della recezione conciliare: Donne e teologia," *Ricerche Teologiche* 13, no. 1 (2002): 211–24.

On the one hand, an internal dynamic is at work in the conciliar tradition, which calls for the reception of the council—of the Council of Trent as well as of Vatican II—in a period of time that must be measured not in years, but in decades and generations. Many years ago, Giuseppe Alberigo highlighted the memoranda sent between 1600 and 1612 by Cardinal Robert Bellarmine to Pope Clement VIII on the progress of the reforms adopted by the Council of Trent. In them, the cardinal worried about the slow start of the application of the council fifty years after its beginning.[4]

But on the other hand, the case of Trent offers an important example that can help us understand the difference between the conciliar texts and their chances of reception. First, there is the issue of the relationship between a council and the era it opens: between the council of Trent and the Tridentine age, between Vatican II and the Church in the modern world. Second, it is necessary to understand the relationship between an epochal council (like Trent and Vatican II) and the theological paths opened by it for the Church in the following period. All this becomes clear if we finally acknowledge that if the real point of reference for understanding Vatican II is the Council of Trent, then in the same way, to understand the period following Vatican II, we must understand the period following the Council of Trent.[5]

For us to reconsider the relationship between the Vatican and some conciliar instances that emerged later, it is time to reevaluate the difference and appreciate the value of the distinction between the

3. See Étienne Fouilloux, "Histoire et événement: Vatican II," *Cristianesimo nella Storia* 13, no. 3 (1992): 515–38; Peter Hünermann, "Il concilio Vaticano II come evento," in *L'evento e le decisioni: Studi sulle dinamiche del concilio Vaticano II*, ed. Maria Teresa Fattori and Alberto Melloni (Bologna: Il Mulino, 1997), 63–92; and Joseph A. Komonchak, "Riflessioni storiografiche sul Vaticano II come evento," in Fattori and Melloni, *L'evento e le decisioni*, 417–40.
4. See Giuseppe Alberigo, *La chiesa nella storia* (Brescia: Paideia, 1988), 218–39.
5. See Massimo Faggioli, *Vatican II: The Battle for Meaning* (Mahwah, NJ: Paulist, 2012).

councils and the postconciliar periods. Church history knows that difference very well, but it is not clear if Catholic theology and the magisterium are fully conscious of it. In a sense, for one to appreciate fully the post–Vatican II period, one must appreciate fully and in a non-ideological way the post–Trent period.

The terminology dividing a "liberal" Protestant Reformation from a "conservative" Counter-Reformation is now part of the ideological and theological controversies of the past. Besides making the well-known distinction between "Catholic reform" and "Counter-Reformation,"[6] it is now necessary to reexamine the distinctions between "Trent," "Tridentinism," and "Tridentine age." From this, we must draw consequences for Catholic theology today to appreciate the council that was celebrated between 1545 and 1563.[7]

The terms *Trent, Tridentinism, Tridentine age, early modern Catholicism,* and *Catholic reform* have something in common, but they do not completely overlap or substitute for one another. Inside the idea of an "early modern Catholicism," there are different and sometimes conflicting cultures:[8] "The fight against religious confessions of the Reformation leads to overshadowing and then to suppressing many of the needs that emerged in the Catholic Reformation and the Council of Trent: the reading of the Bible and the Fathers of the Church, the centrality of personal conscience

6. See Erwin Iserloh, Josef Glazik, and Hubert Jedin, *Reformation, Katholische Reform und Gegenreformation* (Freiburg: Herder, 1967); Hubert Jedin, *Riforma cattolica o Controriforma? Tentativo di chiarimento dei concetti con riflessioni sul Concilio di Trento* (Brescia: Morcelliana, 1957).

7. See Paolo Prodi, "Il binomio jediniano 'riforma cattolica e controriforma' e la storiografia italiana," *Annali dell'Istituto storico italo-germanico in Trento* 6 (1980): 85–98; John W. O'Malley, *Trent and All That: Renaming Catholicism in the Early Modern Era* (Cambridge, MA: Harvard University Press, 2000); John W. O'Malley, *Trent: What Happened at the Council* (Cambridge, MA: Harvard University Press, 2013), 10–11.

8. See Kathleen M. Comerford and Hilmar M. Pabel, eds., *Early Modern Catholicism: Essays in Honour of John W. O'Malley, S. J.* (Toronto: University of Toronto Press, 2001).

in relation to salvation, the multiplicity of spiritual and liturgical experiences."[9]

Immediately after the Council of Trent, a series of acts by Pope Pius IV crystallized the council in an institutional and juridical structure. In December 1563, a congregation of the Roman Curia began work on the interpretation to be given to decrees of the council. The Curia published the *Index Librorum Prohibitorum* (list of prohibited books) and the *Professio Fidei* (profession of the faith) in 1564, the *Catechismus Romanus* (Roman Catechism) and the new breviary in 1566, and the new missal of Pius V in 1570. These acts gave the impression of a Catholicism made more systematic by Trent. But from the ecclesiological point of view, it is clear that the centralized and universalist model adopted by the Roman doctrinal policy of "Tridentinism" was not shaped by the theology of the Council of Trent, which did not debate the question, because Luther did not raise this argument on the ecclesiological relationship between the local church and the universal church.[10]

In other words, it is true that the Catholic Church in the modern age has been shaped by "Tridentinism" certainly no less than by the Council of Trent. It is equally true that the Church of Vatican II in the contemporary world—especially the question of the theology of women and the role of women in the church—is shaped by the dynamics of the conciliar reception, rather than the texts of the Second Vatican Council, which as it is known, is silent on some issues.

---

9. Paolo Prodi, *Il paradigma tridentino: Un'epoca nella storia della chiesa* (Brescia: Morcelliana, 2010), 50.

10. See Giuseppe Alberigo, "From the Council of Trent to 'Tridentinism,'" in *From Trent to Vatican II: Historical and Theological Investigations*, ed. Raymond F. Bulman and Frederick J. Parrella (Oxford: Oxford University Press, 2006), 19–37, esp. 21–23; Massimo Faggioli, "Chiese locali ed ecclesiologia prima e dopo il concilio di Trento," in *Storia della Chiesa in Europa tra ordinamento politico-amministrativo e strutture ecclesiastiche*, ed Luciano Vaccaro (Brescia: Morcelliana, 2005), 197–213.

2. Vatican II as a Paradigm and the Theology of Women

To apply the analogy between Trent/Tridentinism/early modern Catholicism on the one hand and Vatican II/postconciliar Church on the other hand, it is necessary, at this point, to draw a parallel with what happened at the magisterial level during Vatican II and after 1965—a task that is as much for historians of the contemporary Church as for Catholic theologians. But once we have accepted the idea of a gap between three different concepts for a crucial moment in the history of the Church—"the Council of Trent," "Tridentinism," and "early modern Catholicism"—we have to identify similar gaps that surround Vatican II and its age and to frame the question of the "theology of women" and the "role of women in the Church" in one of these gaps.

Now, it is clear that fifty years from the beginning of the council is too early to draw a line between different "conciliar cultures" in a process that is still ongoing. But here we limit ourselves to look at the leap between the council and the postcouncil period as a combination that imperfectly reflects the combination, now classic (but also subject to ideological distortions) of "letter" and "spirit."

If the issue of the theology of women and the role of women in the Church does not belong to the council in its letter, it definitely belongs to the council as its spirit has been passed down and lived in the postconciliar period. A legal or legalistic application of the letter of the council to the demands of the postconciliar period cannot be the only way to address the question of the theology of women and the role of women in the Church, when for many other issues, the phrase "spirit of the council" has been used to legitimize practices and forms of life in the Church that had no role in the discussions of the material, the council, and the final documents of the council.[11] In fact, as it would be wrong to reduce the Council of Trent to its documents, to Tridentinism as an ideology, or to the culture of early modern Catholicism, so it is inappropriate to reduce the object "Vatican II" only to the discussions and documents of the council or the instances that have subsequently emerged thanks to those debates and those documents.

One can speak of a "Tridentine paradigm," thanks in large part to the monocultural or European character of the Catholic Church in the sixteenth to nineteenth centuries. But for Vatican II, it is difficult to speak of a "paradigm" as a mixture of definitions, instructions, and culture. Vatican II is likely to be, rather than a paradigm, a "paradigmatic event"[12] in the sense of a new way of doing theology and of being a Church that has direct consequences for the theology of women.

This way of doing theology and being a Vatican II Church includes several distinctive qualities:

- *Ressourcement* as a return to the sources and a relativization of all other ecclesiastical regulations: "This sacred Council has several aims in view: it desires to impart an ever increasing vigor to the Christian life of the faithful; to adapt more suitably to the needs of our own times those institutions which are subject to change."[13]

---

11. See Massimo Faggioli, "Between Documents and Spirit: The Case of the New Catholic Movements," in *After Vatican II: Trajectories and Hermeneutics*, ed. James L. Heft with John O'Malley (Grand Rapids, MI: Eerdmans, 2012), 1–22.

12. See Lieven Boeve, "Une histoire de changement et conflit des paradigmes théologiques? Vatican II et sa réception entre continuité et discontinuité," in *La théologie catholique entre intransigeance et renouveau*, ed. Gilles Routhier, Philippe J. Roy, and Karim Schelkens (Louvain-la-Neuve: Collège Erasme; Leuven: Universiteitsbibliotheek, 2011), 355–66.

13. Vatican II, constitution on the sacred liturgy *Sacrosanctum Concilium*, par. 1. See Massimo Faggioli, *True Reform: Liturgy and Ecclesiology in* Sacrosanctum Concilium (Collegeville, MN: Liturgical, 2012); Gabriel Flynn and Paul D. Murray, eds., with the assistance of Patricia Kelly, Ressourcement: *A Movement for Renewal in Twentieth-Century Catholic Theology* (Oxford: Oxford University Press, 2012).

- A dynamic circle connecting Scripture, tradition, and magisterium, and a recovery of the *sensus fidei* as an integral part of the conciliar hermeneutical circle: "The work of the inter-ecclesial dialogue comes also from the Spirit that is behind Scripture, tradition, *sensus fidei*, theological research, and magisterium."[14]

- An inculturation of Catholicism as part of the redefinition of its universalism, and the beginning of a new age in which the living space of the Church is essentially the whole world.[15] The universalist paradigm of second millennium Catholicism needs a rebalancing in a more local ecclesiology.

- This entails a detachment from sociocultural patterns that have been taken for granted for centuries also in the ecclesiological "translation" of these patterns about the different ministries in the Church.

- The pastoral nature of the doctrine is based on the open-ended character of the conciliar corpus. This means the reception of Vatican II does not depend only on the texts, nor only on the "spirit" of those texts, but on "a reception that takes necessarily the shape of a conversion."[16]

3. Conciliar Trajectories and Ecclesial Trajectories

Even for gender issues, the "myth of Trent" or the "imagined council" was much more effective than the real Council of Trent, which was not the bearer of male or female precise anthropology.[17]

---

14. See Ormond Rush, *Still Interpreting Vatican II: Some Hermeneutical Principles* (Mahwah, NJ: Paulist, 2004), 69–85, quotation at 78.
15. See Karl Rahner, "Basic Theological Interpretation of the Second Vatican Council," in *Concern for the Church* (New York: Crossroad, 1981), 77–90, quotation at 83.
16. See Christoph Theobald, *La réception du concile Vatican II: Vol. I. Accéder à la source* (Paris: Cerf, 2009), 409.

Similarly, for a council like Vatican II that did not have on its agenda the issue of women in the church, we must ask ourselves honestly what was the relationship, in the first fifty years of the post–Vatican II period, between the "real Vatican II" and the "myth of Vatican II." As there was a Tridentine age symbolized by Carlo Borromeo, the same way there is a "Church of Vatican II," made of "real Vatican II" and of the "myth of Vatican II," of "letter" and of "spirit," which includes a new role for women. If Tridentinism was obviously influenced more by the postconciliar debates with the Protestants and the surrounding culture that dictated by Trent, so it is the same for Vatican II and the issue of women.

But the main difference between the Council of Trent as a council of a European church and Vatican II as the first council of a world Church is also in the scope of the impact of these two events in the history of the church. If for Trent we can differentiate between the council, Tridentinism, and the Tridentine age (and between application and reception of Trent), for Vatican II it is necessary to keep in mind not only the difference between the application of the council and its reception, but also between these two moments and the "trajectories" of the council in the Church and in the contemporary world.[18]

What appear here, in all their consequentiality, are the radical difference between the two great councils of the modern age, Trent and Vatican II, and the difference between Trent and Tridentinism on the one hand, and Vatican II and the postconciliar period on the other hand. The theology of women proves to be a crucial

---

17. See Wolfgang Reinhard, "Il concilio di Trento e la modernizzazione della chiesa," in *Il concilio di Trento e il modern*, ed. Paolo Prodi and Wolfgang Reihnard (Bologna: Il Mulino, 1996); Anna Carfora, "Il concilio di Trento da evento storico a categoria simbolica," in *Anatemi di ieri, sfide di oggi: Contrappunti di genere nella rilettura del concilio di Trento*, ed. Antonio Autiero and Marinella Perroni (Bologna: EDB, 2011), 79–90.

18. See John W. O'Malley, "Introduction: Trajectories and Hermeneutics," in Heft with O'Malley, *After Vatican II*, x–xxii.

case of reception, if not *the* case of the conciliar reception, for its ability to reveal an essential difference between the two councils and the two decisive periods of postconciliar theology and the Catholic Church over the past five hundred years. Vatican II means a new consciousness of the Church, a new ecclesiology, a new way of doing theology, and especially new subjects of doing theology and new places of doing theology. In this sense, the periodizing value of the Second Vatican Council is clear not only for the history of the Church, but also for the history and theology of Christianity as a "global history," especially from the point of view of the case of the theology of women and the role of women in the Church.

The Council of Trent differed from Vatican II in terms of the direction in which its authority flowed. The Council of Trent and Tridentinism were a top-down "application" of the council by Rome to the local churches. Vatican II, because of its own dynamic (rather than the conscious intention of the bishops, theologians, and laity) cannot work following a "center to the periphery" ecclesiological model.[19] In the words of Yves Congar, Vatican II gave birth to a "kind of decentralization of the *urbs* [Rome] on the *orbis* [world], given that the *orbis* almost took possession of the *urbs*."[20]

Vatican II is not a "paradigmatic event," but rather a programmatic council: "Vatican II did not leave us all with the answers; *it left us with a new way of being faithful to the past*. If we do want to take an insight from 'exemplarism,' then Vatican II is *an exemplar for the way it itself is to be interpreted*. And just as *Dei Verbum* teaches that Scripture 'must

---

19. See Giuseppe Alberigo, "L'ecclesiologia del concilio di Trento," *Rivista di storia della chiesa in Italia* 18 (1964): 227–42; Giuseppe Alberigo, "Applicazione e ricezione del concilio di Trento," in *La chiesa nella storia* (Brescia: Paideia, 1988), 218–39; "Concezioni della chiesa al concilio di Trento e nell'età moderna," in *Il concilio di Trento: Istanze di riforma e aspetti dottrinali*, ed. Massimo Marcocchi, Claudio Scarpati, Antonio Acerbi, and Giuseppe Alberigo (Milan: Vita e Pensiero, 1997), 117–53.

20. Yves Congar, *Le concile de Vatican II: Son Église, Peuple de Dieu et Corps du Christ* (Paris: Cerf, 1984), 54.

be read and interpreted in the sacred spirit in which it was written,' so too Vatican II must be interpreted with the same Spirit-inspired creativity that it itself exhibited."[21] In the case of the issue of women and Catholic theology, it is clear that the reception of Vatican II is not a simple "application" of the council, and that the issue of women in Catholic theology definitely belongs—and is most probably the key issue—in the long-term trajectories of Vatican II.

21. Rush, *Still Interpreting Vatican II*, 78.

13

The Future of Vatican II

The Vision of the Council beyond the "Narratives"

The legacy of Vatican II is much more than the "documents" of
Vatican II. But especially in the Western world, and specifically in
the North American context, Vatican II fell victim of a clash of
narratives that focuses on certain texts in an approach that is more
theological-political than theological and that dismisses history from
the hermeneutical horizon. A first necessary step to reclaim Vatican
II is liberating the memory of the council from those narratives.
History serves the theological tradition of the Church much better
than ideology.[1]

---

1. This chapter was originally published as "The Future of Vatican II: The Vision of the Council
beyond the 'Narratives,'" in *Vatican II: A Universal Call to Holiness*, ed. Anthony Ciorra and
Michael Higgins (New York: Paulist, 2012), 7–26.

1. From the End of the Council to the "Clash of Narratives"

During the last public session of Vatican II, on December 7, 1965, Pope Paul VI after the celebration of the Mass read his speech about the religious value of the council that was coming to an end. The main line of thought was summed up in a thesis that today should resonate more often in the public discourse of the Church: "It must be truthfully asserted that the Catholic religion and human life are connected in a friendly alliance and that both strive for the human good. For the Catholic Church exists for the human race; it is as it were the life of the human race."[2]

This attitude of renewed friendship between the Church and the human is part of the message of Vatican II and truly part of the theological reception of the council. In a Church that values so much the experience of *paradosis* (tradition) and of reception, the historical experience of the ecumenical councils has always been a history of reception, but it is also one of forgetting. The Catholic Church is no less subject than other earthly powers to the grinding of history. The Holy Spirit speaks to the Church in history, and in history the Church filters the teachings of ecumenical councils, ponders their meaning, and understands what is left by this history of tradition: what needs to be rediscovered and what is to be left in the archives of expired ideas no longer able to translate the gospel to all of humanity, which needs and deserves to hear it.

Looking at Vatican II and its message for the Church today means looking at the history not only of the council itself but also of its reception and interpretation in these last fifty years.[3] The texts

---

2. Paul VI, in *Acta Synodalia Sacrosancti Concilii Oecumenici Vaticani II: Cura et studio Archivi Concilii Oecumenici Vaticani* (Vatican City: Typis Polyglottis Vaticanis, 1970–99), vol. 4, no. 7, p. 661. See also Peter Hünermann, "The Final Weeks of the Council," in *History of Vatican II*, ed. Giuseppe Alberigo, English version ed. Joseph A. Komonchak (Maryknoll, NY: Orbis, 2006), 5:474.

3. See Massimo Faggioli, *Vatican II: The Battle for Meaning* (Mahwah, NJ: Paulist, 2012).

of Vatican II would not survive outside of the fertile ground of theological and pastoral reflection on those very texts. As Bernard Häring said about the last day of Vatican II, December 8, 1965, "The council begins today."[4] That was true for December 8, 1965, as it is for every day.

That is why is not surprising—actually, it is reassuring—to look at the early history of the post–Vatican II period and see that there was, and very early on, an interruption between the enthusiasm of the celebration of the final days of Vatican II and the first steps of its reception and interpretation.[5] In a way, the naïve enthusiasm for a supposedly easy "fresh start" for Catholicism had long disappeared, even before the conclusion of the council in 1965. As Yves Congar wrote in the very first page of his council diary, written the first day after Vatican II, December 9, 1965 (my translation): "What a desk! I have stacks of books and journals everywhere: on the table, on the chairs, on the floor! What a job!!!"[6] He was just talking about his desk, but in a way he was already talking also about the agenda of the Catholic Church after Vatican II.

2. The First Few Years of the Age of Vatican II

For some historians of the post–Vatican II era, the age of "euphoria" lasted only ten years, until 1975, followed by a decade of "contestations," and then concluded with the current period of "restoration" that had begun well before 2005.[7] For some others, the "honeymoon" between Vatican II and the *ad extra*, the world

4. See Bernard Häring, *Il concilio comincia adesso* (Alba: Edizioni Paoline, 1966).
5. See John W. O'Malley, *What Happened at Vatican II* (Cambridge, MA: Belknap Press of Harvard University Press, 2008); and Giuseppe Alberigo, ed., *History of Vatican II*, vol. 5, English version ed. Joseph A. Komonchak (Maryknoll, NY: Orbis, 2006).
6. "Quelle table! Il y a des piles de livres et de revues partout: sur la table, sur les chaises, par terre! Quel boulot!!!" Yves Congar, *Mon journal du concile*, presented and annotated by Éric Mahieu (Paris: Cerf, 2002), 2:517.

outside, had ended already in 1968, the peak of the sixties, at least in the Western Hemisphere, with its student protest movements, counterculture, and rise of political violence.[8]

But also from an intra-Catholic perspective, it can be argued that the honeymoon between the council, and modern culture lasted even less than ten years. The first celebration of the newly created Synod of Bishops came in 1967. Before the second session of the synod could gather in 1969, during the summer of 1968, Paul VI's encyclical *Humanae Vitae* had become the symbol of the first crisis in the renewed relationship between Church and modern world.[9] It became clear that the interpretation of Vatican II would be touched by modern Catholicism's new emphasis of on moral issues.[10]

All that said, and no matter what our periodization is, it is undeniable that at the beginning of the 1970s, Vatican II had already become the underlying platform for the renewal of Catholicism in different fields: liturgy, biblical studies, ecclesiology, ecumenism, and interreligious dialogue. Changes in Catholic theology also entailed changes in the structure of the Catholic Church—or this is what many thought at the time.[11] The seventies were the first—and so far the last—decade of cautious decentralization of Roman Catholicism:[12] decentralization of the balance of power in the Church as an

7. See Étienne Fouilloux, "Essai sur le devenir du catholicisme en France et en Europe occidentale de Pie XII à Benoît XVI," *Revue théologique de Louvain* 42 (2011): 526–57.

8. See Denis Pelletier, *La crise catholique: Religion, société, politique en France, 1965–1978* (Paris: Payot, 2002).

9. See Lisa Sowle Cahill, "Moral Theology after Vatican II," in *The Crisis of Authority in Catholic Modernity*, ed. Michael J. Lacey and Francis Oakley (New York: Oxford University Press, 2011), 193–224; and Leslie Woodcock Tentler, "Souls and Bodies: The Birth Control Controversy and the Collapse of Confession," in Lacey and Oakley, *The Crisis of Authority in Catholic Modernity*, 293–315.

10. About this, see John T. Noonan Jr., *A Church That Can and Cannot Change: The Development of Catholic Moral Teaching* (Notre Dame, IN: University of Notre Dame Press, 2005).

11. See *Vatican II: Assessment and Perspectives; Twenty-Five Years After (1962–1987)*, ed. René Latourelle (New York: Paulist, 1988–89).

12. See Heribert Schmitz, "Tendenzen nachkonziliarer Gesetzgebung. Sichtung und Wertung," *Archiv für katholisches Kirchenrecht* 146 (1977): 381–419.

institution, and displacement of the centers where Catholic theology was thought, taught, and lived.[13] The clash with the Lefebvrian schism made clear already in the mid-1970s that Catholic theology was not to be reduced to nostalgia for a historically determined political and social ideology of European Catholicism—one that often overlapped with the political worldview of fascism and with the conspiracy mind-set, including anti-Semitism and theological anti-Judaism.[14] With the first pope of the post–conciliar period (the same pope who had brought the council to a conclusion), Paul VI, Vatican II experienced its first decade of reform, renewal, and experiments.

But failure and disappointments have strangely become, in the eyes of many, more visible than the many successes of the council. Vatican II seems subject to a midlife crisis; today, when Catholics and theologians form their judgment about Vatican II, the risk is to focus more on the failures than on the successes. It is also true that in some quarters of neoconservative Catholicism, failures have become more important and cherished than successes. But Church historians know how the Council of Trent was talked about after fifty years from its conclusion. The state of the reception of Vatican II is now, at fifty years of age, certainly not worse than the application of the Council of Trent at the beginning of the seventeenth century.[15]

That is why, no matter how successful these reforms and experiments were, Pope Paul VI has become, especially for the ultranostalgic and ultraconservative fringe of Catholicism, the uncomfortable paradigm of a "reformist pope,"[16] if not (as Paul VI is

---

13. See Jean-Pierre Jossua and Johann Baptist Metz, eds., *Fundamental Theology: Doing Theology in New Places* (*Concilium* 5, no. 115 [1978]; New York: Seabury, 1979); J. Audinet et al., eds., *Le Déplacement de la theologie* (Paris: Beauchesne, 1977).

14. See Daniele Menozzi, "Opposition to the Council," in *The Reception of Vatican II*, ed. Giuseppe Alberigo, Jean-Pierre Jossua, and Joseph A. Komonchak (Washington DC: Catholic University of America Press, 1987), 325–48.

15. About the council of Trent as a paradigm, see Paolo Prodi, *Il paradigma tridentino: Un'epoca della storia della Chiesa* (Brescia: Morcelliana, 2010).

for the Lefebvrites) the bogeyman of Catholicism facing modernity. The historiographical and theological silence about Giovanni Battista Montini–Paul VI (just like the silence about John XXIII, except from a few specialists of Vatican II) is a very clear sign of the theological zeitgeist in the Catholic Church of today. This harsh judgment of the popes of Vatican II involves and assumes for some an even harsher judgment of the council that John XXIII announced in 1959 and Paul VI led until its end in 1965.

3. From John Paul II to Benedict XVI

A new phase in the reception of Vatican II began in 1978 with the election of John Paul II, the last pope who had been a council father of Vatican II. The caution of Catholic theologians in assessing John Paul II's legacy regarding the reception of Vatican II has more to do today with the fear of fueling the ongoing neoconservative backlash than with the length and complexity of his pontificate.[17] The difficult position of Vatican II theologians in assessing John Paul II's contribution to the reception of Vatican II is now between the generous but often also confusing "conciliar nominalism" of John Paul II and the active effort of reinterpretating the council in a minimizing way brought about by the Roman Curia and the willing entourage of Pope Benedict XVI more than by Pope Benedict XVI himself.

It is undeniable that the vulgarized and tabloid-like propaganda about Pope Benedict XVI's interpretation of the council lends itself

---

16. See Andrea Riccardi, *Il potere del papa da Pio XII a Giovanni Paolo II*, rev. ed. (Roma-Bari: Laterza, 1993).

17. See George Weigel, *The End and the Beginning: Pope John Paul II; The Victory of Freedom, the Last Years, the Legacy* (New York: Doubleday, 2010), to be compared now with the counternarrative offered by the founder of the Community of St. Egidio, Italian Church historian Andrea Riccardi, *Giovanni Paolo II: La biografia* (Cinisello B.: San Paolo, 2011), English translation forthcoming.

perfectly to feeding the theological side of the "culture wars," especially in the West and on the North American continent. The phenomenon of political conversions to Catholicism in the North Atlantic scene (America and Europe) is not immune from this debate and does in fact influence it.[18] For theological pundits and ultraconservative Catholic bloggers, the theology of Vatican II seems to function sometimes as collateral—an openly negotiable thing in the Church of the "nonnegotiables"—not only for the relationships within the Church and its various souls but especially for relations with the various parties of nostalgia: for Lefebvrists as well as for converts who have chosen Catholicism as the home of choice for their neoconservative worldview.[19] In this sense, it is no coincidence that the focus of the interpretation of the council during the pontificate of Pope Benedict XVI was clearly centered on "political-ecclesiastical considerations."[20]

Now, fifty years after the beginning of Vatican II, in some Catholic quarters there is a sense of disappointment about the failed promises of the Church and of the council. The historiographical work on the council tells us that this disappointment is related to the vast underestimation by council fathers and theologians active at the council of the work that needed to be done after its conclusion. However, what seems to be the prevailing sentiment—a parallel to the underestimation of the first generation—is an underestimation of the work already done by the council for the renewal of Catholicism.

18. Cf. Joseph P. Chinnici, "An Historian's Creed and the Emergence of Postconciliar Culture Wars," *Catholic Historical Review* 94 (2008): 219–44; Joseph Chinnici, "Reception of Vatican II in the United States," *Theological Studies* 64, no. 3 (2003): 461–94; see also T. J. Shelley, "Vatican II and American Politics," *America*, October 13, 2003.

19. See Giovanni Miccoli, *La Chiesa dell'anticoncilio: I tradizionalisti alla riconquista di Roma* (Roma-Bari: Laterza, 2011).

20. See Lieven Boeve, "'La vraie réception de Vatican II n'a pas encore commencé': Joseph Ratzinger, Révélation et autorité de Vatican II," in *L'autorité et les autorités: L'herméneutique théologique de Vatican II*, eds. Gilles Routhier and Guy Jobin (Paris: Cerf, 2010), 13–50.

The simple fact that the Catholic Church cannot simply understand itself and present itself to the world of today without Vatican II was made evident in the controversial lifting of the excommunications of the Lefebvrite bishops in January 2009, the fiftieth anniversary of the announcement of the council.[21]

The coincidence of that anniversary in 2009 with the lifting of the excommunications of the four bishops ordained by Marcel Lefebvre has focused a new kind of attention on the council and has created a situation that is leading to a new understanding of its significance. The debate on the meaning of the council entered a new stage there. Not only have bishops' conferences and individual bishops spoken out, and, understandably, representatives of Jewish communities around the world, but so have political leaders in parliaments and similar bodies, even if sometimes discreetly. Their reactions have forced the Holy See to acknowledge the central point at issue: the meaning of Vatican II. This is because the followers of Lefebvre have proclaimed from the beginning their refusal to accept the council and particularly to accept certain elements of its corpus. Their only reason for existence is their rejection of the council.

In the horizon of the contemporary Church, contemporary politics, and international public opinion, the Second Vatican Council has shown itself to be a guarantee of citizenship for the Catholic Church in today's world. This guarantee has been identified in public opinion with the definitive rejection of anti-Judaism and anti-Semitism because they are elements of a premodern and antidemocratic political culture. This guarantee also has been identified with other specific elements in the way the council broke with the Catholic Church of the "long nineteenth century"[22]:

21. See Massimo Faggioli, "Il Vaticano II come 'costituzione' e la 'recezione politica' del concilio," *Rassegna di Teologia* 50 (2009): 107–22.
22. O'Malley, *What Happened at Vatican II*, 53–92.

religious freedom and freedom of conscience, ecumenism, interreligious dialogue, and collegiality and co-responsibility in church government. It is no coincidence that these core elements of the political reception of the council are exactly the ones rejected by the Lefebvrites as the heresies of the council.[23]

The efforts to analyze the council in absolute and strict continuity with the past are often tied to ideological positions that advocate a reactionary Catholicism as the only hope for the survival of Western civilization, embodying a "neo-Maurrassism"[24] that has replaced the Communist threat with the "clash of civilizations."[25] In the light of the reaction to the lifting of the excommunications of 2009, it has become clear that denying the discontinuities of the council with the past could easily backfire. The astute argument made by the conservative (but far from neoconservative) political scientist Samuel Huntington, who argued that the process of democratization might have more to do with the Second Vatican Council than with the spread of free markets, is today as valid as ever.[26]

Truth be told, the actual role of Vatican II in contemporary Catholic theology is twofold. On the one hand, the ongoing debate on the Lefebvrites and their views on Vatican II becomes thus almost paradoxically a reassuring reminder that it is impossible to go back to the pre–Vatican II era. On the other hand, the current underestimation (if not expulsion) of Vatican II in some Catholic quarters is no different from the underestimation of the consequences

---

23. About this, see Faggioli, *Vatican II: The Battle for Meaning*, 24–35.
24. French Catholic author Charles Maurras (1868-1952), was the leader of Action Française, a Catholic political-cultural group condemned by Pius XI in 1926 for its ultra-nationalist views: see Emile Perreau-Saussine, *Catholicism and Democracy. An Essay in the History of Political Thought*, trans. Richard Rex (Princeton: Princeton University Press, 2012).
25. See Samuel P. Huntington, *The Clash of Civilizations and the Remaking of World Order* (New York: Simon & Schuster, 1996).
26. See Samuel P. Huntington, *The Third Wave: Democratization in the Late Twentieth Century* (Norman: University of Oklahoma Press, 1991).

of the discovery of vaccines against smallpox and polio. What is disturbing, especially in the last few years, is that theological pundits have credited younger generations of Catholics with having a detached or even skeptical view of Vatican II that symbolizes polarization, culture wars, and division in the Church—something the young people allegedly feel the need to distance themselves from, as if the common ground they seek could only be a ground as distant as possible from Vatican II.

The invasion and spread of the simplistic distinction of the polarity between continuity and discontinuity in the ecclesial debate is certainly one of the most disturbing elements of today's scenario.[27] The subtext of this sharpened distinction and opposition between continuity and discontinuity is not only a mutual exclusivity of the two parts of the expression but also the implication of the catholicity of continuity and the "un-catholicity" of discontinuity and change in the Church.

The identification of Vatican II with "continuity with the tradition" in opposition to "discontinuity and rupture" is probably the most serious challenge for the correct understanding and reception of the council in the Church today. This challenge has become possible in an ecclesial environment where the debate seems more and more inclined to shift toward an institutional hermeneutic of the council, in which the issue of the juridical authority in the Church trumps the issue of the authority of the ecumenical council.[28]

---

27. See, for example, Matthew L. Lamb and Matthew Levering, eds., *Vatican II: Renewal within Tradition* (New York: Oxford University Press, 2008).

28. See François Nault, "Comment parler des textes conciliaires sans les avoir lus?," in Routhier and Jobin, *L'autorité et les autorités*, 229–46.

4. The Vision of Vatican II beyond the Narratives

An ever-present temptation of the scholars of Vatican II is the instinct to play the "guardians of the temple," especially when the generation of the bishops, theologians, and Catholics who made Vatican II is fading away. But there is a reason to continue the research on the history and the theology of the council. The current clash of narratives on Vatican II cannot transport an intellectual disputation between theologians animated by pastoral concerns onto a pundit-dominated stage, where sound bites and catchphrases substitute for real concern for the issues surrounding knowing, understanding, interpreting, and receiving the council.

The clash of narratives on Vatican II that tends to identify Vatican II with the sixties has somehow pushed the council itself into the background. But in fact, there is a vision of Vatican II that goes beyond the disputation about the narratives on the council. Our view of Vatican II cannot be distracted by the ongoing clash of narratives, especially when we know that between the various narratives and the serious historiographical work on Vatican II, there is a gap that makes the different positions often unable to understand each other.

What remains is the vision of Vatican II—a vision that is complex, as complex as the analysis of the corpus of the final documents of Vatican II.[29] The effort to form a vision becomes helpless when it is detached from an understanding of their historical developments. It is now time to offer here a few insights based on an intertextual and intratextual interpretation of the documents in light of the history of the event Vatican II.[30]

29. See Hans Jochen Hilberath and Peter Hünermann, eds., *Herders Theologischer Kommentar zum Zweiten Vatikanischen Konzil* (Freiburg i.B.: Herder, 2004–05).

30. About the development of the debate, see Massimo Faggioli, "Concilio Vaticano II: Bollettino bibliografico (2000–2002)," *Cristianesimo nella Storia* 24, no. 2 (2003): 335–60; "Concilio Vaticano II: Bollettino bibliografico (2002–2005)," *Cristianesimo nella Storia* 26, no. 3 (2005): 743–67; "Council Vatican II: Bibliographical Overview 2005–2007," *Cristianesimo nella Storia*

5. Vertical and Horizontal in Vatican II

In a recent two-volume work, the German-French Jesuit Christoph Theobald has described the documents of Vatican II as bidirectional, having a vertical axis and a horizontal axis that fundamentally represent the overall vision of the council.[31] The vertical axis of all the major documents of Vatican II represents a spiritual dimension, and the horizontal axis is their social dimension. But some of the final documents have the function of expanding the global message of the council in one direction or the other.

The key documents building the vertical axis are the Dogmatic Constitution on Divine Revelation *Dei Verbum*, the pastoral constitution *Gaudium et Spes*, and the declaration on religious freedom, *Dignitatis Humanae*. Thanks to these three documents, says Theobald, the Church can once again "have access to the source," that is, the revelation in God's word. In this sense, the vision of Vatican II is essentially *ressourcement*, the quest for a new access to the same source but after a hermeneutical reframing (recadrage) of Catholic theology in light of a Church in transition from its European and Western paradigm toward the paradigm of a world or global Catholicism, after the first transition from Christianity as a Jewish religion to a Hellenistic-Mediterranean religion in the first centuries. The vertical axis of the vision of Vatican II cannot survive without a deep understanding of the new cultural geography of Catholicism. Vatican II, the first global-ecumenical council, assumes this new paradigm starting from the very identity of its participants.

29, no. 2 (2008): 567–610; "Council Vatican II: Bibliographical Overview 2007–2010," *Cristianesimo nella Storia* 32, no. 2 (2011): 755–91; "Council Vatican II: Bibliographical Survey 2010–2013," *Cristianesimo nella Storia* 34, no. 3 (2013): 927–55.
31. See Christoph Theobald, *La réception du concile Vatican II*, vol. 1, Accéder à la source (Paris: Cerf, 2009).

The vertical axis means, for access to the Bible and the tradition, a new emphasis away from *revelation as instruction* and toward *revelation as communication*, the involvement of all the Church members in bringing the Scripture into the life of the Church, and a necessary role of reception also for the paradosis, the transmission of the Scripture. The same vertical axis means, for the relationship between Church and world, an acute awareness of the signs of the times and the need for the Church and every Christian to discern and make a decision, thus calling every Christian to the need to look at the climate he or she lives in, and to seek truth as the reason for the right to religious freedom in light of the revelation.

The second dimension is the horizontal axis built by the council documents. This horizontal dimension gives foundation to the reframing operated by Vatican II and that constitutes the vision of Vatican II as a new relational understanding of the Church. This relational dimension of the Church grounds the ecclesiology of Vatican II after the era of apologetics and of hierarchical idolatry or, in Yves Congar's words, "hierarchology" (*Lumen Gentium*), builds the pastoral and missionary dimension of the Church (*Gaudium et Spes* and *Ad Gentes*), its ecumenical and interreligious dimensions (*Unitatis Redintegratio* and *Nostra Aetate*), and the liturgy according to *Sacrosanctum Concilium* as the center of Christian life and of the Church in its local realization. Communication with God is nothing if it is not reflected in a human way of communicating and relating horizontally. The two ecclesiological constitutions and *Nostra Aetate* give theological expression to this horizontal orientation: ecumenism, interreligious relations, the Old Testament and the relations with the Jews, atheism, and modern culture.

For Theobald, the vertical and horizontal dimensions of the council documents meet in the ecclesiology of Vatican II, especially in *Lumen Gentium*. Mission and conversion of the Church in the pilgrimage of the people of God does not identify itself statically with the Church of Christ, but needs constant reform (the subsistit in, "subsists in" of *Lumen Gentium* 8). The ecumenical dimension, institutional framework of the Church, and its eschatological orientation lived in the liturgy build the connection between the two axes.[32]

6. *Ressourcement* and *Rapprochement*

Crossing the paths of the different council documents, we can identify another couple of ideas that are crucial and common to the message of Vatican II: *ressourcement* and *rapprochement*.

The idea of *ressourcement* is at the heart of the constitutions on revelation and on liturgy. The idea of *ressourcement* drives Catholic theology to the rediscovery of the first source of the Christian message—Scripture—and of the early sources of an undivided Christianity: Tradition (with a capital *T*), the fathers of the Church, and liturgy. *Ressourcement* wanted to give back to the fathers of the Church the influence that they had had in the education of the leadership of Catholicism and that had been lost in favor of neo-scholastic theology and also had become suspected of modernistic heresy at the beginning of the twentieth century.[33]

Ressourcement puts at the center of theology what needs to be at the center, and it reorganizes everything else with a compass that uses the category of "historicity" in theology in order to make theology free from history and at the same time more faithful to a Tradition dynamically understood. The idea of development in theology thus

---

32. Ibid., 1:476–82.
33. About this shift in theology between the nineteenth and the twentieth centuries, see also Avery Dulles, *Models of Revelation* (New York: Doubleday, 1983), 36–67.

finds itself not automatically excommunicated or blessed, but examined in light of the development's coherence with the very sources of theology and theology's main operating principle, the pastoral character of the doctrine, *salus animarum* (the salvation of souls).

In this sense, Vatican II is an event not only for what it accomplished, but also for what it decided to reject. For example, the council fathers did not accept the early proposals coming from some European bishops aiming at giving Catholics not the Bible, but a purified and selective collection of biblical texts, an anthology with only selected and untroubling passages from a few books of the Bible. Vatican II decided not only to put the Scripture back into the hands of the faithful, but also to draw the epistemological consequences of this decision for the whole balance of Catholic theology.[34]

Liberating theology and the faithful from the shadow of the suspicion of antibiblicism is today an almost forgotten fact, especially in European Catholicism, as is forgotten the accomplishment of the liturgical reform as the most important reform in Roman Catholicism in the last five centuries.[35] The idea of liturgy as a source for Christian theology and Christian life made that reform as important back then as it is controversial in some Catholic quarters. It is thus clear that belittling its accomplishments is possible only if we forget the role of liturgy in Catholic theology in the twentieth century, before the council and after the council.[36]

Along with *ressourcement*, the second crucial idea of Vatican II is *rapprochement*—re-approaching, reaching out, and reconciliation. The

34. About this, see Riccardo Burigana, *La Bibbia nel concilio: La redazione della constituzione "Dei Verbum" del Vaticano II* (Bologna: Il Mulino, 1998).

35. About this, see Massimo Faggioli, *True Reform: Liturgy and Ecclesiology in Sacrosanctum Concilium* (Collegeville, MN: Liturgical, 2012).

36. See Andrea Grillo, *La nascita della liturgia nel XX secolo: Saggio sul rapporto tra movimento liturgico e (post–) modernità* (Assisi: Cittadella, 2003).

idea of *rapprochement* is at the core of the very idea of calling an ecumenical council after World War II. The watershed of the two world wars called Church leaders and theologians, very early on, to make a shift toward a theology and a Church that could contribute to the idea of a fundamental unity of humankind. One of the main aims of the council announced by John XXIII was to summon the Church and celebrate its unity in a new relationship with the outer world.[37] But Vatican II was meant to be a "celebration" in the most profound liturgical sense:[38] not a mere display of false unanimity, but a living experience of communion within the Church and with the world through the interaction of different cultural sensibilities, historical backgrounds, and theological orientations.

The liturgical movement and the theology of Vatican II reflected the impact of the dialogical principle in twentieth-century Western philosophy: Husserl, Buber, Levinas, and Gadamer.[39] The liturgical reform expressed the deep theological aspiration of the Church to shape itself in the form of Jesus as "the universal brother of all human beings, who died for all men without exception" (le Frère universel de tous les humains; mort pour tous les hommes sans exception), in the words of Charles de Foucauld (1858–1916), a French Catholic religious and priest living among the Tuareg in the Sahara in Algeria.

Vatican II continued the tradition of unity expressed through liturgy, but through an understanding of *rapprochement* that expressed more clearly the attempt of Vatican II to make of the Church "a sacrament of reconciliation" for humankind.[40] The idea of *rapprochement*, a term used many times by the pioneer of ecumenism

37. For the fundamental idea of "unity" related to Vatican II, see John XXIII, *encyclical Ad Petri Cathedram*, June 29, 1959; and John XXIII, opening speech of Vatican II, *Gaudet Mater Ecclesia*, October 11, 1962.
38. See Giuseppe Alberigo, "Sinodo come liturgia?," *Cristianesimo nella storia* 28, no. 1 (2007): 1–40.
39. See Werner Stegmaier, "Heimsuchung: Das Dialogische in der Philosophie des 20. Jahrhunderts," in *Dialog als Selbstvollzug der Kirche?*, ed. Gebhard Fürst (Freiburg i.B.: Herder, 1997), 9–29.

and liturgist Dom Lambert Beauduin,[41] is not part of the corpus of Vatican II in a material way, but it belongs fully to the aims of Vatican II. *Rapprochement* in the theology of Vatican II means seeking a new unity among peoples, nations, and cultures (in the constitution *Gaudium et Spes*), among different religions and faiths (in the declaration *Nostra Aetate*), among Christian churches (in the decree on ecumenism *Unitatis Redintegratio*), and within the Catholic Church (constitutions on the liturgy *Sacrosanctum Concilium* and on the Church *Lumen Gentium*)—and above all, *rapprochement* with God through a renewed understanding and practice of the sacraments.[42] In John O'Malley's words, if the Church of Vatican II is visible through its new "style," much of its style is represented by *rapprochement* as the style of the Church,[43] as the end of the era of polemical apologetics as the only proof of catholicity.

7. Church and World in the Twenty-First Century

In evaluating the vision of Vatican II, we must always consider the temptation to take one specific period of the history of the Church as the "golden age." On another anniversary of Vatican II, the twentieth anniversary in 1982, the theologian of the council, Marie-Dominique

---

40. See Peter Smulders, "La Chiesa sacramento della salvezza," in *La Chiesa del Vaticano II: Studi e commenti intorno alla Costituzione dommatica Lumen gentium*, ed. Guilherme Barauna (Florence: Vallecchi, 1965), 363–86; and Jan L. Witte, "La Chiesa 'sacramentum unitatis' del cosmo e del genere umano," in Barauna, *La Chiesa del Vaticano II*, 491–521. For the use of "sacramentum" in the ecclesiological debate at Vatican II, see Daniele Gianotti, *I Padri della Chiesa al concilio Vaticano II: La teologia patristica nella* Lumen Gentium (Bologna: EDB, 2010).

41. See Raymond Loonbeek and Jacques Mortiau, *Un pionnier, Dom Lambert Beauduin (1873–1960): Liturgie et unité des chrétiens* (Louvain-la-Neuve: Collège Érasme, 2001), 1:907–9. See also Jacques Mortiau and Raymond Loonbeek, *Dom Lambert Beauduin visionnaire et précurseur (1873–1960): Un moine au coeur libre* (Paris: Cerf, 2005).

42. About this, see Peter Hünermann, "Kriterien für die Rezeption des II. Vatikanischen Konzils," *Theologische Quartalschrift* 191, no. 2 (2011): 126–47.

43. See O'Malley, *What Happened at Vatican II*, 305–7.

Chenu, OP, reminded us, "Vatican II produced texts so rich that their application went necessarily beyond the letter of the texts."[44] This was true not only of Vatican II, but also of the Council of Trent, and reminds us that whatever the clash of interpretations about Vatican II will bring us, much of what Vatican II was has become reality in the Catholic Church. Much has been done; much still needs to be done; its major accomplishments cannot be undone anymore.

For the few anti–Vatican II Catholics, the council carries the guilt of having put to an end the "golden age" of a religion that in their mind was righteously and healthily reluctant to engage with modernity. The price for that golden age of intellectual stability and moral certainty was a sense of self-righteousness that came from a staunch opposition to a "world" metaphysically understood and seen as necessarily evil, though in a political and counterrevolutionary sense more than in a Paulinian understanding of the relationship between the Christian and the danger of "conforming to the mentality of this world" (Rom. 12:2).

On the other side, in some quarters of more liberal Catholicism, the simple mention of Vatican II triggers a "veterans' sentimentality" of the ones who were there or who had seen that moment and think it is gone. They feel that such a golden age was too brief and too good to last, and that it has been betrayed because this is what always happens in the Catholic Church. Their sociological approach to Vatican II as a purely cultural event sometimes takes for granted the theological value of the council.

Both perspectives are not only too pessimistic; they also miss one of the major points of Vatican II, which was exactly the rejection of the idea of a golden age in history. For all of the council's theological appreciation of history and historicity as sources for theology, the

44. Marie-Dominique Chenu, "Un concile prophétique," *Le Monde*, October 12, 1982.

only golden age Vatican II had in mind was the one of the gospel, which we can approach theologically through *ressourcement*. Fidelity to the gospel, not to a golden age (whenever that age was), is one of the key ideas of the council as an event of a world church. This reorientation of Catholic theology entails a new relationship to the idea of culture and makes of Vatican II a countercultural council, if only for the refusal of Catholicism either to reduce itself to a "culture" or to tie itself to a historically connoted culture.[45]

This is what makes Vatican II a true compass (as is written in the spiritual testament of John Paul II) for the future of the Church:

> As I stand on the threshold of the Third Millennium "in medio Ecclesiae," I would like once again to express my gratitude to the Holy Spirit for the great gift of the Second Vatican Council, to which, together with the whole Church—and especially with the whole Episcopate—I feel indebted. I am convinced that it will long be granted to the new generations to draw from the treasures that this 20th-century Council has lavished upon us. As a Bishop who took part in the Council from the first to the last day, I desire to entrust this great patrimony to all who are and will be called in the future to put it into practice.[46]

On a world map whose visible and invisible boundaries have significantly shifted in the last fifty years, Catholicism can call itself a world church because of its new freedom received by the council in terms of relationship between theology and cultures.

The vision of Vatican II is crucial not only for the survival of the Church in the age of the culture wars, but also for the viability of theology in modernity. On one side, clearly long overdue were the shifts about biblical hermeneutics, theology and modern science, interreligious and the ecumenical dialogue. On the other side, for other theological issues, Vatican II opened a path toward the future

---

45. See O'Malley, *What Happened at Vatican II*, 311.
46. "Testament of the Holy Father John Paul II," available at the Holy See website, http://www.vatican.va/gpII/documents/testamento-jp-ii_20050407_en.html.

of the Church: a more communional and less juridical ecclesiology, a new understanding of the relationship between laity and ministry, and Church reform.

It is thus clear that Vatican II was not only a "reform council," but also a "paradigmatic event" for the life of the Church and its inner vitality.[47] The aggiornamento, the bringing up to date of Catholic theology represents still today an example of both courage and foresight, in the way these reforms were debated and decided. Vatican II is the latest, not the last, moment of representation of conciliarity in the Church and a testimony of the link between conciliarity and reform.[48]

With Vatican II and after Vatican II, the theological reflection has rediscovered synodality and conciliarity as basic features of Christianity, Catholicism included. The council has once again demonstrated that nineteenth-century ultramontanism was a phenomenon typical of the siege mentality that shaped Catholicism in the long nineteenth century, and that conciliarity and collegiality are processes, not just one-time events. Vatican II reminds us that councils and synods are the places and moments par excellence where Christian churches have reached an ecclesial consensus in matters of faith and discipline in particular moments of their history.[49]

Secondly, in its paradigmatic character, Vatican II is shaping Catholic theology so that theology after Vatican II need not limit itself to a "theology of the interpretation of Vatican II."[50] This is

---

47. See Boeve, "'La vraie réception de Vatican II n'a pas encore commencé': Joseph Ratzinger, Révélation et autorité de Vatican II."

48. See Giuseppe Alberigo, "Concili e rappresentanza," in *Repraesentatio: Mapping a Keyword for Churches and Governance*, ed. Massimo Faggioli and Alberto Melloni (Berlin: LIT, 2006), 99–124.

49. See Alberto Melloni and Silvia Scatena, eds., *Synod and Synodality: Theology, History, Canon Law and Ecumenism in New Contact* (Münster: LIT, 2005).

50. See Laurent Villemin, "L'herméneutique de Vatican II: Enjeux d'avenir," in *Vatican II et la théologie*, ed. Philippe Bordeyne et Laurent Villemin (Paris: Cerf, 2006), 247–62.

where the current battle fought in some quarters for the meaning of Vatican II reveals its futility. Vatican II is essential for the Church because the council is not about itself, but rather is about recentering theology in the very roots of the Christian revelation without losing sight of the signs of our times.

It is no surprise that many of the new features of the Catholic Church after Vatican II surpassed the letter of the council documents; this is true both for the liberal and the conservative interpretation of the council. This also reveals one of the key aspects of the vision of Vatican II, the real common ground of Catholicism in an ideologically polarized era: the fundamental shift from the Church as an institution to the Church as a movement, in which the "new Catholic movements" are only one visible face of the new dimensions of being Church.[51]

This is where the vision of Vatican II becomes movement. Vision with no movement is destined to remain private; a movement with no vision is simply a physical phenomenon. The vision of Vatican II has changed the Church, and the new feature of the Church as a movement is nothing less than undeniable evidence of the many fruits of the council.

---

51. See Massimo Faggioli, *Breve storia dei movimenti cattolici* (Rome: Carocci, 2008). English expanded edition: *Sorting Out Catholicism: A Brief History of the New Ecclesial Movements*, trans. Demetrio S. Yocum, (Collegeville, MN: Liturgical, 2014).

PART IV

A Council for the Global Church

14

Catholicism

From a European Church to Global Catholicism

The relevance of Christianity for Europe[1] goes far beyond the scarce figure of the European churchgoer in comparison with the "desperately godly" America on one side and the secularization of culture, schools, and the media in Europe on the other.[2] One of the ironies of the contemporary discourse on religion is the fact that businesspeople seem to believe in the future of European Christianity much more than European theologians and European Christians do.[3] But the fact is that European Christianity, particularly European

---

1. This chapter was published originally as "Europe and the Modern World in the Catholic Narrative during the 1960's: Migration, Decolonization and De-Europeanization," in *The Heart of Europe: The Power of Faith, Vision and Belonging in European Unification*, ed. Katharina Kunter (Hannover: Wehrhahn, 2011), 127–39.
2. See George Weigel, *The Cube and the Cathedral: Europe, America, and Politics without God* (New York: Basic, 2005); and Grace Davie, *Europe: The Exceptional Case; Parameters of Faith in the Modern World* (New York: Orbis, 2002).
3. See John Micklethwait and Adrian Wooldridge, *God Is Back: How the Global Revival of Faith Is Changing the World* (New York: Penguin, 2009). Micklethwait and Wooldridge, both journalists for *The Economist*, forecast that the American model of Christianity will have a future influence on Europe.

Catholicism, still has to absorb the epochal changes that happened in the cultural features of the Christian faith in Europe in the 1960s. So far, the debate has been influenced by ideological and generational factors that are now much less relevant and decisive for a real understanding of the issue at stake.

Given the focus in the public debate on the sociologically and politically immediate impact of the development of secularization, few have tried to elaborate the relationships between Europe, religious traditions, and Catholicism in the twentieth century from a historical, and not theological-political, point of view.[4] But not looking at Christianity and Catholicism from a historical perspective is a secure recipe for intellectual disaster. Accordingly, it is time to summarize and analyze, from the beginning of the changes that took place around the 1960s,[5] some developments in Europe's role in the self-characterization of the Church with respect to its broader cultural heritage, its theological tradition, and its political and diplomatic orientation.

1. The New Frontiers of Catholic Culture

In many respects, the twentieth century has been for Catholicism the first century of its "catholicity"—save for the *Entgrenzung*, the un-limitation of Christianity to Jewish culture conducted by the apostle Paul.[6] The time when the cradle of Catholic theology, culture, and leadership was geographically located and ideologically locked in

---

4. On the other side, see Hans G. Kippenberg, Jörg Rüpke, and Kocku von Stuckrad, eds., *Europäische Religionsgeschichte: Ein mehrfacher Pluralismus* (Göttingen: Vandenhoeck & Ruprecht, 2009).

5. Notwithstanding the deconstructionist view of the 1960s offered recently by Gerard J. DeGroot, *The Sixties Unplugged: A Kaleidoscopic History of a Disorderly Decade* (Cambridge, MA: Harvard University Press, 2008).

6. See Giuseppe Alberigo, "Il concilio Vaticano II e le trasformazioni culturali in Europa," in *Transizione epocale: Studi sul Vaticano II* (Bologna: Il Mulino, 2009), 601–27.

continental Europe seems far away. From the Greek *logos* to medieval Thomism and neo-Thomism, the intellectual history of Catholicism is simply unthinkable without the contribution, or better, "monopoly" of the Old Continent. It comes as no surprise that for all the ecumenical councils from the eleventh century to the First Vatican Council (1869–1870), the representation of non-European bishops was limited to a small attendance in terms of non-European Catholic Churches represented as well for their relevance to the agenda of the council.

Nevertheless, things changed soon after Vatican I. A few years before the "modernist crisis," at the beginning of the twentieth century, the impact of the soon-condemned "Americanism" left footprints deeper than usually believed.[7] The change in the culture of Catholicism was not just a matter of secularization in Europe having lost its grip on the Roman Catholic tradition. There is no doubt that the materialistic and consumerist culture of post–World War II Europe left its mark on the self-representation of Catholic Europe, but the roots of cultural change are to be found elsewhere.

On one side, the official philosophy of European Catholicism, Thomism, underwent a major transformation from the beginning of the twentieth century and gave birth to the passage from neo-scholasticism to post–Scholastic Thomism.[8] On the other side, the terrible experiences of the two Europe-centered world wars came to full maturation in the sixties, when the generation of Catholics born at the beginning of the century understood the impact of European culture on Catholicism and vice versa.[9]

---

7. See the classic work by Thomas McAvoy, *The Great Crisis in American Catholic History, 1895–1900* (Chicago: University of Chicago Press, 1957).

8. See Gerald McCool, *From Unity to Pluralism: The Internal Evolution of Thomism* (New York: Fordham University Press, 1989).

9. See Yves Congar, *Journal de la Guerre 1914–1918*, annotated and commented on by Stéphane Audoin-Rouzeau and Dominique Congar (Paris: Cerf, 1997); Marie-Claude Flageat, *Les Jésuites français dans la Grande Guerre: Témoins, victimes, héros, apôtres* (Paris: Cerf, 2008).

The influence of the major cultural shift of European Catholicism's theological and philosophical culture signaled a particularly deep change in French- and German-speaking Catholic theology. The acceptance of human sciences in the "canon" of Catholic culture—which had been countered by a merciless repression by the Vatican anti-modernist campaign at the beginning of the century—bore fruit between the end of World War II and the late sixties. European theologians such as Yves Congar, Marie-Dominique Chenu, and Edward Schillebeeckx (Dominican theologians who had survived the pre–Vatican II repression against the "new theology" and the internal struggle about the approach to Thomism that had started in the 1940s) and the Jesuit Karl Rahner shared a fundamentally Thomistic epistemology and openness to the modern world. During the first session of Vatican II, Congar visited southern Italy, not far from Aquinas's place of birth, and entered in his journal, "What I saw explained to me how it was that St. Thomas paid so much attention to the Arabs, to the *Gentiles*. I perceived St. Thomas *filled with an extremely open and active attention* to the world which surrounded him. He experienced there a perceptible revelation of a whole world of great culture."[10] Rahner did not see the necessity of a change in the relationship between theology and philosophy, but rather the need of a change in the cultural identity of philosophy: "The West need not abandon its own synthesis of theology and philosophy in favour of an attempt to hand on the, as it were, naked message of Christianity without the so-called 'overlay' of Western philosophy. . . . This does not mean, however, that the Western world should be allowed to extend its traditional philosophy in a traditional way into a world-philosophy."[11]

10. Yves Congar, *My Journal of the Council*, trans. Mary John Ronayne, OP, and Mary Cecily Boulding, OP, ed. Denis Minns, OP (Collegeville, MN: Liturgical, 2012), entry of December 9, 1962, p. 248 (emphasis in Congar's text), orig. pub. as *Mon journal du concile*, ed. Éric Mahieu (Paris: Cerf, 2002).

The image of an immutable Catholicism as *societas perfecta* (a perfect institution) made room for a growing awareness of the historical dimension of the Christian tradition, not only in French theology but also in German Catholicism,[12] and for the need to rediscover the history of the Catholic Church, that is, what really happened (*wie es eigentlich gewesen ist*).[13] The sociological need for an understanding of religion as a social phenomenon became more accepted also in the Catholic intellectual milieu,[14] and Catholic thought became more familiar with the new area of religious studies, called in German *Religionswissenschaften*—the sciences of religion.[15] European Catholicism's encounter with the plurality of religious experiences was extremely different from the diversity of the religious and cultural landscape of America,[16] but pluralism passed anyway from being observed from an exotic and colonialist point of view and began being part of Catholic culture and education.[17]

11. Karl Rahner, "Philosophy and Theology," in *Theological Investigations*, vol. 6, *Concerning Vatican II* (London: Darton, Longman & Todd; New York: Seabury, 1974), 79–80.

12. See, for example, *Zeitgeschichtliche Katholizismusforschung: Tatsachen, Deutungen, Fragen; Eine Zwischenbilanz*, ed. Karl-Joseph Hummel (Paderborn: Schöning, 2004); Étienne Fouilloux, "Histoire et sociologie religieuse en France depuis un siècle," in *Religious Studies in the 20th Century: A Survey on Disciplines, Cultures and Questions*, ed. Massimo Faggioli and Alberto Melloni (Berlin: LIT, 2007), 197–218.

13. It is helpful to remember the shock caused by Hubert Jedin's four-volume *Geschichte des Konzils von Trient* (Freiburg i.B.: Herder 1950–75) and by the early-1960s essays by Ernst Wolfgang Böckenförde, republished in *Kirche und christlicher Glaube in den Herausforderungen der Zeit: Beiträge zur politisch-theologischen Verfassungsgeschichte 1957–2002* (Münster: LIT, 2003).

14. See Benjamin Ziemann, *Katholische Kirche und Sozialwissenschaften 1945–1975* (Göttingen: Vandenhoeck & Ruprecht, 2007); Henri Godin and Yvan Daniel, *La France, pays de mission?* (Paris: Cerf, 1943); and the pioneering work of Fernand Boulard, *An Introduction to Religious Sociology: Pioneer Work in France*, preface by Gabriel Le Bras (London: Darton, Longman and Todd, 1960), orig. pub. as *Premiers itinéraires en sociologie religieuse* (Paris: Éditions ouvrières, 1954).

15. See Hans G. Kippenberg, *Die Entdeckung der Religionsgeschichte: Religionswissenschaft und Moderne* (Munich: Beck, 1997).

16. See, for example, John Courtney Murray, "E Pluribus Unum: The American Consensus," in *We Hold These Truths: Catholic Reflections on the American Proposition* (Lanham, MD: Rowman and Littlefield, 2005), 43–58.

17. See, for example, Franz König (Archbishop of Wien, 1956–1985), ed., *Religionswissenschaftliches Wörterbuch: Die Grundbegriffe* (Freiburg i.B.: Herder, 1956).

2. Between *Ressourcement* and *Nouvelle Théologie*

A decisive element of the passage from a heavily European Catholicism toward a "world Catholicism" was the contribution of the "revival movements" in the first decades of the twentieth century. The biblical movement, the patristic revival and *ressourcement*, and the ecumenical movement based in Europe and North America had survived the modernist crisis at the beginning of the twentieth century[18] and the condemnations of Pius XII and had managed to bring to the fathers and theologian-experts of Vatican II the core of their historical-theological reflections for the renewal of the Catholic Church.[19]

The biblical revival introduced into the Catholic Church the drive for direct access to the Bible for every faithful person.[20] The liturgical renewal stressed the need to reset the balance of the life of the Church around the liturgy and to renew the liturgical language in order to strengthen spiritual life also through a development of the principle of "adaptation" to and "inculturation" with the local cultures of the individual Catholic churches.[21] The ecumenical movement had suffered some severe setbacks from Rome from the 1920s on, but at the local level, it had slowly broken the taboo of official relations between Catholics, Protestants, and Orthodox Christians.[22]

---

18. See Emile Poulat, *Histoire, dogme et critique dans la crise moderniste* (Paris: Casterman, 1962).

19. About the Catholic movements, see Massimo Faggioli, *Breve storia dei movimenti cattolici* (Rome: Carocci, 2008), trans. Demetrio S. Yocum as *Sorting Out Catholicism. A Brief History of the New Ecclesial Movements* (Collegeville, MN: Liturgical, 2014).

20. See Riccardo Burigana, *La Bibbia nel concilio: La redazione della constituzione "Dei Verbum" del Vaticano II* (Bologna: Il Mulino, 1998); François Laplanche, *La crise de l'origine: La science catholique des Évangiles et l'histoire au XXe siècle* (Paris: Albin Michel, 2006); Bernard Montagnes, *Père Lagrange, 1855–1938: The Story of Father Marie-Joseph Lagrange, Founder of Modern Catholic Bible Study* (New York: Paulist, 2006), orig. pub. as *Marie-Joseph Lagrange: Une biographie critique* (Paris: Cerf, 2005).

21. See Annibale Bugnini, *The Reform of the Liturgy, 1948–1975* (Collegeville, MN: Liturgical, 1990); Maria Paiano, *Liturgia e società nel Novecento: Percorsi del movimento liturgico di fronte ai processi di secolarizzazione* (Rome: Edizioni di Storia e Letteratura, 2000).

The patristic renewal had advocated the return to the great tradition of the fathers of the Church (Latin and Greek fathers), prior to European Christendom and the myth of a Catholicism necessarily European from a theological point of view.[23]

The Catholic Church thus arrived at the end of Pius XII's pontificate and the eve of Vatican II in a complex situation. An extremely Rome-centered and Curia-controlled theology was officially still based on neoscholastic guidelines for its theological and spiritual identity, but the so-called revival or renewal movements somehow independent from the "traditional" Catholic culture were gaining audience in the theological and ecclesiastical milieu. These revival movements directly or indirectly contributed to the council debate on ecclesiology, which became the main issue debated at Vatican II. The passage from a juridical ecclesiology (according to which the Church is "juridically a perfect institution") to a more spiritual ecclesiology (the Church as "mystical body of Christ") also marked the end of the dominance of Canon Law (heavily influenced by the juridical tradition of the Roman Empire)[24] and of the way Catholicism conceived itself as an institution.[25]

After the condemnation of *nouvelle thèologie* and Pius XII's silencing of the major Catholic theologians in 1950 through the encyclical *Humani Generis*, the encounters between European Catholicism and the humanities unfolded and contributed to the development and recognition of that same "new theology" in the wake of the Second Vatican Council (1962–1965).[26] In this major

22. See Étienne Fouilloux, *Les catholiques et l'unité chrétienne du XIXe au XXe siècle: Itinéraires européens d'expression française* (Paris: Centurion, 1982); and Mauro Velati, *Una difficile transizione: Il cattolicesimo tra unionismo ed ecumenismo (1952–1964)* (Bologna: Il Mulino, 1996).

23. See Étienne Fouilloux, *La Collection "Sources chrétiennes": Editer les Pères de l'Eglise au XXe siècle* (Paris: Cerf, 1995).

24. On the new awareness of the role of Roman law in the history of the institutions of the Western Church, see Jean Gaudemet, *L'Église dans l'Empire Romain (IVe–Ve siècles)* (Paris: Sirey, 1958).

25. See Otto Semmelroth, *Die Kirche als Ursakrament* (Frankfurt a.M.: Knecht, 1953).

event, the relationship between Catholicism and Europe changed through a theological development of some of the cultural movements Catholicism received and acquired.[27]

Between 1962 and 1965, Vatican II assembled for the first time twenty-five hundred bishops and hundreds of theologians from all over the world, representatives of a Church that had begun to shape itself not long before as a "world church" from a cultural and theological point of view. The new ecclesiology summarized other theological developments in the de-Europeanization of Catholicism immediately before and around Vatican II, such as the new impact of missions on the body of Catholicism. Once perceived as mere recipients of a theology "exported" from Europe, the mission churches located in Latin America, Africa, and Asia became far more active in proposing different, and not less but more "catholic" (universal), religious practices and theological insights. This process occurred with the beginning of decolonization, gradually severing the churches' ties with the colonizing Western empires and their heirs.[28]

The idea of the Church as a "world Church," according to Karl Rahner's definition,[29] gradually became a manifest for Vatican II Roman Catholicism. It implied not only a different relationship with

26. See Étienne Fouilloux, *Une Église en quête de liberté: La pensée catholique française entre modernisme et Vatican II (1914–1962)* (Paris: Desclée de Brouwer, 1998); Giuseppe Alberigo, ed., *History of Vatican II*, 5 vols., English version ed. Joseph A. Komonchak (Maryknoll, NY: Orbis, 1995–2006).

27. See John W. O'Malley, *What Happened at Vatican II* (Cambridge, MA: Belknap Press of Harvard University Press, 2008), 53–92.

28. See Samuel P. Huntington, *The Third Wave: Democratization in the Late Twentieth Century* (Norman: University of Oklahoma Press, 1991); Adrian Hastings, *The Church in Africa: 1450–1950* (Oxford: Clarendon; New York: Oxford University Press, 1994); Jean Comby, ed., *Diffusion et acculturation du christianisme (XIXe-XXe siècles): Vingt-cinq ans de recherches missiologiques par le CREDIC* (Paris: Karthala, 2005).

29. See Karl Rahner, "Der Welt der Weltkirche: Die dritte Epoche der Kirchengeschichte hat begonnen," in Karl Rahner, *Horizonte der Religiosität: Kleine Aufsätze*, ed. Georg Sporschill (Vienna: Herold, 1984), 119–23.

the different cultures of Catholicism and with other churches born in Christian Europe, but also a new relationship with non-Christian religions and with those parts of the world dominated by ideologies and weltanschauungs opposed to Christianity:[30] "In a world increasingly wracked with discord, hatred, war, and threats of war, the result was a message that was counter-cultural while at the same time responsive to the deepest human yearnings. Peace on earth. Good will to men."[31]

3. The Political Cultures of Vatican II: From European Christian-Democratic Parties to a "Global Vatican Diplomacy"

The 1960s hosted a shift also in the European character of political Catholicism. After World War II, the flourishing of Christian-Democratic parties in Western Europe represented a clear break from the post–1789 "intransigent" tradition of European Catholicism toward political democracy, its forms and spirit.[32] But from the very beginning—already during the war[33]—the new attitude toward the development of political Catholicism was also meant, especially by the Vatican, to counter the major threat to the freedom of the West, that is, a Soviet-backed communist expansion in Europe and in

---

30. See Josef Sinkovits and Ulrich Winkler, eds., *Weltkirche und Weltreligionen: Die Brisanz des Zweiten Vatikanischen Konzils 40 Jahre nach Nostra Aetate* (Innsbruck: Tyrolia, 2007); Hans Hermann Henrix, ed., *Nostra aetate—Ein Zukunftsweisender Konzilstext: Die Haltung der Kirche zum Judentum 40 Jahre danach* (Aachen: Einhard, 2006).
31. O'Malley, *What Happened at Vatican II*, 311.
32. See Jean-Marie Mayeur, *Des partis catholiques à la démocratie chrétienne: XIX–XX siècles* (Paris: Colin, 1980); Karl-Egon Lönne, *Politischer Katholizismus im 19. und 20. Jahrhundert* (Frankfurt a.M.: Suhrkamp, 1986).
33. See Peter C. Kent, *The Lonely Cold War of Pope Pius XII: The Roman Catholic Church and the Division of Europe, 1943–1950* (Montreal: McGill University Press; London: Queen's University Press, 2002); Michael Phayer, *Pius XII, the Holocaust, and the Cold War* (Bloomington: Indiana University Press, 2008).

countries that could be allies in pursuing a Communist scenario for the continent.[34] This connection between political Catholicism and anti-communist geopolitics of the Catholic Church peaked in the 1950s.[35] At the beginning of the 1960s, it was already weakened. The death of Pius XII and the election of John XXIII in 1958 on the one hand, and the first steps of the détente by John F. Kennedy and Nikita Khrushchev on the other, represented the end of the short golden age for the dream of a "new European Christendom." The Second Vatican Council concluded the tight connections between the geopolitics of the Western world with the social-political agenda of the Vatican.[36]

The event of Vatican II represented not only a major theological shift but also the beginning of a series of issues for a Western and European geopolitics at odds with the "global agenda" of the Catholic Church. This meant rising tensions between the firm political alliances of the Western European states with the U.S.-led coalition on one side and the strategic option for a Vatican *Ostpolitik*, the diplomatic offensive of the Vatican towards Russia and Communist-ruled Eastern Europe.[37] The involvement of the Catholic Church in the scenario of an East-West relationship assumed a new meaning after Vatican II, making the Church more independent and at the

---

34. See Gerd-Rainer Horn and Emmanuel Gerard, eds., *Left Catholicism 1943–1955: Catholics and Society in Western Europe at the Point of Liberation* (Leuven: Leuven University Press, 2001); Gerd-Rainer Horn, *Western European Liberation Theology: The First Wave (1924–1959)* (Oxford: Oxford University Press, 2008).

35. See Philippe Chenaux, *Une Europe vaticane? Entre le plan Marshall et les traités de Rome* (Brussels: Ciaco, 1990); Wolfram Kaiser, *Christian Democracy and the Origins of European Union* (Cambridge: Cambridge University Press, 2011).

36. See Alberto Melloni, *L'altra Roma: Politica e S. Sede durante il Concilio Vaticano II (1959–1965)* (Bologna: Il Mulino, 2000).

37. See Michael Feldkamp, *Die Beziehungen der Bundesrepublik Deutschland zum Heiligen Stuhl 1949–1966: Aus den Vatikanakten des Auswärtigen Amts* (Cologne: Böhlau, 2000); Andrea Riccardi, *Il Vaticano e Mosca 1940–1990* (Roma-Bari: Laterza, 1992); and Karl-Joseph Hummel, ed., *Vatikanische Ostpolitik unter Johannes XXIII. und Paul VI. 1958–1978* (Paderborn: Schöning, 1999).

same time more conscious of its role for the continent and for the whole world.[38]

In this sense, Vatican II changed the face of Catholicism not only from a cultural point of view, but also from a geopolitical point of view. That is why the much-feared (or in some quarters hoped for) "revision" of the role of Vatican II for the future of Catholicism would imply not only a huge theological issue but also a political issue, in particular for the relationship between the modern world and the Catholic Church, between the new interpretation of the European roots of Christianity and the Catholic Church as a global player. The communist threat also represented an opportunity to rescind geopolitical alliances that tied too tightly the political and cultural destinies of the Catholic Church and the West.[39] This major geopolitical shift in the agenda of the Catholic Church could have not been possible without the cultural and theological changes that blossomed in post–World War II Catholicism and that changed the language of Catholicism in the decade called the sixties.

4. Is European Christianity Over?

Christianity and Catholicism have an extremely complex relationship with Europe. The geopolitical dimension of this relationship is often overlooked by observers of the future of Christianity, but also by its officials, Church leaders, and theologians.

There are no definitive conclusions on the subject of the relationship between Europe and Catholicism in the last half century.

---

38. See Hans-Jakob Stehle, *Die Ostpolitik des Vatikans 1917–1975* (Munich: Piper, 1975); Agostino Casaroli, *Il martirio della pazienza: La Santa Sede e i paesi comunisti (1963–1989)* (Turin: Einaudi, 2000); Jozef Mindszenty, *Erinnerungen* (Frankfurt a.M.: Ullstein, 1974); and Alberto Melloni, ed., *Il filo sottile: L'Ostpolitik vaticana di Agostino Casaroli* (Bologna: Il Mulino, 2006).
39. See Philippe Chenaux, *L'Église catholique et le communisme en Europe (1917–1989): De Lénine à Jean-Paul II* (Paris: Cerf, 2009).

Yet it is well known that the issue of the relevance of Catholicism for the discourse on the "soul of Europe"—its identities, its cultures, its future—could not have been more emphasized in recent years. Especially during the passage from John Paul II to Benedict XVI's pontificate, this relationship has been studied and employed mostly from a geopolitical and statistical standpoint—that is, the future of Catholicism before a secularized Europe, in relation to the demographically growing churches (Catholic and non-Catholic) in Africa and the Americas, and most of all in comparison with Islam.

On the one hand, Europe seemed to be a given in the debate about the future of Catholicism (seemingly a more global and ex-European Catholicism). On the other hand, Catholicism seemed to be a given in the debate about Europe (Catholicism as a relic or a dangerous, unexploded bomb in the heart of the European Union). In fact, in recent years, the public debate on the relationship between Christianity and Europe has been splitting between the advocates of "European Christendom" on one side[40] and the advocates of the "Next Christendom in the Global South" on the other.[41]

Strange as it may sound, beyond the nuances of academic debates, many seem to agree in articulating their view of Europe and Christianity in the recent, pre–Vatican II past. European neoconservatives see it as a golden age, and "globalists" see it as a relic. Reality seems to be much more complex, still developing, and capable of midterm and long-term trends that are right now impossible to detect. Nevertheless, from a historical point of view, it is possible to offer three basic conclusions.

---

40. See Joseph Ratzinger–Benedict XVI and Marcello Pera, *Without Roots: The West, Relativism, Christianity, Islam*, foreword by George Weigel (New York: Basic, 2006).

41. See Philip Jenkins, *The Next Christendom: The Coming of Global Christianity* (Oxford: Oxford University Press, 2002). On the other side, the same Jenkins has argued that "Europe remains a stronger Christian fortress than people realize." Philip Jenkins, "Europe's Christian Comeback," *Foreign Policy*, June 2007, http://www.foreignpolicy.com.

A first conclusion is that, as a matter of fact, Catholicism is still very European, and Europe is still very much influenced by Catholicism—maybe more than Europe is ready to admit. The very geography of the boundaries of the European Union should be telling us something about the *longue durée*, long duration of major trends of Christianity and of Catholicism in the history of Europe. The ecclesiastical institutions of Catholicism (bishops and dioceses, Catholic political parties, Church-controlled associations, pontifical universities, etc.) have always been less relevant and necessary for U.S. Catholics than for European Catholics, so the destiny of American Catholicism is not tied to the fortune of those institutions. That could be true in some measure also for the Catholic part in the soul of Europe. The fact that the institutions of the Catholic Church (bishops, parishes, theological education, Catholic welfare) in Europe have become much weaker than in the past centuries does not mean that Catholicism in Europe is necessarily making its way out of the European scene, given the historical and cultural complexities of Europe as a continent, a market, a political union, and a culture with shared values and common experiences. The question therefore, has more to do with the face of future Christianity and future Catholicism in Europe than with the mere survival of Christianity and Catholicism in Europe.[42]

A second element to consider is that, from the contemporary European perspective, the Second Vatican Council has shown itself to be a guarantee of citizenship for the Catholic Church in today's world. This "guarantee" has been identified in public opinion, with the definitive rejection of anti-Judaism and anti-Semitism as being elements of a premodern and antidemocratic political culture, as well as in the Church's relationship to democratic culture, in appreciation

42. See John L. Allen Jr., *The Future Church: How Ten Trends Are Revolutionizing the Catholic Church* (New York: Doubleday, 2009).

of the modern liberties rejected by Pius IX's *Syllabus* in 1864, in collegiality and co-responsibilities, and in the commitment to ecumenism and interreligious dialogue. Europe is ready to accept the contribution of Catholicism as long as it remains faithful to some "constitutional" elements of Vatican II: religious freedom and freedom of conscience, ecumenism, interreligious dialogue, and collegiality and co-responsibility in church government. (It is no coincidence that these core elements for the council's "political reception" are exactly the ones rejected by the Lefebvrites as the heresies of the council.) This nucleus is not "constitutive" of the rich corpus of Vatican II, but it is "constitutional" because these discontinuities are the new face of Catholicism, not only for Catholics but also for the world at large and Europe especially.[43]

A third element is represented by the need to acknowledge the relationship between the interpretation of the Second Vatican Council and the "politics" of those who by their words and deeds are at the moment interpreting it: theologians, of course, but also lay men and women, politicians, diplomats, intellectuals, and artists. That implies, first of all, an acknowledgment of the need for a serious consideration of the political culture of the council, especially for everyone interested in understanding the potential of Catholicism's contribution to the soul of Europe. The actual mind-set of the leadership of Catholicism seems to be driven by a lack of awareness about the geopolitical and cultural implications of Vatican II for the role of Catholicism in Europe, in the Western Hemisphere, and in the global world. It is clear now that declaring the centrality of the "Christian roots" of Europe is not enough for us to understand the

---

43. On this, see Massimo Faggioli, "Vatican II Comes of Age." *Tablet*, April 11, 2009; and Massimo Faggioli, "Die kulturelle und politische Relevanz des II. Vatikanischen Konzils als konstitutiver Faktor der Interpretation," in *Exkommunikation oder Kommunikation? Der Weg der Kirche nach dem II. Vatikanum und die Pius-Brüder*, ed. Peter Hünermann (Freiburg i.B.: Herder, 2009), 153–74.

complexity of the relationship between the Church and Europe and their possible futures.

15

The Church of Vatican II and the Common Ground

Catholicism and Citizenship

Catholicism carries, by its very name "Catholic," a special responsibility of keeping a sense of unity that is at risk in our times. My experience of a European Catholic who came to America a few years ago made me painfully aware of this risk.[1]

1. Examining the Issue of a "Common Ground" from a European Window

The legacy of Cardinal Joseph Bernardin (1928–1996) is particularly close to the interest of Catholic scholars who study Vatican II and its impact on the relationship between the Catholic Church and the modern world, which is *the* issue of post–Vatican II Catholicism.

---

1. This chapter was originally a lecture delivered for the 14th Joseph Cardinal Bernardin Annual Lecture at the University of South Carolina (Columbia, SC, October 7, 2013).

For anyone looking honestly at the role of the Catholic Common Ground Initiative and at Cardinal Bernardin's leadership in the Church, it is difficult, if not impossible, to make the case that Vatican II really changed nothing in the life and doctrine of the Church, or that Vatican II can be labeled a "liberal sellout" of Catholicism. There is no doubt that Cardinal Bernardin was one of the most representative bishops of the post–Vatican II Church, and he was undoubtedly the most representative North American bishop of the age of Vatican II, akin to what Saint Charles Borromeo of Milan was for Italian Catholicism after the Council of Trent in the sixteenth and seventeenth centuries.

I am trying to address this issue as an Italian citizen who married an American woman, moved to the United States in 2008, and started a family in America. Cardinal Bernardin is one of the great makers of American Catholicism, and I take no little pride when I remember his Italian roots.

The opportunity to address this issue is a great responsibility, because it requires a very delicate balancing act. One must try to keep a scholarly distance from the object—the Catholic Common Ground Initiative and current political cultures—and, at the same time, be faithful to the mission of a theologian to make a responsible contribution to the situation as it is today, both ecclesially and politically. It also necessary for me to maintain a methodologically useful "European perspective" on the issue of the relationship between theology and political discourse, but at the same time not conceal that my perspective has changed and is still evolving because of my experience in the United States and in its scholarly, Catholic, and political communities.

First of all, a few words regarding my European perspective, and I shall begin with my birthplace. I grew up in a region in northern Italy and studied and worked for almost twenty years at the

University of Bologna, my alma mater and the oldest university in Europe, founded in the year 1088. In the second half of the twentieth century, the political landscape of Bologna was representative of many European countries in which the Catholic Church was active in the middle of a political environment split between a strong Communist Party and an equally strong—and explicitly and formally Church-backed—Christian Democratic Party. In this European setting (Italy and Western European in general), not all Catholics voted for the Christian Democratic Party; the percentage of Catholics who were members or voters of the Christian Democratic Party was steadily declining. (Today the "Christian Democratic Party" can be found only in Germany, and it is not completely different from the one that ruled Germany immediately following World War II.)

Political polarization was not reflected in a theological polarization within Catholicism, especially after Vatican II, in any of these European countries. In the political system and cultural environment of the 1960s, when European Catholicism was still the "canon," the standard for world Catholicism, Vatican II represented—especially in Italy—an opening, a kind of thaw that made it possible to build bridges between two different political cultures: the socialist-Marxist and the Catholic social doctrine. These cultures had much in common, at least in the special kind of Communist Party that was the Italian Communist Party, since many of its members and voters were Catholic.

Therefore, it is not difficult to understand why the issue of polarization in different political cultures within American Catholicism is so important for me—as a recent immigrant, a Catholic, and a scholar—in a country where the historical and political experience of Catholicism is so unlike the European one.

2. "Common Ground" and Theological-Political Polarization

The question is whether or not the very idea of a "Catholic common ground" can survive current political cultures. This question presents us with other questions related to the issue of polarization in the Catholic Church and in the political cultures of Catholics. The first question concerns the roots of this polarization: Does a political or a theological fault line divide Catholics? Or are these two fault lines that overlap, making it difficult to tell if political polarization is a reflection of theological polarization, or vice versa?

A second question derives from the first one and concerns the existence of a Catholic common ground: Is there a "Catholic common ground"? Is there a relationship between the shrinking political common ground and the shrinking ecclesial common ground? I am convinced that there is a common ground and that the reason (reason in the sense of *motive*) for the ongoing polarization is not theological, but political. Nevertheless, there are also theological responses to this political polarization, which in my judgment constitute mortal risks for the future of the "catholicity," that is, for the catholic character of Catholicism, and not only for the Common Ground Initiative. As a theologian, I feel called to answer this particular question that has political consequences. To explain this, I will proceed with a historical-comparative analysis that includes the recent history of the Catholic approach to politics and a comparison between the American and European scenarios.

2.1. Contemporary Catholicism and Political Cultures

It is worthwhile, first of all, to remember that the idea that Catholics *can* have a political culture, and even different political cultures (plural), is a very recent acquisition for the Catholic Church and

Catholic magisterium. The march of Catholics toward democracy was a long one, and until recently, Catholics were not even supposed to have a political culture. After the shock of the revolutions of the late-eighteenth and midnineteenth centuries, politics was seen as *the* fruit of the modern world's separation from the moral guidance of the only true Church. Catholic politicians were allowed to entertain commerce with the modern world only de facto—as a practical necessity, because sometimes for the hierarchy, it was too embarrassing to be involved directly with a political realm when they did not acknowledge its legitimacy. However, in many cases, embarrassment could be overcome, and Vatican international politics trumped the political orientations of Catholics. For example, the rise of Italian Fascism was a consequence of the fact that Catholics were not allowed to have political cultures or a political party of their own.[2]

Only during Vatican II do we see this scenario change with the acknowledgment that modernity "exists" and that Catholics live in the Church but also in society and in a political community that had in recent times become democratic—one of the "signs of the times" that the Church had to look at. Vatican II was inspired by a fundamental call to unity—ecumenical and interreligious unity—and the fathers and theologians of Vatican II saw in modernity a moment of advancement toward unity and the Church as one of the agents of the promotion of this unity: "The Church recognizes that worthy elements are found in today's social movements, especially an evolution toward unity, a process of wholesome socialization and of association in civic and economic realms. The promotion of unity belongs to the innermost nature of the Church" (Council Vatican II, constitution *Gaudium et Spes*, par. 42).

---

2. About this, see recently Lucia Ceci, *L'interesse superiore: Il Vaticano e l'Italia di Mussolini* (Roma-Bari: Laterza, 2013).

Nevertheless, the Catholic Church's discovery of partisan politics was not only due to its greater awareness of different legitimate political cultures that Catholics could embrace. It also concerned the fact that the Catholic Church elaborated at the Second Vatican Council (1962–1965) a set of principles that Catholics must represent in the public arena—and in a democratic public arena that can be called a "social democracy," a democracy whose goal is not procedural but must be measured in its ability to meet the demands of a human dignity that the Church proclaims as closely connected to the "social nature" of the human person (Council Vatican II, declaration *Dignitatis Humanae*, par. 3).[3]

Vatican II's view on the Catholic understanding of the relationship between the individual human person and the social-political dimension—that is, what we can call the "political culture of Vatican II"—not only draws on the recent experience of the Christian Democratic parties in post–World War II Europe, but also draws on the traditional social doctrine of the Church, all the way back to the "idea of rights" that first appeared in Thomas Aquinas and medieval Canon Law.[4] Vatican II envisioned an agreement on the "ends" and the fairness of the means to the ends that are made of consensus and political implementation—that is, of compromise.

However, there is little doubt that the process of decolonization and of democratization after World War II profoundly influenced the political culture of Vatican II. As the late political scientist Samuel Huntington famously said, it is one of the great ironies of world

---

3. See here the work of a European historian working in the United States, such as Tony Judt, esp. *Thinking the Twentieth Century*, with Timothy Snyder (New York: Penguin, 2012).

4. See here the seminal works by Brian Tierney, *Foundations of the Conciliar Theory: The Contribution of the Medieval Canonists from Gratian to the Great Schism* (Cambridge: Cambridge University Press, 1955) and *The Idea of Natural Rights. Studies on Natural Rights, Natural Law, and Church Law, 1150–1625* (Atlanta: Scholars, 1997); and Kenneth Pennington, *The Prince and the Law, 1200–1600: Sovereignty and Rights in the Western Legal Tradition* (Berkeley: University of California Press, 1993).

history that the Catholic Church became the most important advocate of democracy and religious freedom in the world today.[5]

An integral and undisputed part of Vatican II is the Catholic acceptance of democracy not just as the lesser evil when compared with dictatorship, but as the system in which religious freedom is respected. The post–Vatican II magisterium developed this and discussed a "legitimate plurality" of political choices, as Pope Paul VI said in his apostolic letter *Octogesima Adveniens*: "While recognizing the autonomy of the reality of politics, Christians who are invited to take up political activity should try to make their choices consistent with the Gospel and, in the framework of a legitimate plurality, to give both personal collective witness to the seriousness of their faith by effective and disinterested service of men" (Paul VI, apostolic letter *Octogesima Adveniens*, May 14, 1971, par. 46).

2.2. Catholicism and Political Cultures Today

Today the words *legitimate diversity* sound outdated to American liberal Catholics clashing with the hierarchy of bishops who they perceive as politically partisan. On the other side of the spectrum, the idea of a legitimate diversity is more and more alarming for Catholics worried about the political unanimity of Catholics around the so-called nonnegotiable values. Will this change or become worse?

In light of the consequences of the election of Pope Francis in 2013, we must ask ourselves whether or not the polarization will soon disappear with the end of the long transition in the post–Vatican II Church represented by the pontificates of John Paul II and Benedict XVI. The resignation of Benedict XVI in February 2013 marked the end of a long transition of popes who were not popes of Vatican

---

5. See Samuel Huntington, *The Third Wave: Democratization in the Late Twentieth Century* (Norman: University of Oklahoma Press, 1991).

II, but neither really popes of the post–Vatican II Church (as Pope Francis is), and with this, maybe also some of the typical features of a Catholicism focused on the "anthropological challenges" that arise from the changing moral universe of modernity.

Even so, there is reason to believe that in American Catholicism, some issues will continue to be central in the intra-Catholic debate. We have seen some of these in the last few weeks with the reception (and the rejection, in some quarters) of Pope Francis's first interview in Jesuit magazines.[6] Only a few weeks before, the debate between the editorials of the Jesuit *America* magazine and *Commonweal* concerning the politics of Catholics in the United States showed the importance of political rhetoric in the intra-ecclesial discourse in American Catholicism.[7]

Scholars of political discourse in America write that "the use of the term 'common ground' peaked during the 1992 presidential election campaign and then fell below the media horizon."[8] It is not clear to me if this is true also in the Church, the 1990s representing the peak—that is, the beginning and the quick end—of the shared idea of a common ground. Nevertheless, we know what happened in the Church in the following years. One of the most helpful books for understanding the plight of American Catholicism, *A People Adrift* by Peter Steinfels (2003), opens with an account of Cardinal Bernardin's funeral on November 20, 1996, in Chicago. Immediately following the account of the harsh reception of Bernardin's initiative by some very powerful American cardinals and bishops, the first chapter of

6. See "Intervista a Papa Francesco," *Civiltà Cattolica* 3918 (19 settembre 2013), anno 164, pp. 449–77, trans. as "A Big Heart Open to God," *America*, September 19, 2013.
7. See Matt Malone, SJ, "Pursuing the Truth in Love," editorial, *America*, June 3–10, 2013, http://americamagazine.org/issue/pursuing-truth-love; and editorial, "America's Politics," *Commonweal*, August 29, 2013, https://www.commonwealmagazine.org/americas-politics.
8. James R. Kelly, "Truth, Not Truce: 'Common Ground' on Abortion, a Movement within Both Movements," in *The American Culture Wars: Current Contests and Future Prospects*, ed. James L. Nolan Jr. (Charlottesville: University Press of Virginia, 1996), 228.

Steinfels's book, entitled "The Battle for Common Ground," identifies in the reception (or lack of reception) of the Second Vatican Council one of the major causes of polarization in the Church. Steinfels identifies four different hermeneutics of Vatican II:

1. Vatican II as a tragic mistake or heresy (the traditionalist interpretation advocated by the Lefebvrites of the SSPX);
2. Vatican II as a victim of erroneous and biased interpretations (the conservative interpretation);
3. Vatican II as a necessary moment of change, reform and reconciliation between the Church and the modern world (the interpretation of liberal Catholicism);
4. Vatican II as a betrayed revolution (the ultra-liberal or radical interpretation).[9]

Steinfels's categorization dates to 2003, approximately ten years ago. Now, ten years later, we can say that these different interpretations of Vatican II have become more entrenched and deeply ingrained in our ecclesial discourse. In my recent book on the interpretations of the council, *Vatican II: The Battle for Meaning*, I attempted to trace a spectrum of theological issues around which different "conciliar" or "anticonciliar" identities revolve, and to separate the theological issues from the ideological spin of different but compatible theological sensibilities. That said, I cannot help but see that our different readings of Vatican II (or invocations of the "spirit of Vatican II" versus total indifference to Vatican II) result in different behaviors in the Catholic Church in the Western world. Our different interpretations of Vatican II are more or less linked to

9. See Peter Steinfels, *A People Adrift: The Crisis of the Roman Catholic Church in America* (New York: Simon & Schuster, 2003).

the same theological reading of the last few decades in the Church and in society at large, such as these examples:

- The cloud of mutual suspicion between theologians and the bishops;
- The creation of a professional theological association alternative to the "mainstream" associations of Catholic theologians (the Academy of Catholic Theology vis-à-vis the Catholic Theological Society of America);
- The growing disconnect between the culture of "ordinary Catholics" and the culture of the Catholic seminaries, especially after the apostolic visitation of 2005–2006;
- The return of Latin masses on Catholic campuses and in some Catholic parishes;
- The generational dynamic within U.S. Catholicism that requires an intergenerational dialogue on many issues—for example, a dialogue between those nostalgic for the "spirit of Vatican II" and the advocates of an anti–Vatican II discourse that is sometimes very visible also among the advocates of a postpartisan Catholic Church;
- The appeal to "collegiality" in the Church versus a monarchical Church led by the magisterium;
- The growing difference in the political orientations of Catholics according to their ethnicity and social background, while at the same time, the American Catholic hierarchy has been very effective at building consensus within itself by eliminating alternatives and diversity of voices.

If we want to understand the depth of these fault lines, we must read within the context of the more general changes in the political cultures of the Western world in which the Catholic Church and its most public figures operate:

- The end of Communism in Russia and Eastern Europe, which also weakened the concept of politics as relevant for human destiny and gave way to economicism;
- The decline of the West and of its relevance for world Catholicism, and conversely, the decline of the role of Catholicism in the destinies of the Western world;
- The crisis of politics no longer being perceived as a possible solution to concrete problems;
- The rise of a privatized and libertarian culture (a fruit of the triumph over Communism) which did as much as the fall of Communism to remove the idea of a "common good";
- The growing marginalization of larger portions of the population from the political process, and the parallel "big sort," that is, the clustering of like-minded Americans (for which there is a new term: *homophily*, meaning "love of the same").

All of these elements differ profoundly from the basic elements of the "culture of Vatican II" in the 1960s and the theological and political cultures of the Church of Vatican II. One wonders if the polarization in the Church is not a response to the radical changes occurring in the general world outside—*ad extra*, after a council like Vatican II, which dedicated much of its work to the *ad extra*.

If this were true, however, some features of the political behavior of Catholics would be visible in many different Catholic churches, not only in the Catholic Church in the United States. But Cardinal Bernardin recognized that problem very soon, and we know that the Catholic Common Ground Initiative started after Bernardin, then Cardinal archbishop of Chicago, saw the polarization affecting many of the parishes of his diocese. In fact, there is a distinct American problem, which I will now try to address, because the growing polarization and the need for a common ground are part of the picture of global Catholicism but also must be understood in their specificity.

2.3. Catholicism and Political Cultures in America

American Catholicism has a special (I am not sure if I want to use the word *exceptional*) history, and this history has created a uniquely vibrant and important Catholic Church with unique characteristics. I will try to list here briefly only the ones that are relevant to the issue of polarization and common ground.

The first and most obvious element is the mingling of religion and politics in the United States, despite (or thanks to) the influence of the First Amendment in the formation of the "civil religion" of the American people.[10] The personal position of the individual in politics says much about her or his position in religion, and vice versa. The history of many denominations in the United States is a history of adjustment and change according to the changing relationships between these two elements. Sometimes Catholicism would like to think of itself as above this American phenomenon, but it is not.

The second largest religious group in America is former Catholics. But notwithstanding the ever-growing masses of what Martin Marty called "the American Catholic Alumni Society," Catholics in America have not left the Church as much as European Catholics have. In other words, the rise of a critical mass against (or questioning) the Church as an institution has become part of the internal debate and

10. See here the studies by Robert N. Bellah (1927–2013) for the idea of "civil religion.": "Civil Religion in America," *Journal of the American Academy of Arts and Sciences* 96/1 (1967): 1–21.

not, as in Europe, part of the debate between a more clerical or clergy-led Catholicism and a more secular landscape.[11]

The Catholic Church in the United States has lived in close contact with a democratic environment, specifically in a democracy that is not "consensual" like European democracies based on multiparty alliances: it is a "competitive" democracy—that is, with two alternative political parties. In this democratic/competitive environment, the Catholic Church came to age a few decades ago also by absorbing democracy—that is, not by rejecting democracy, as was the case in European Catholicism, even regarding the ethos of participation in the Church. Participation in the U.S. Church is driven often by competitive, alternative views more than by consensual instincts. In this, it is clear why the "nonnegotiable values" became so important for American Catholicism (more than for anyone else in global Catholicism). Now we might be witnessing a new wave of democratization (to paraphrase Samuel Huntington's book *The Third Wave*),[12] but the kind of democratization that became part of the Catholic Church in the United States is a particular democratic culture. In other words, democratic ethos has become part of the culture of the Church, but in the United States, this has created more competition than consensus, with all the ecclesial actors (hierarchy, laity, theologians, Catholic think tanks, universities, etc.) taking part in this competition as competitors. The function of the consensus builder has been visibly lacking at all levels of the Church, and this is why many bishops explicitly rejected the Catholic Common Ground Initiative.

A third element is that while there are many scholarly studies on the impact of electoral systems on the political behavior of a country,

11. See Albert O. Hirschman, *Exit, Voice, and Loyalty: Responses to Decline in Firms, Organizations, and States* (Cambridge, MA: Harvard University Press, 1970).
12. See Huntington, *The Third Wave*.

and there are many studies on the *political behavior* of Catholics in the United States, there are very few on the electoral system's impact on the *political cultures* of Catholics in a given country. In very simple terms, the existence of a two-party political and electoral system has given birth in these last few decades (through many passages) to something very close to a two-party Catholic Church. In other countries with a significant population of politically active Catholics, you do not have a two-party Church, because these Catholics live in multiparty systems, in which different theological identities are much more difficult to attract and to absorb into the political discourse and partisan narratives.

This element of the two parties is unintelligible in its impact on American Catholics if we do not acknowledge the fact that American politics became more polarized: "Republican" means "conservative," and "Democrat" means "liberal." Also, our Church politics became more polarized: "Vatican II" means "liberal Catholic," while invoking "magisterium" means "conservative." This is, of course, possible only if we accept an extremely simplified (more political than theological) understanding of terms such as *ecumenical council* and *teaching of the Church.*

A fourth element is that the polarization of American Catholics in a polarized politics is part of a picture in which a nonconfessional but Christian Democratic party has always been conspicuously absent. In most European countries with a large Catholic population, political compromise (in the noble sense of the word) has always been part of the political reception of the magisterial documents of the teaching office of the Church—for example, the excommunication of Communists in 1949 and its impact on Italy, and the reception of *Humanae Vitae* and of the teachings on the so-called "life issues."[13]

13. See Wolfram Kaiser, *Christian Democracy and the Origins of European Union* (Cambridge: Cambridge University Press, 2007).

3. The Need for the Common Ground Initiative Today

Cardinal Bernardin's Catholic Common Ground Initiative is part of the history of American Catholicism and has recently become perceived as an acceptable and sought-after initiative only by certain types of Catholics, following the retreat of some of its inaugural members who were closer to the conservative and traditional side of U.S. Catholicism.[14] Nevertheless, the Catholic Common Ground Initiative belongs to the whole Church, not only to the Church in the United States, and there are several reasons to argue not just for its survival, but to see a more pressing need for it now more than ever and not only because of the shrinking common ground in our Church and in our society.

First of all, the Common Ground Initiative is crucial in a time when the idea of Catholic social teaching has become vague at times, according to the political cultures of different countries or of different "quarters" within one Catholic Church. Advocated in the name of many different issues (life issues, business ethics, workers' rights, etc.), "Catholic social teaching" has sometimes become a blanket that can cover any possible interpretation of the moral message of the Church, not only in terms of the concrete applications of the principles but also of the principles themselves.

Second, the changing demographics of American Catholicism will alter also the dynamics of an entrenched debate. On one side, the expectations and contributions of recent immigrants to the U.S. Church will modify the paradigm of the political alignments in the Church. I am not sure how it will modify the paradigm, given the many differences of opinion between Cubans and migrants from

---

14. See Cardinal Joseph Bernardin and Archbishop Oscar H. Lipscomb, *Catholic Common Ground Initiative: Foundational Documents* (Eugene, OR: Wipf and Stock, 2002).

Mexico or the Dominican Republic on, for example, the role of government.

Third, the Catholic Common Ground Initiative will play a different role in our ecclesial discourse because of the election of Pope Francis. In other words, this might well be the end of the "culture wars"—or at least in the Church of Pope Francis, it will be more challenging to wage culture wars and say this is a faithful reception of the papal teaching. Pope Francis has put an end to any endorsement of an ideologization of the gospel at the service of a conservative agenda, and he is equally distant from an "Americanist" (liberal, libertarian, and individualistic) view of Catholicism.[15] As a "social Catholic," Pope Francis has clearly stepped back from a set of issues that put Catholic *naturaliter*, naturally in two different camps through a kind of a bipartisan mutual exclusion: the use of the triad abortion-contraception-homosexuality as a test for entering, staying in, or leaving the Church; the weaponization of sacraments; and the ideologization of the Catholic tradition as naturally conservative or naturally liberal. No one expects Pope Francis to call conservative Catholicism an "exhausted project" (as Cardinal Francis George of Chicago famously did with liberal Catholicism),[16] but the social radicalism of Pope Francis is for sure exhausting the spin doctors active in Catholic think tanks, just as he is going to disappoint liberal Catholics who expected from him an endorsement of their agenda.

4. Vatican II and the Temptation of a Sectarian Church

In light of these recent events in the world Church, the need for an initiative claiming the existence of a Catholic common ground seems

---

15. See Michael L. Peppard, "Francis the Liberal? If He Is One, What Kind Is He?," *Commonweal*, September 30, 2013, https://www.commonwealmagazine.org/francis-liberal.
16. See Francis George, "How Liberalism Fails the Church," *Commonweal*, June 17, 2004.

more necessary because the swinging pendulum of the Church (in its language, style, and approach to issues) requires a stabilizing factor. That is, it needs a "place" that can give Catholics the opportunity to articulate their contribution to the "change" factor in the Church without being absorbed by the rhetoric of "competitive theologies" fighting for the upper hand.[17] In particular, in this time of change in the Church, the rediscovery of a common ground will be even more necessary now—that is, when for many Catholics attached to the social-political language of the last two pontificates, it is particularly difficult to articulate, under Pope Francis, a language for a "faithful dissent" with the magisterium of the Church (it will suffice to take a look at some articles published online shortly after the election of Pope Francis and throughout his pontificate by the theological journal *First Things*).

One last thing needs to be pointed out, which is maybe the most important issue behind the ongoing debate on Catholics and political polarization in America. I believe that the Catholic Common Ground Initiative and other initiatives bringing Catholics back to the public square are the best possible response to the ever-insisting calls for a Catholic retrenchment into an alternative universe, from the political dimension of "government," "state," into a world of small communities, more traditional and radical than what conventional politics can offer Catholics today. In the first chapter of his book *Migrations of the Holy*, DePaul University theologian William Cavanaugh writes, "The Nation-State is not the keeper of the common good." In the conclusions of the chapter, Cavanaugh states the following:

The nation–state is neither community writ large nor the protector of

---

17. About this, see Mark S. Massa, "Beyond 'Liberal' and 'Conservative': The Internal Sectarian Threat to U.S. Catholicism," in *Inculturation and the Church in North America*, ed. T. Frank Kennedy, SJ (New York: Herder & Herder / Crossroad, 2006), 127–43.

smaller communal spaces; rather, it originates and grows over against truly common forms of life. . . . The problem, as MacIntyre notes, is that the nation-state presents itself . . . as the keeper of the common good and repository of sacred values, so that it demands sacrifice on its behalf. . . . The urgent task of the Church, then, is to demystify the nation-state and to treat it like a telephone company. . . . The Church must 'complexify' space, that is, promote the creation of spaces in which alternative economies and authorities flourish.[18]

My friend Cavanaugh is not alone in this. More recently, Michael Baxter made a similar argument in *America*: "The lesson to be learned is this: those who set out to manage the modern state get managed by the modern state." In the conclusion of his article, Baxter launches a similar attack against the modern state:

The modern state must be resisted because it is corrosive to the practices and virtues necessary for genuine political community. Only small-scale, practice-based communities, MacIntyre argues, can support the kind of practical reasoning aimed at achieving the common good. Only a *polis*, as envisioned by Aristotle and re-envisioned by Aquinas, can sustain the moral and intellectual life through these dark and difficult times. Providentially, this task of constructing local forms of community has been taken up by increasing numbers of Catholics. Troubled by a sense of political homelessness in America, disaffected with both liberal and conservative ideologies, they have turned from state-centered, partisan politics and devoted themselves instead to the political life of local communities wherein the common good may be embodied: unions, worker co-ops and neighborhood organizations; agrarian projects and charter schools; ecclesial communities of prayer, friendship and works of mercy; houses of hospitality for the poor, unemployed, elderly, disabled, unwed mothers and immigrant families.[19]

As a European Catholic living in America, convinced that health care is a universal right and shocked every day by the political debate

18. See William T. Cavanaugh, *Migrations of the Holy: God, State, and the Political Meaning of the Church* (Grand Rapids, MI: Eerdmans, 2011), 41–42.
19. Michael Baxter, "Murray's Mistake," *America*, September 23, 2013.

on gun control (just to name two obvious examples), I understand the leaning to give up politics, state, government, and all that. I most surely admire the conviction of Catholics who want to rebuild ecclesial communities and fellowship of social services. But that entails a refusal to enter into a dialogue with other Catholics and others in general in search for a common ground.

Moreover, there are, in my opinion, many problems with this call to make of an acutely perceived "political homelessness in America" a detour into a depoliticization of Catholics in the sense of a withdrawal of legitimacy from the *polis* as we know it:

1. The nation-state and its political realm are not dying.[20] The idea of replacing the space for the *zoon politikon*, political animal, from the nation-state to small communities, even if it were workable in practice, would call for a total reversal of Catholicism's recent approach of to the "global" issues of our time.[21]

2. The Catholic delegitimization of the nation-state will make the situation worse for Catholics and non-Catholics. Some might benefit from this retreat from the nation-state into small communities, but many others are just not able to do so spiritually, physically, and financially.

3. Even if we were able to do this, the withdrawal from the nation-state would be rife with consequences. The withdrawal from the nation-state here in America might lead us to the early communities of Christians in a society that never had an "established" Church. But in a European scenario, the withdrawal from the nation-state to a period before the Peace of

20. Alan Wolfe, "The Nation-State Is Not Dying," *Chronicle Review*, September 3, 2013.

21. See David Hollenbach, *The Global Face of Public Faith: Politics, Human Rights, and Christian Ethics* (Washington, DC: Georgetown University Press, 2003).

Westphalia in 1648 would bring back the wars of religion that
ravaged Europe for at least a century.

4. A retrenchment of Catholicism in the form of a resistance
against the modern state implies a radical rethinking of the
Catholic view of the "political," paradoxically augmenting the
"Americanist" taste of Catholicism and making the polarization
even more serious.

5. This retrenchment would get Catholicism intellectually and
spiritually into a sectarian mind-set that is impossible to
reconcile with the "universal" claim typical of the Catholic idea.

As a historian, I do not need to be convinced of the destructiveness
of public power and its temptation to absorb every aspect of life in
a manner that is not even comparable to the times of the empires.
I know very well the level of ambiguity in the recent Catholic
magisterium (the teaching of Vatican II included) about the deep
nature of political power and the power of the nation-state.
Nevertheless, I also believe that the modern state is the last anchor
against much more destructive forces, and I fear that Catholic
theology might become soon victim of an antipolitical sentiment that
contradicts recent papal teaching about service in political life as a
very high form of charity.[22]

All this is to say that the idea of a Catholic common ground in
the public square is important not only for bridging current political
cultures and the polarized environment permeating also the Catholic
Church. The idea of a Catholic common ground represents a reality
check against possible alternatives that can be entertained only at

22. About this, see the consistent tradition of the teaching of the Catholic Church, especially in
Paul VI and John Paul II in the post–conciliar Church. Pope Francis confirmed this tradition in
his apostolic exhortation: "Politics, though often denigrated, remains a lofty vocation and one
of the highest forms of charity, inasmuch as it seeks the common good" (*Evangelii Gaudium*, 24
November 2013, par. 205).

unimaginable costs. Engagement in political dialogue can be a sign of solidarity, respect, and love for the entire human family bound together by myriad challenges in the late 20th century. The relationship between Catholicism and citizenship in the world of today needs to be rediscovered: not because our politics demands it, but because Catholic faith requires it.

The crisis of Cardinal Bernardin's Catholic Common Ground Initiative is therefore part of a broader landscape where politics has become "populistically unpopular." The crisis of the Catholic Common Ground Initiative is part of the crisis of the idea of politics as a form of charity. In a sense, the Catholic Church is one of the last defenders against the potentially humanizing effect of politics, and against the potentially dehumanizing effect of a community of Christians apocalyptically withdrawn into the desert.

16

Conclusions

Pope Francis and the Shift in the Debate on Vatican II

Vatican II stands, at fifty years from its conclusion, between event and reception, and this particular moment in the life of the Christian theological tradition can be understood only in a historical perspective. In a sense, this is the only claim of this book, which follows and comes at the end of an important season in the studies on the Second Vatican Council.[1]

This is the core of this book that started with a section focusing on the history of the debate on the council in relation to some key features of that event (the conciliar debate as a source of legitimacy and the "constitutional" value of the conciliar teaching for the Church). A look at the history of the conciliar documents and at

---

1. For the development of the debate on Vatican II, see Massimo Faggioli, *Vatican II: The Battle for Meaning* (New York: Paulist, 2012); and the literature overviews published in *Cristianesimo nella Storia* every two to three years, the most recent update being "Council Vatican II: Bibliographical Survey 2010–2013," *Cristianesimo nella Storia* 24, no. 3 (2013): 927–55.

the debates behind, before, and after the promulgation of those texts is a first step toward recognizing and identifying the trajectories of Vatican II going beyond the usual polarization between conservative and liberal interpretations of Church teaching. Useful as these characterizations may be for an initial perception of the cultures of references behind those interpretations, the liberal/conservative cast does not do justice to theological ideas that precede (by many centuries) the birth of this parliamentarian geography of ideas.

The second step is to acknowledge the relationship between ecclesiology and intertextuality at Vatican II. The textual dimension of Vatican II is essentially intertextual and indissoluble from the context of the debate in the council, plenary and commissions, about those texts. If it is true that the ecclesiological issue is at the center of the whole Vatican II, that is, the macro issue of Vatican II, then it is also true that the ecclesiological constitutions of Vatican II are not sufficient to comprehend the ecclesiological turn of the council. The liturgical reform, the evolution of Church teachings on political issues such as religious liberty, a new understanding of the position of the Church vis-à-vis the modern and contemporary world—all these are part of the ecclesiology of the Church of Vatican II.

The third step is to reassess the value of those teachings: Vatican II and the agenda of the Church. One implication of the paradigmatic shift at Vatican II from a metaphysics theology to a more historical understanding of the truths of Christian faith is that the conciliar teaching is not abstract, but something that must be understood in the world of today—not in an essentialist perspective, but with a look at the ways the Church of Vatican II has (or has not) been able to reform itself in order to be a credible witness of the changes announced by the council.

Finally, the last two chapters make a statement about the nature of the Church's mission in the world of today in light of Vatican II:

a council for the global Church. The permanent value of Vatican II has been confirmed to me in my personal intellectual and spiritual journey from Europe to America. I found that the council is the most important point of passage from a Europe-centered Catholicism to a global Catholicism, and the council is a solemn moment of rejection of the temptations to make of the Catholic Church an inward-oriented community.

This itinerary in some of the most important legacies of Vatican II has proceeded historically, not only because its author is a historical theologian who approached Vatican II first of all as a Church historian. It is the very nature of the object that compels the scholar to proceed this way. If indeed there is anything that the history of the debate on Vatican II in these last fifty years teaches us, it is that the wavelength of the conciliar idea is a long one.[2] Before the real preparation of Vatican II after the announcement of January 25, 1959, Vatican II was prepared in the minds of the best theologians of the twentieth century (including the future pope John XXIII) between World War I and World War II. In a similar way, the Church received Vatican II in the first few years after the end of the council, but there are waves—moved by the energy of the profound meaning of those documents and of that event—that are still coming toward us. The energy that moves these waves is not exhausted. Understanding this key dynamic of the Church as a living body is possible only through a historical-theological lens, and not through the news cycle that sometimes engulfs the ecclesial discourse.

The history of Vatican II and of the postconciliar debates is important because it gives us the coordinates of deep ecclesial rifts, of powerful long-term movements, and of a specific Catholic

---

2. See Hermann Josef Sieben, *Die Konzilsidee im 19. und 20. Jahrhundert* (Paderborn: Schöningh, 1993) and the other volumes by the same author on the conciliar ideas in antiquity, in medieval times in the Latin world, and between the Reformation and *Aufklärung*, the Enlightenment (included the Catholic European Enlightenment).

geopolitics that becomes visible only in conciliar-synodal moments. We have seen this at the Extraordinary Synod of Bishops on family and marriage of October 2014, but it is true for the whole conciliar tradition. The teaching of councils that we thought forgotten come back to us in unexpected ways; the renewed debate on collegiality and synodality in the Church of Pope Francis is a clear evidence of this.[3]

Nevertheless, it is undeniable that a reflection on the history of Vatican II and its aftermath is "countercultural" (I use this adjective reluctantly because of all the possible ideological implications). On the one hand, Vatican II took place only fifty years ago, but it was the council of a Church that was still very European, with non-European Catholic Churches still largely led by a European missionary episcopate. The Church of today is much more global, and a noncritical appeal to Vatican II can disguise the temptation to re-Europeanize the Catholic Church. On the other hand, similarly suspicious are the appeals to Vatican II as a generational event, in which the "cultural" content of that moment (for example, "the golden sixties") becomes more important than the theology of the documents and debates of Vatican II. It's no wonder that younger generations of Catholics are allergic to these nostalgic celebrations of the conciliar event. On top of that, there is the ever-alive rejection of Vatican II in some Catholic quarters that associate Vatican II with a naïve acceptance of modernity by a radicalized and politicized theological intelligentsia, as if secularization were something that happened because of and after Vatican II and not something Catholics had been talking about already in the 1930s and 1940s.

The "dangerous memory of Vatican II" (to paraphrase the famous dictum by Johann Baptist Metz about the "dangerous memory of

---

3. See Francis Oakley, "Authoritative and Ignored: The Overlooked Council of Constance," *Commonweal*, October 24, 2014, pp. 20–23.

Jesus Christ") is especially dangerous for the ones who forget—or pretend they do not know that there are conciliar cycles that return in the life of the Church. That's why scholars of Vatican II saw in the election of Jorge Mario Bergoglio–Francis to the papacy something that eluded those who had dismissed the council as an anomaly in the way Catholicism works. Words, symbols, and acts of the 2013 conclave and of the beginning of Francis's pontificate were clearly an echo of the 1958 conclave and of the beginning of John XXIII's pontificate.[4]

There is something especially relevant in this moment of reception of Vatican II at fifty years, that is, a fundamental shift in the status of the council as point of reference for Catholic theologians and Church leaders. If there is no question that all the successors of John XXIII were "Vatican II popes" (Paul VI brought the council to a conclusion, John Paul I and John Paul II were council fathers, and Benedict XVI was one of the most important theological *periti* at the council), then it is also true that in the post–Vatican II years, there was a tendency to label with Vatican II much or everything that was being enforced in the Church by the magisterium. In other words, a kind of "Vatican nominalism" was evident, so that at some point, the reference to Vatican II in official magisterial documents became a litmus test and not a real marker of the theological references of that document.

With Pope Francis, the first post–Vatican II pope who was not at Vatican II in any capacity (and actually was ordained priest only in 1969), "Vatican II nominalism" is over. The election of Francis on March 13, 2013, has indubitably changed the landscape of the Church and especially of the debate on Vatican II. The fact that Jorge Mario Bergoglio–Francis is a Vatican II Catholic—and, in a sense, the first post–Vatican II pope—has changed the nature of the debate

4. About this, see Massimo Faggioli, *Pope Francis: Tradition in Transition* (New York: Paulist, 2015).

on the council. In the pontificate of Francis, we see Vatican II going largely unnamed by the pope, except on some particular occasions. This lack of direct mention of Vatican II by a post–Vatican II pope like Francis is not indicative of a dismissal of the council by the Argentine pope; on the contrary. It may have to do with the fact that when Vatican II is mentioned (especially in the English-speaking world), it is still captive to polarizing narratives. But the fact that Francis rarely mentions Vatican II has to do for sure with the *sensus ecclesiae* that he interprets as pope: the Church at fifty years from Vatican II has reached a point in the reception of the council when the conciliar trajectories need no labeling. Ecumenism, interreligious dialogue, an ecclesiology of the Church "that goes forth," a Church of mercy and for the poor—all this is unquestionably the theology of Vatican II in act. Vatican II was an act, and the reception of Vatican II is an act. Looking for it only in written documents reveals a scant understanding of the profound nature of that moment—and of the Church in general. Francis showed that Vatican is still a "compass" (as John Paul II wrote in his testament). Without reference to the council, it is impossible to recognize in his basic traits not only the Jesuit Jorge Mario Bergoglio–Pope Francis but also the very basic features of Catholicism, a Church that became theologically global thanks to Vatican II.

A creative act of interpretation of Vatican II was Francis's decision to celebrate the Synod of Bishops on the same topic twice in twelve months between October 2014 and October 2015. The synod that was celebrated in the Vatican in October 2014 was a synod that resumed the interrupted dialogue in the church of the post–Vatican II era. The "Where were we?" of Pope Francis was clear in his opening speech of the synod on the evening of October 4, 2014, which was very similar to the "moonlight speech" of John XXIII on the evening of the opening day of Vatican II, October 11, 1962. Francis talked about "the joys and hopes," evoking *Gaudium et Spes*; referred to Church history as *magistra*, as a teacher; and invoked the wind of Pentecost.[5]

There is a profound reception of Vatican II by Pope Francis and a rejuvenation of conciliar theology at fifty years. Much of what Pope Francis has said and done is witness that Vatican II cannot be reduced to documents. Vatican II is not documents, but it is an event whose "performative" value can only be performed in gestures. Vatican II cannot be enslaved to a closely guarded official and institutional hermeneutic of texts. The debate on Vatican II is not anymore expedient for determining power dynamics in the Church. The interpretation of Vatican II as an exercise of textual exegesis made in a historical vacuum is not only a reduction of its meaning: it is also the subtlest form of rejection of the council.

---

5. Address of Pope Francis during the prayer vigil for the Synod on the Family, organized by the Italian Bishops Conference in Saint Peter's Square, October 4, 2014, available at https://w2.vatican.va/content/francesco/en/speeches/2014/october/documents/papa-francesco_20141004_incontro-per-la-famiglia.html.

Index

Acerbi, Antonio, 23, 238, 252, 264

Adolphus, Lalit, 22, 106

Agagianian, Grégoire-Pierre XV, 73

Aggiornamento, 24, 50, 101, 104, 156, 253, 286

Ahern, Kevin, ix, xii

Alberigo, Giuseppe, 4, 19, 22-24, 26, 27, 30, 39, 42, 51-55, 58, 61, 66-70, 72, 74, 75, 81, 87, 90, 92, 106, 108, 111, 119, 126, 128-131, 146, 150, 151, 161, 170, 172, 184, 186, 188, 196, 197, 231, 232, 235, 238, 253, 257, 259, 264, 268, 269, 271, 282, 286, 292, 298

Aletti, Jean-Noël, 42

Alfrink, Bernard, 207, 236

Allen, John L. Jr., 303

Antón, Angel, 203, 213

Arnandez, Richard, 125

Attanasio, Salvator, 21, 95

Aubert, René, 23

Audinet, Jacques, 271

Audoin-Rouzeau, Stéphane, 293

Augustine of Hippo, 126, 128

Autiero, Antonio, 263

Aymans, Winfried, 215

Bärsch, Jürgen, 109

Bäumer, Remigius, 86

Baldisseri, Lorenzo, 227

Baldovin, John, ix, 102, 144, 249

Balthasar, Hans Urs von, 17, 131

Baraúna, Guilherme, 105, 130, 283

Bartholomew I, Patriarch of Constantinople, 33

Barros Camara, Jaime de, 236

Battlogg, Andreas, 59

Baxter, Michael, 324

Bazzell, Pascal D., 179

Beauduin, Lambert, 118, 188, 283

Becker, Karl Josef, 28

2015. 11. 09   44.00 (30.90)